HAILE SELLASSIE I
THE FORMATIVE YEARS
1892-1936

Provinces

1 GERA
2 JANJERO
3 KULO KONTA
4 WALLAMO
5 GOLDIYA
6 SHEWA GIMIRA
7 BENESSO
8 GURAFERDA

0   100 MILES

HAILE SELLASSIE I
THE FORMATIVE YEARS
1892-1936

HAROLD G. MARCUS

The Red Sea Press, Inc.
Publishers & Distributors of Third World Books

11-D Princess Road
Lawrenceville, NJ 08648

P. O. Box 48
Asmara, ERITREA

The Red Sea Press, Inc.

Publishers & Distributors of Third World Books

11-D Princess Road
Lawrenceville, NJ 08648

P. O. Box 48
Asmara, ERITREA

Copyright © 1987, 1995, 1998 Harold G. Marcus

First Red Sea Press, Inc. Edition 1996
Second Printing 1996
Third Printing 1998

Cover Design & Illustration by Carles J. Juzang

Library of Congress Cataloging-in-Publication Data:
Marcus, Harold G.
       Haile Sellassie I : the formative years, 1892-1936 / Harold G.
Marcus.
        p. cm.
       Originally published: Berkeley : University of California Press,
1987.
       Includes bibliographical references and index.
       ISBN 1-56902-007-8 : $49.95. -- ISBN 1-56902-008-6 (pbk.) : $18.95
       1. Haile Sellassie I, Emperor of Ethiopia, 1892-1975. 2. Ethiopia-
-History--1889-1974. 3. Ethiopia--Kings and rulers--Biography.
I. Title.
DT387.7.M37   1995
963'.055'092--dc20
[B]

94-48486
CIP

Dedicated to

Norman Singer and Owen Jervis, two men who changed my life,

and to

Florence and Jerry Marcus and Barbara and Peter Morano,
brothers and sisters,

and to

Rose Linsky, my extraordinary aunt

CONTENTS

Illustrations follow page 108

PREFACE

Over a decade ago, a kindly friend advised me not to undertake a biography of Haile Sellassie. He claimed that any study of the emperor, especially one written soon after his demise, would not be treated fairly. Readers, my friend said, would respond to the subject, not to the scholarly reconstruction of his life and times. The emperor was just too controversial, and we were too close to the events that led to his denouement and the subsequent Ethiopian crisis. Haile Sellassie was a political icon to some, a monster to others, and to all a legend. Every Ethiopian, each foreigner who met him, knew and viewed the emperor differently. I was warned gently that every statement I made, each fact used, and all my ideas would be subjected to the most intense personal scrutiny and judged in terms of memory, impression, and folklore. Worse, my scholarship would be selectively used by Ethiopia's warring political factions for corroboration of their positions.

My friend's concerns were sincere and serious, and, for a time, his arguments deterred me from attempting the Haile Sellassie book.

Yet the research I subsequently accomplished, the dissertations my students wrote, and my own scholarship underscored the emperor's centrality in Ethiopia's last half century. As the architect of the modern state, he had managed his country's entry into the world, in the process becoming a global figure. His achievements demanded serious study, especially in light of the current political controversies about the significance of his reign. Given the scholarly challenge, my friend's well-meaning admonitions lost their substance, and I decided to write Haile Sellassie's biography, the first part of which is offered here.

The endeavor has taken me to archives and libraries in Washington, London, Paris, Rome, Khartoum, and Addis Abeba, where I was received with kindness and cooperation. My dialogue with the documents has not been matched by conversation with informants. I regret this lapse, but Ethiopia's decade-long catharsis negated my efforts to work there with the aged informants who might usefully have provided data and insights for the present book. I do not believe, however, that their testimonies would have changed the analysis of Haile Sellassie presented in this volume.

I tend to agree with Edwin R. A. Seligman that not all history can be explained in terms of economic factors, even if they "exert a preponderant influence in shaping the progress of society."[1] Peter Worsley, though a materialist, has pointed to the importance of culture in the political economy within which individuals work out their destinies and, if powerful enough, shape the fate of others.[2] "Men," Karl Marx advised, "make their own history, but they do not make it just as they please; they do not make it under circumstances chosen by themselves, but under circumstances directly encountered, given and transmitted from the past."[3] In this light, Haile Sellassie appears a uniquely gifted political genius who acted on a stage not of his own construction. He could select the *dramatis personae* and adapt some of the script, but not the play's main features.

His role approximated Europe's absolutist rulers of the transitional period between feudalism and capitalism. Like his Western counterparts, Haile Sellassie introduced a standing army, a permanent bureaucracy, new forms of taxation, uniform laws, and the mechanisms of a national economy. He also came to control the landed aristocracy, whose authority he redefined and whose functions he redirected to strengthen his increasingly centralized state. The emperor supported his programs through more efficient exploitation of the existing modes of agricultural production, in whose interstices merchant capitalism grew in cooperation with the ruling elites.[4] Even though the Ethiopian absolutist social formation anticipated a more advanced method of production, it contained elements of social organization that characterized earlier centralized empires.

As had the Egyptian pharaoh, the Chinese emperor, and the Persian king of kings, Haile Sellassie constructed a bureaucracy in which talent, skill, achievement, and, above all, loyalty to the ruler counted more than ethnic or social origins. The emperor's men ensured that the crown received a continuous flow of resources to maintain the machinery of royal and bureaucratic authority. Together with their patron, "they strove to concentrate in their own hands, the main centers of power and control in the country"; they codified and unified law, regularized revenue collection, and standardized administrative practices. The bureaucrats also helped to portray the ruler as the heir to ancient cultural traditions, whose importance would be strengthened through his governance. The king and his men fostered belief in ancient prescriptions through educational, cultural, and religious institutions. Uninterested in any new and secular legitimation based on social groups or universalist values, the ruler continued to base his authority on traditional or charismatic themes and on the mystification surrounding the monarchy.[5]

As this study reveals, Haile Sellassie built a bureaucratic, absolutist monarchy that related to the world capitalist economy. Yet, however much such an abstraction helps us to understand the complexities of a period of long personal rule, it would have meant little to the emperor himself, involved as he was in the daily business of power and authority. Haile Sellassie viewed himself as the embodiment of Ethiopia's proud sovereignty and independence. His national vision derived from his early experiences as the heir of Ras Makonnen, a military ruler whose army kept order and whose officers constituted an oligarchy that exploited a polyglot, non-Christian population. Haile Sellassie naturally regarded this political order as normal and in the best interests of Ethiopia's peoples. He governed, as had his immediate predecessors, by acting as the country's balancer of power, a method that worked well in a customary government that mediated between the ruling classes and the masses. His limited Western education directed him toward change, however, and he introduced modern institutions whose functions he never clearly understood. He found them useful, however, because they added to imperial power and to the authority of the central government that acted in the emperor's name.

Haile Sellassie always worked behind the scenes, manipulating actors and events to his advantage. His political goals were obvious, even if his tactics were concealed. He was always involved, though always proclaiming his innocence, his inaction, his isolation from events. He never admitted his nature as a politician but posed as a tool of fate, ready to do God's will or the will of the people. His apparent noninvolvement in politics only underscores the obscurity in which he maneuvered; the emperor's deft hand was invariably apparent in retrospect, and his careful planning became as obvious as his success. He was such a good actor, however, that even thoughtful persons never understood that Haile Sellassie was always offstage directing the action in his favor.

Economics also played its part. The emperor was lucky to be able to exploit southern Ethiopia, which the articulation of capitalism had made into his empire's richest region. The process had begun before World War I, when land was measured and classified as fertile, semifertile, and poor, depending on the availability of settled population, who lost title to their holdings and became sharecroppers. Cash crops as such and money came to dominate Ethiopia's political economy, and control over coveted appointments to the south added greatly to the emperor's wealth and power and to the resources of the state. Haile Sellassie was able to educate a cadre of "Young Ethiopians" to strengthen the central government, to transform Addis Abeba, his ramshackle capital, into a leading city, and to begin securing Ethiopia's frontiers from encroachment by adjacent colonial powers.

Ever jealous of his country's sovereignty and independence, the emperor also directed Ethiopia's trade and other activities away from its traditional European partners toward Japan and America, both of whom he believed supported his country's independence. By so doing, he robbed France of a good economic reason to protect

Ethiopia from Italy; he alienated Great Britain; and he permitted Italy to contemplate his nation's conquest. Mussolini regarded Ethiopia's progress, especially after 1928, when Haile Sellassie gained indisputable power, as potentially threatening Somalia and Eritrea and as marking Italy's failure to transform the Solomonic Empire into a Roman colony. During 1930–1932, domestic political considerations drove him to consider an attack on Ethiopia, and by 1934–1935, the European situation permitted the aggression. By then, Ethiopia was without allies and without the means to counter the Fascists. Haile Sellassie learned, as would other leaders, that collective security was the opiate of small, defenseless countries. Although the emperor would suffer defeat, despair, and exile, he would return in 1941, as a phoenix, to restore the status quo ante.

This volume is a culmination of many years' work, and its faults are all mine. Blameless are those of my friends and colleagues whose criticisms helped bring the book to completion: Patrick Gilkes, James McCann, Tessema Ta'a, Donald Lammers, and John Coogan. I want to thank Admiral Henri Labrousse, president of the Ethiopian Studies Association of France, for providing me with essential bits of information and thus saving me a trip to Paris, alas. I offer a special appreciation to Susan Drabik, who put up with me in Africa, Europe, and North America during the manuscript's long gestation, and who helped me through some particularly difficult paragraphs and sentences, dragons against which her sharp lance of a pen was proof. For the National Humanities Center, which provided succor and shelter as I transformed manuscript into book, I present my deep gratitude. To the Social Science Research Council, to Hays/Fulbright, and to Michigan State University, I say keep up the good work of supporting research, reflection, and scholarship. Thank you very much for your confidence in me.

Harold G. Marcus
National Humanities Center, January 1986

TERMS

GLOSSARY

Abba	Literally "father"; a priestly title.
Abuna, Abun	Metropolitan of the Ethiopian church; a title also given to Ethiopia's suffragan bishops.
Alaka	Teacher-leader; a priestly title.
Ato	Literally "sir"; now "Mr."
Awrajja	The largest subprovincial administrative unit.
Balabbat	Literally "one who has a father"; a local-level official who mediated between the people and the government.
Bejirond	Treasurer.
Bitwoded, Bit.	Literally "beloved"; a title of nobility equivalent to earl.
Blatta, Blattangeta	A title given to learned men and councilors.
Dejazmach, Dejaz., Dej.	Literally "commander of the gate"; a title of nobility equivalent to count.

Derg	Literally "committee"; a term now almost exclusively associated with Ethiopia's present military government.
Dubat	An irregular force of Somalis in the Italian army.
Duce	Italian for "leader"; the term associated with Mussolini and often used as a literary device.
Etchege	The administrative head of the Ethiopian church.
Fitawrari, Fit.	Literally "leader (general) of the vanguard"; a title of nobility equivalent to viscount.
Gabbar	A serflike farmer.
Gasha	A nonstandard unit of land measure, between thirty and fifty hectares.
Gerazmach, Geraz.	Literally "commander of the left"; a title of nobility equivalent to baron.
Gibbi	Any large structure such as a palace or a villa; term associated with Menilek's Grand Palace in Addis Abeba.
Kenyazmach, Kenyaz.	Literally "commander of the right"; a title of nobility equivalent to baron.
Lij	Literally "child"; a title reserved for the children of the high-ranking nobility.
Makwanent	The high nobility as a body.
Nagadras, Nag.	Literally "chief of the merchants," with authority to collect market taxes and customs.
Neftenya	Literally "one who owns a gun"; more specifically a northern soldier-settler in southern Ethiopia to whom the government granted rights over land and people.
Negus	King; title for a few provincial lords of high birth or special merit who governed under the direct authority of the negus negast, king of kings or emperor. Haile Sellassie never granted the title, and writers, myself included, have used the term *negus* as a literary device to refer to the monarch.
Ras	Literally "head"; a title of nobility equivalent to duke.
Woizero, Woiz.	Literally "lady"; now used for Mrs.

NAMES

I have rendered place names as they are presented in the most recent maps published by the Ethiopian Mapping Agency. I know this explanation will displease those who believe that we should continue to use better-known European versions of Ethiopian names because they have been used for generations. Nevertheless, I think that forms such as Mitsiwa and Wichale, although imperfect, are considerably better in terms of orthography than Massawa or Ucciali.

I have also used the spellings *Menilek* and *Haile Sellassie*, rather than the conventionally accepted *Menelik* and *Haile Selassie*. First, my rendering of Menilek more precisely approximates the Amharic spelling and is steadily winning favor. Second, Haile Sellassie was the spelling used by the emperor's palace and by the university that bore his name. I note that the eminent Ethiopianist Professor Edward Ullendorff followed this usage in his translation of the first volume of Haile Sellassie's autobiography (see Bibliography). It is a sensible spelling in terms of its Amharic version, although there is also a case to be made for *Sellasie*, a choice that undoubtedly would have sent readers and others into utter confusion.

HAILE SELLASSIE I

CHAPTER ONE

Beginnings,
1892 - 1916

In the fall of 1936, exiled amid the Georgian elegance of Bath, the ever practical Haile Sellassie sold off most of the silver salvaged from his palace in Addis Abeba and, with the help of Empress Menen, transformed a more humble property into a "tasteful English home." There, using "a simple chair as a throne," the emperor received his visitors and, with the help of a small staff, authored an autobiography vindicating his life and activities through the Italo-Ethiopian crisis of 1934–1936.[1] The volume dealt only sparingly with Haile Sellassie's childhood and youth, and its austere and remote tone revealed a man who obviously believed that life began only when he was born to power in 1916, as the heir apparent to Empress Zawditu. The public man provided little about his private life and almost nothing about his feelings, emotions, and sensibilities about people and events. His reserve stemmed partly from the rules of life in a culture that regards most visible signs of emotion as indecorous but also partly from a conscious decision made in 1930, upon accession to the Solomonic throne, to become the perfect monarch. For Haile Sellassie, the decision meant living self-consciously as the embodiment of Ethiopia's sovereignty, scarcely revealing his personality and humanity. He had few unguarded moments, he rarely made immediate judgments, and he seldom acted spontaneously.[2] Obviously, therefore, his two-volume autobiography, published in 1973 and 1974, provides none of the homely facts so important to the biographer, an insufficiency that makes it difficult to recapitulate Haile Sellassie's childhood and the development of his personality.[3] Enough scattered information is available, however, to outline his first years without fear of serious distortion.

Haile Sellassie's father was Ras (duke) Makonnen, one of Ethiopia's leading figures, a skillful politician and friend and relative of Emperor Menilek II, whose reign (1889–1913) was characterized by expansionism and economic growth. During the 1880s, the ras played an important role in imposing imperial rule over eastern Ethiopia and was named governor of Harerge province, through which moved much of the empire's commerce to and from Gulf of Aden ports. Makonnen, by nature open to innovation and new ideas, entered into contact with Europeans and other foreigners who increasingly came to Harer, the provincial capital, to profit from Ethiopia's economic consolidation under Menilek. They found the governor an intelligent man with an attractive personality, good looks, and the exquisite politeness characteristic of the Ethiopian aristocracy. He impressed them with his desire to learn about the outside world, and his many questions elicited as much accurate information as could be expected from his largely untutored interlocutors. He separated the data from the dross and came to appreciate the geopolitical and economic forces shaping the world, especially the industrialization and modernization of Europe. He learned most from Father André Jarosseau (called by the Ethiopians Abba [Father] Andreas), a shrewd and ingratiating person who quickly became Makonnen's confidant and adviser. The ras soon became Ethiopia's leading Europeanist, a status Menilek recognized in 1890 when he sent Makonnen to Rome to negotiate an important treaty. While in Europe, the ras came to appreciate Ethiopia's urgent need for development, modernization, and education.

If Haile Sellassie's father had seen the shape of the future, his mother, Yishimabet, was surely pleased with the status quo. The daughter of an obscure, petty nobleman from Welo,[4] she had used her great beauty and charm to win the heart of a man descended maternally from the great king Sahle Sellassie of Shewa (r. 1813–1847), Menilek's grandfather. So smitten was Makonnen that he divorced his common-law wife, the mother of Haile Sellassie's half brother, Yilma, and married Yishimabet in 1876, "according to Christian custom." Only Tafari Makonnen, her tenth and last child, born on 23 July 1892, near Harer at Ejersagoro, survived into adulthood. In 1930, he decided to use his baptismal name, Haile Sellassie, the "Power of the Trinity," as his regnal appellation. By then, Yishimabet had been dead thirty-six years, leaving little behind to her son but some of his delicate good looks. Nurturing was left to Ras Makonnen, who arranged to have Tafari raised with his second cousin Imru (later ras; d. 1981), also born in 1892.

The two youngsters became lifelong companions and friends,[5] and Imru's father, Fitawrari (general) Haile Sellassie Abayneh, was Tafari's real parent. Makonnen's son recalled the surrogate with affection, whereas he invariably referred to his father with formality and deference. The professions of deep filial love reflected his sense of propriety, as he scarcely knew Ras Makonnen, whose heavy responsibilities often kept him away from home. Yet the ras's personality—a good mix of shrewdness, gentility, sophistication, and political acumen—provided the boy with an apt role model. From his father, the son also learned to hide his tenacity of spirit and ambition behind diffidence, deference, and gentle grace. Makonnen taught his scion to respect learning, especially the modern education then seeping into Ethiopia. The ras recognized that the country had to change with the times, or fall prey to imperialism. He was determined that his son would learn the new lore and become one of Ethiopia's agents of modernization.[6]

After desultory tutoring in French by Dr. Joseph Vitalien, the Martinique physician who ran the local hospital, the boy was sent to the Capucin school run by Jarosseau. Makonnen charged the priest: "If I die be his father. I give him to you and God will do the rest." Moved to tears, Abba Andreas agreed and immortalized the event by having "the little Tafari [photographed] with [my] pectoral cross . . . on his neck as a sign of adoption." The Frenchman later remembered his ward as an intelligent child, quick to learn, with a sweet disposition and a natural affection for his teachers. With his cotton clothing and unshod feet, however, he differed little from the other lads who daily struggled with Western education.[7]

Tafari relished being one of the boys during the hurly-burly of his childhood, and he even enjoyed church school, where he learned to be a good Christian by studying Geez, Amharic, and the Psalms of David. The three years of traditional education came largely through rote, and Tafari's mastery here left him with a well-organized mind and awesome recall. He liked his predominantly Amhara classmates and always proudly declared, "Our upbringing was like that of the sons of ordinary people, and there was no undue softness about it."[8] The divergence came from his continuing exposure to European education.

After 1903, he was tutored by a Capucin seminarian and later priest, Abba Samuel, whom Jarosseau hoped would provide an intellectual model for Tafari. The young cleric was, by all reports, a profound intellectual who followed in the tradition of his academic father, Alaka (teacher-leader) Wolde Kahen, an early Catholic convert. The emperor remembered his tutor as "a good man who possessed great knowledge, who applied himself to learning and teaching, who in goodness and humility gathered knowledge like a bee from anyone, [and] was devoted to the love of God and his neighbour." According to Henri de Monfried, Jarosseau hoped that the spirit of "the Sages of Greece" present in Samuel would help Tafari develop into the "sublime man" promised by his youthful personality. Samuel remained at Tafari's side, a strong and positive influence until 1915, when he died.[9]

Even this capsule history of Tafari's education reveals its paradoxical nature. It comprised an inadequate mélange of traditional and modern learning imparted by teachers of various credos and levels of pedagogy. The boy was raised and disciplined as an Ethiopian but was exposed to Western language, logic, and lore. Throughout his long career, Tafari worshiped the Zeus of modernism, but more directly propitiated the household gods of Amhara parochialism. He was also a victim of his environment: Harer was the capital of a conquered province in a largely subjugated empire; most of the inhabitants spoke languages other than Amharic, the rulers' tongue, and followed Islam or a traditional religion; and they were his father's subjects. Tafari was the heir of a military ruler, whose army kept order and whose officers formed an oligarchy that exploited the provincial economy. The pattern of subservience and superiority had much in common with the Roman Empire, and Tafari was *civus Romanus,* a member of a culturally and religiously self-conscious elite that considered itself superior and born to rule. The oligarchy and the other Semitic-speaking, Christian northerners in the army, church, police, and administration constituted a ruling cadre not without compassion or a vision of a better life for themselves and their subjects—but only within the context of the colonized and the colonizer.[10]

Tafari naturally regarded Ethiopia's political and social stratification as normal. He daily observed his father and other elitists governing, administering, and judging. He watched expeditions marching out of Harer toward remote regions to collect the tribute apparently due those who had modern weapons and a disciplined, hierarchical social organization. Absorbing the prejudices and paternalism of his class, he came to believe that the Amhara governed in the best interests of the empire's anarchic peoples.[11] Indeed in 1905, at age thirteen, Tafari joined the ruling class when he was named dejazmach and made titular governor of a small region southwest of Harer. Ras Makonnen celebrated his son's formal entry into the empire's elite by hosting a reception and feast, during which he publicly proclaimed Tafari his heir and entrusted him to his officers, some of whom came to the awful conclusion that their leader "knew that the time had come for us to be separated by death."[12]

During the year left to him, the ras familiarized his son with the workings of provincial government. Constantly at the ras's side, the youth was permitted to ask questions and to offer advice, experiencing a hitherto unknown daily intimacy with his father. Perhaps this unusual but cherished closeness led Haile Sellassie later to claim a love relationship with Ras Makonnen, all but contradicted by the obviously unintended portrayal in his autobiography of an emotionless tie based on filial respect and paternal responsibility. The boy certainly derived much from his father, not the least a persona to imitate throughout his career. Ras Makonnen, according to no less an authority than Emperor Menilek, had the good fortune "to be loved and to be feared," to be "sagacious" in judgment, "merciful and understanding" in the application of the law, and charitable and benevolent, "doing all this [as] part of his resolve to please God without being vainglorious."[13]

God required the soulful presence of this remarkable man during his fifty-second year, in 1906. In January, en route to Addis Abeba, the ras fell seriously ill from typhoid. His officers took him to the holy place of Kulubi, where he was isolated, even from Tafari. On 20 March, the dying man entrusted all his financial papers to the British consul, admonishing him to "guard them well, and give them to my son when things have returned to normal." A little later, he worried, "Oh, if only I could have lived for a few years more, until the time when he would be able to stand up for his own rights." In order to ensure the boy a few more years of protection, Makonnen wrote Menilek, consigning Tafari to his care, mentioning that in the next life he would ask how he had acquitted the charge.

When Tafari was finally summoned to his father's bedside, the ras was too weak to talk but managed to place his hand in benediction on the shoulder of the kneeling youth. He motioned Tafari to sit nearby, where the boy spent the night, a witness to the pain and suffering of his father's passing at dawn on 21 March.[14] After the body had been washed and wrapped in new, white homespun, it was taken to Harer, where, just before dawn the next day, Makonnen's death was announced by cannon and rifle fire, trumpets, and ululations.

The ras's palace quickly filled with townspeople paying their condolences to Tafari, who stood on a dais surrounded by relatives and high officials. Abba Andreas stayed by his side for three hours while mourners filed past, including soldiers who recalled their dead leader by acting out some of his moments of bravery in twirling, leaping dances full of symbolism and emotion. Men of all ranks showed their despair by baring their chests, their sympathy by embracing Tafari, and their homage by kissing his feet and hands. Visibly moved and close to tears, the youth continued to receive mourners until exhaustion forced him to rest.[15]

Perhaps he dreamed about a future in which he had succeeded his father. Doubtless Jarosseau, ever the romantic when considering his godson, already had whispered words of inspiration and ambition to

Tafari. Indeed the boy considered himself a reasonable candidate for the Harer post, and a few days after Makonnen's funeral, he sent Abba Andreas the model of his first seal as governor, with the request that it be sent to France for engraving.[16] Menilek, however, refused to name an inexperienced youth to lead one of Ethiopia's more important provinces. Its governor had to be a diplomat able to deal with the three adjacent European dependencies; an administrator skilled at handling a heterogeneous population; a superior soldier, given the province's many unreconciled peoples; and a shrewd businessman and tax collector. Meanwhile, the emperor was being hectored by Empress Taitou, whose niece was married to Dej. Yilma, Tafari's older half brother. For Menilek, Yilma was the ideal choice: his appointment would quiet his nagging wife, keep Harerge in Makonnen's family, and ensure that the province had an experienced administrator.[17]

Tafari did not learn of the decision until after a magnificent ceremony in Addis Abeba, on the forty-day anniversary (Teskar) of Makonnen's death. The emperor gently asked him to remain in the capital as one of his young gentlemen-in-waiting, then confirmed him as dejazmach, named him titular governor of nearby Selale, and permitted him to continue his education in the newly established palace school.[18] Tafari accepted, ordered his armed escort back to Harer, and wisely permitted the palace priests to rebaptize him, according to Orthodox rite, to allay suspicions that his relations with Catholics, especially with Abba Samuel, had brought him to apostasy.[19] He wanted above all to make a success of his palace stay. Tafari needed the time there to make contacts, especially with those whom he would find at the palace school; to meet national personalities and to impress them; to obtain experience in statecraft, administration, and politics; and to absorb the sophistication of the capital city.

By Ethiopian standards, Addis Abeba has always been a remarkable place. In 1906, as today, it defined progress, innovation, and change for the entire nation. In Menilek's time, the city had a population of about fifty thousand and featured modern telephone and telegraph services; some brick and stone buildings, among them an imposing central post office; at least one paved road and one bridge; and hotels, cafés, and a few electrified buildings, including legations, the villas of leading men, and the imperial palace, which also boasted piped water and flush toilets.[20] There was also a relatively large foreign community led by the emperor's several advisers, the twenty or so diplomats assigned to the royal court, and a like number of rich Asian merchants who controlled the import-export trade.

Their agents included scores of Asians, Greeks, and Armenians, who traveled to southern and eastern Ethiopia to purchase hides, grains, oil, seeds, coffee, and other primary products in international demand. They transacted most of their business in imperial garrison towns, which had quickly become market centers catering to the needs of local people and to an expanding population of soldiers, officials, technicians, craftsmen, and northern settlers, following the central state's increasing economic exploitation of its peripheries. From the provincial centers, petty traders fanned out into the countryside, collecting commodities in exchange for finished goods, unwittingly of course acting as agents of innovation and economic integration. In order to obtain coveted textiles and manufactured products, hitherto subsistence agriculturalists shifted some of their activities to cash crops, especially coffee, and began to become peasants. The central state followed closely behind both regional and local traders, imposing taxes and otherwise forcing the local population further into the market sector, thus continuing the process of economic change.[21]

The small Addis Abeba government was especially attentive to Ethiopia's foreign trade because customs dues paid for the state. Moreover, ministers and monarch enjoyed receiving gifts from businessmen who wanted favors and concessions, and government figures thus participated, often as silent partners, in the commerce going on around them. Finally, as some provincial lords became adept at extorting money from passing traders or themselves became merchant-princes, the palace received increased tributes, which governors presented to Menilek on their periodic visits to pay homage, to receive orders, or to reconfirm imperial trust. During residence in the capital, members of the makwanent (the high ruling class) daily came to the palace to offer their services and advice, to be seen, to gossip, to scheme for advancement for themselves and their protégés, to settle legal cases, and generally to politic.[22] Tafari participated in this welter of activity for eight crucial months, observing much that influenced him subsequently. He learned that it was appropriate for high officials to participate in business or to take gifts from those who sought concessions or cooperation. Tafari would so amplify this tradition that he became wealthier than Menilek had ever been. He also developed the old man's method of rule into a high art.

Menilek kept his authority by acting as Ethiopia's balancer of power, personally giving and taking, approving or rejecting, dismissing and appointing, ruling in favor or judging against, agreeing or not yielding, participating or remaining aloof. Tafari would exploit the same techniques, which he would learn to manipulate perfectly. The system worked well in administering a society that lived according to custom, but it became increasingly dysfunctional as modern institutions developed. Ethiopian traditional government mediated between the ruling class and the masses; modern government regulates institutions, in which groups of people are organized. Haile Sellassie's limited education directed him toward change, but he could not manage the institutions he established to modernize Ethiopia.

Some of Tafari's ideas about innovation probably came from Menilek. The monarch had an unquenchable curiosity about modern technology, gadgetry, and weaponry. He was never embarrassed to ask questions or to try devices presented to him. He was not, however, even semieducated in the Western sense; he neither spoke nor read a European language. Although he understood Ethiopia's geopolitical situation, he had only the vaguest sense of the shape of the modern world; and although he valued contemporary weaponry, he could not appreciate the infrastructure and social organization necessary to produce modern weapons. Menilek was pragmatic, however, about being emperor and, above all, prized ideas that added to his power. He therefore was first attracted to modern communications to facilitate the growth of the central state, not to develop commerce. Tafari similarly regarded roads and airplanes, even if he could couch his appreciation in the language of modernization.

Neither mentor nor novice comprehended the vast social changes sweeping the Western world, nor was either man likely to have questioned the social construction of Ethiopia's political economy. Menilek had fostered, indeed had built, the Ethiopian empire-state with flamboyance and humor. With sincerity and devotion, Tafari accepted the social, economic, and political infrastructure as given, to be exploited after deliberation and calculation. His approach to the empire was emotionally more in keeping with the stance of the Ethiopian ruling class than was the impulsive and creative view of his cousin, Lij Iyasu, the emperor's grandson and heir.

The scion of Ras Mikael of Welo, the crown prince was a physically larger, more open, and more instinctual person than the diffident and subtle son of Ras Makonnen. Yet the lads were often together at court or on the playing fields, where Iyasu was successful in athletics and Tafari proved best in such disciplined sports as horsemanship and shooting. While Tafari devoted himself to the classroom, his cousin was carousing in the capital's bars and brothels. Although the two did not understand each other very well, they managed to get along, and Menilek often paired them for escort duty in his retinue.[23] Tafari's service and good behavior did not, however, win him Harerge after pneumonia killed Dej. Yilma in October 1907.

Tafari's name quickly began circulating as the possible successor, but in April 1908, Menilek posted his confidant, Dej. Balcha, a highly skilled general, to the province.[24] Tafari's youth had worked against him once again, but the emperor made him governor of Darassa, an awrajja (subprovince) in Sidamo vacated by Balcha's move. "Therefore I had to abandon my studies . . . to take care of the business of government."[25] He moved to Darassa with three thousand of his father's soldiers and several of Makonnen's trusted officers, among them Fit. Haile Sellassie Abayneh and his son Imru.[26]

Tafari recalled his governorship as "a time of perfect joy, as I encountered no trouble whatsoever" from either staff or subjects. He was not on the job long enough for problems to develop, since reports of Menilek's worsening illness drove him to the capital in April 1909.[27] The emperor had been visibly ailing from advanced syphilis since 1904, although the disease did not become debilitating until late 1907, when he formed a nine-member cabinet to reduce his workload. A mild stroke in June 1908 impelled the ministers to draft a contingency decree naming a regency council. Although his condition grew worse, Menilek stubbornly clung to power, permitting Empress Taitou to act for him.[28]

Ever ambitious, always meddling, the empress gained a stronger position in January 1909, when Menilek suffered a stroke that finally crippled his reason, if not his body. The old man was lucid often enough to prevent any serious opposition to the empress, who quickly went about the business of acquiring partisans throughout Ethiopia, especially those who would insist that Lij Iyasu accept her authority. She was opposed by Ras Tesemma Nado, the designated regent, by the ministers who sought to place Iyasu on the throne, and by those who disliked her.

Tafari was around the palace, waiting daily on the emperor, when some of the Shewan elite began to plot the empress's retirement. He refused to join the conspiracy, an act of loyalty that quickly became known, convincing Taitou that she had found a potentially important ally. During one of the emperor's lucid moments, she praised Tafari's steadfastness in face of malcontents, who, she declared, wanted Lij Iyasu's immediate accession. Since the young dejazmach had refused to name any conspirators, he further demonstrated his reliability in delicate situations, and he won political capital on both sides of the succession struggle. He was, as he put it, "biding my time . . . and thinking that I could not fail to obtain the governorship [of Harer] whenever it might be God's will to show me favour." [29]

Haile Sellassie invariably described his advancement as "God's will," but he clearly believed that the Lord helped those who helped themselves. He characteristically organized his own success, and more than anything else his cunning and planning accounted for his good luck. By mid-1909, he had made himself politically acceptable to Menilek, Taitou, Lij Iyasu, and even those who opposed the empress. Nobody in Addis Abeba would hinder his appointment to Harer, even if Taitou made it for political reasons. Balcha, of course, howled in outrage, but the empress hid behind Menilek. Even after the emperor was no longer *corpus mentis* following a massive stroke on 28 October 1909, Taitou's enemies had to cooperate with her for a time or risk the total paralysis of government. Consequently, Tafari's appointment went through even as the empress was overthrown on 21 March 1910. [30]

His commission was confirmed by Ras Tesemma, now regent and head of government, but not before he brought Tafari and Iyasu together to negotiate "a covenant . . . to prevent anything from happening that might be an obstacle in his [the regent's] work." Ras Makonnen had endowed his son with the requisite "Solomonic" bloodline; this and the solvent of military power constituted the two criteria for emperorship. Obviously Tesemma sought to ensure that God's will would not move Tafari into competition for the crown.

In a palace chapel, before the highest church and state authorities, Tafari vowed he would not seek "by trickery or rivalry, Ledj Iyasu's throne"; and the heir declared that he would not regard his cousin ipso facto as a competitor and order his "destruction on account of . . . rivalry." Before leaving Addis Abeba, Tafari had reservations about the permanence of the new order and paid his respects to possible reaction: "Although it was a very delicate time for taking leave of Empress Taitou, I felt that my conscience would reproach me if I went without saying goodbye; hence I went to the palace, took my leave, and set out on my journey."[31]

The new governor entered Harer on 12 May 1910, welcomed by an enthusiastic crowd of Ethiopians, Asians, and Europeans; "a living mosaic of nationalities, of colors, of different features, all had become one at this moment through the same expression of joy." Tafari, soon to be eighteen, appeared scrawny but mature, "his youth hidden under a brown beard." Tempered by a smile reminiscent of Ras Makonnen, his narrow face radiated a combination of intelligence, precocity, elation, and melancholy—the last, according to Jarosseau, a reflection of the early loss of both parents. After formal greetings from leading dignitaries, Tafari visited Harer's main church, to offer a heartfelt prayer of thanksgiving. The night was given over to feasting, but early the next morning, Tafari began the serious business of shaping his administration.[32]

His immediate goal was to soften the harsh exploitation of the previous two, largely militaristic, regimes by restoring Ras Makonnen's more moderate taxes, which had sustained a flourishing economy. Tafari accordingly searched for "a method by which it was possible to govern by reconciling peasants and soldiers and to please them as in my father's time." He began by limiting the obligations of the peasantry to their immediate overlords, whose authority was also reduced. Then he undertook a complete survey of Harerge's resources in order to gather the data necessary for tax reform.[33]

Tafari's men found that only seventy thousand subjects in the province were able to pay the currently high taxes and still have enough for their families. After halving the obligations, the dejazmach established a semiautonomous court system to ensure equity and divided his administration into twelve subgovernates, whose leaders were responsible for seeing that soldiers received their rations and subjects due process. Since the military and traditional officialdom received fewer payments in kind, they were "not at all pleased," in sharp contrast to the peasants, who, "since the yoke of government and taxes were lightened for them, . . . all set out to do their work with a calm heart."[34] As long as Ethiopia remained a traditional state, Tafari's enactments were progressive; over the longer run, however, as Ethiopia became part of the world economy, positive change could occur only through a transformation of the system of production. Haile Sellassie could not bring himself to interfere with the political economy bequeathed to him by Menilek and Makonnen, especially since it permitted the development of a merchant and agricultural capitalism that sustained urbanization and the development of centralized authority.[35] Tafari's reorganization of Harerge's administration reflected the long-term economic trend that he would exploit to reform provincial and central government and to build Addis Abeba.

Meanwhile, he worked hard to satisfy the regency regime that he was no threat to Lij Iyasu. In 1911, he married Woizero (lady) Menen, Ras Mikael's granddaughter and therefore the crown prince's niece. Obviously such a liaison was politically expedient, although it should be remarked that Menen was an attractive woman of twenty-two, in whom Tafari found only "goodness . . . no evil or malice." The union was dignified through the sacrament of marriage in a church ceremony, rendering divorce difficult if not impossible. The nuptials took place on 3 August 1911, followed by a splendid feast at Tafari's palace. The couple was blissful during the next year, though events in Addis Abeba were worrisome.[36]

On 10 April 1911, Ras Tesemma died after a series of strokes. When the heir refused to accept the authority of a new regent, the ministers constituted themselves as a regency council with Lij Iyasu as chairman, thus releasing the sixteen-year-old from personal supervision. From the beginning of his de facto reign, the prince revealed himself as undoubtedly bright, even visionary, but politically unrealistic. His dream of a ruling elite in which religious and ethnic affiliation did not matter contradicted the social situation in the empire. He was also undisciplined and found administration so boring that he took long holidays in the country and surrounded himself with amusing but sycophantic courtiers, opportunistic to a man. He also dedicated considerable time to women, whom he pursued with the energy he should have devoted to affairs of state. Bereft of its head, the central administration deteriorated during the years 1911–1913, while provincial governments remained as strong as their leaders, in some cases powerful enough to ignore Addis Abeba's orders and evade taxes.[37]

Tafari did not join in humiliating Iyasu's government. He remitted his taxes on time and periodically went to the capital to confirm his fidelity.[38] He believed, however, that his cousin's lackadaisical attitude was responsible for the increasing anarchy, corruption, and violence. Iyasu's ideas about ethnic and religious conciliation seemed to Tafari a dangerous dalliance with Islam. The heir stubbornly refused to consider that his actions were self-defeating because they caused Christian alienation.[39] His activities did not become a scandal until the outbreak of World War I, when he sought to benefit from the strife and to promote his internal policies.

In August 1914, Addis Abeba had troops near the Eritrean border to keep order in Tigray, where there had been a rebellion. Iyasu hoped that Rome would enter the war on the side of the Central Powers, whereupon his forces would invade the colony, eject the Italians, and restore Ethiopia's coastline. When the Italian government shrewdly opted for the Allies, the prince withdrew his army but continued to hope that he could profit from the war. He and some of his advisers were impressed with the early successes of Austria-Hungary, Germany, and Turkey. Istanbul directed a virulent propaganda war against the Allies among their subjects in the Horn of Africa, and Iyasu saw an opportunity to unite Somalis and Ethiopians to eject the hated colonizers. The prince consequently saw his policy of equality between Muslim and Christian as sweet reason itself, even as its implementation continued to alienate the church and worry Tafari, in whose province Iyasu decided to demonstrate the wisdom of his idea.[40]

Iyasu made long visits to Harer, where he spent much time in the central mosque and with Muslim subjects. He inaugurated a program of taxing the Christian gentry for the benefit of the Muslim masses. He appointed a Muslim foreigner as nagadras (director of customs and markets) in Harer and Dire Dawa, robbing Tafari of a lucrative source of income, hardly the act of a friend.[41] Iyasu explained that he sought to reduce the tyranny under which Muslims lived and to lessen the exploitation they suffered. He wanted to transform himself into a more national and neutral figure, not inflexibly identified with the Christian ruling caste. He wanted to reconcile Ethiopia's Muslims to their Christian compatriots, thereby reducing the empire-state's chronic unrest, benefiting the economy, and permitting a program of modernization.[42] He sought to release the energies and creativity of his empire's Muslim population, which, "up to now, has been abandoned and persecuted."[43] He offered them brotherhood: "though we differ in religion and tribe, I would wish all of us to be united through a nationalist sentiment . . . cooperation with the rest of your Ethiopian brothers will keep your country united and her frontiers secure."[44] His task was nation building, not imperial exploitation. His message of brotherhood and social equality threatened those who ran the empire-state.

Harer, Iyasu explained to Jarosseau, was the logical place to begin his new deal: he had less to fear here from the clergy or the Shewan aristocracy, and once his program showed the anticipated excellent results, he would then "little by little . . . impose the same regime on the entire empire."[45] Although he did not say so, the prince had decided that members of the Amhara cadre were expendable in the face of national needs as he defined them. Tafari understood that he was the first sacrifice, but he could do little to counter, since Iyasu and his father, Ras Mikael, had changed Ethiopia's political landscape.

Most of the ministers, with the exception of Fit. Habte Giorgis, the minister of war, owed their jobs to the prince. By 1915, at least two-thirds of Ethiopia was governed by Iyasu's appointees, and the trend was to eliminate or demote Menilek's administrators. A good many disappointed and unhappy aristocrats were living out their frustrations and rancor in Addis Abeba; given the proper leadership and the right opportunity, they were available as potential rebels.[46] Yet Iyasu thought little about the capital and its denizens. Between June 1915 and April 1916, while the prince was touring and being lionized in predominately Muslim eastern Ethiopia, he decided to move ahead with his policy of national reconciliation. Although we do not know why he so concluded, the first indication of a new direction for Ethiopia was the dispatch from Harer, during October 1915, of an eight-camel caravan of ammunition to Seyyid Muhammed Abdullah, the Somali leader, who had mobilized his people against the British and the Italians by "using Islam as the cementing force." [47] A deeply disturbed Tafari reported the news to Addis Abeba and the foreign missions.

Events recently had gone against the edgy dejazmach. On 7 June 1915, he and nine of his retinue had gone boating on Lake Haramaya, about twenty kilometers northwest of Harer. On return from the far shore, near the center of the lake, the old boat began to leak. Bailing failed, and the passengers were soon awash. "As the lake was wide and it was impossible to cross it by swimming," seven drowned. Among them was the heroic Abba Samuel, who exhausted himself keeping his protégé's head above water until help arrived. Everyone's eyes were on Tafari, who was coughing up water: "our soul had barely been prevented from getting separated from our body . . . [and] we were unable to recognize anyone or to speak." [48] In the confusion, Samuel slipped unnoticed to his death. Possibly embarrassed, Haile Sellassie did not acknowledge his mentor's sacrifice in his autobiography, testifying instead that someone swam from the shore to his rescue. This treatment is odd, as the autobiography was written only two decades after the event, and Samuel had been Tafari's teacher, companion, councilor, adviser, and secretary. Perhaps the spare treatment stems from Haile Sellassie's conscious effort to retain a protective wrap over his private life and emotions.

In Harer, meanwhile, Iyasu had replaced the Amhara police with Arabs, Somalis, and Oromos, which deeply distressed the province's Christian population. [49] Then, on 13 August 1916, as part of his program of Islamizing the provincial government, the prince reassigned Tafari, in Addis Abeba since May, to Kefa. [50] As the first of his kind to be affected by Iyasu's revolution, the dejazmach inevitably would become intimately involved with any movement to dethrone the prince. [51] Haile Sellassie wanted history to record that he had little to do with the plot, even if he accepted what destiny and "the leaders of Ethiopia" demanded, a pose that accorded well with the monarch's self-characterization as a tool of fate or God. Royal wishes aside, it is hard to believe that Tafari had little to do with the planning of the coup. Iyasu thought him involved when his agents reported the scheme in early September 1916, and he ordered his cousin to Kefa immediately while banishing others from the capital. Tafari ignored the command, remaining in the center of play, anticipating that the prince would make a mistake that would spark a coup.[52] Meanwhile, he worried about the safety of his son and heir, Asfa Wossen, born on 27 July in Harer, now a Muslim redoubt.[53]

Iyasu had arrived in the city on 7 September, foolishly remaining there rather than traveling to Addis Abeba to ensure that the plotters retired to the provinces. In Harer, the prince was acclaimed by the province's Muslims while Tafari's disgruntled troops and other settlers watched with barely disguised distaste. There was similar alienation in Addis Abeba, where the conspiracy went forward, fueled, as Tafari had foreseen, by Iyasu's continuous gaffes. Reports circulated that the heir was constructing a regional Muslim front, that he was arming non-Christians, and that he had worshiped in mosques. Iyasu was quoted as saying that the sultan of Turkey had granted him sovereignty over the coastal strip from Berbera in British Somaliland to Mitsiwa (Massawa) in Italian Eritrea, and that he hoped shortly to occupy these territories. If the Europeans resisted, he boasted, they would be swept into the sea, a threat that quickly found its way to London, Paris, and Rome. The reports confirmed earlier Allied fears that Iyasu had compromised the neutrality of Ethiopia, which now became a threat to their war in the Middle East against Turkey and Germany.[54]

On 12 September, the Allies sent a note to the Foreign Ministry, complaining about Iyasu's belligerency. They demanded an immediate explanation and declared an arms embargo against Ethiopia.[55] Their strong denunciation of the prince raised less anxiety in Addis Abeba than the disturbing intelligence that he had armed a substantial Somali army, which, on parade in Dire Dawa, presented an Ethiopian flag bearing the Red Crescent and the Muslim Creed. In Addis Abeba, anti-Iyasu propaganda stressed that his continued leadership would plunge Ethiopia into war with the Allies and also lead to civil strife fueled by class, ethnic, and religious struggles.[56] The heir's apostasy seemed confirmed when he failed to return to the capital in late September to prepare for the Feast of the Holy Cross, a celebration that also marked the end of the long rainy season. In Harer, on 25

September, Jarosseau recorded a Latin testament in his diary that
Iyasu had become a Muslim. For the priest, the evidence was convincing: the prince had four wives or concubines, including several
Muslims; he prayed in the Muslim fashion; and he sent gifts to
mosques and shrines devoted to Muslim saints.[57] The priest's appraisal conformed exactly to the thoughts expressed at a meeting of
aristocrats in Addis Abeba on 27 September 1916.

In the precinct used by the monarch as a court of last resort,
Ethiopia's leading politicians, clergy, and citizens had gathered to
discuss the country's future. There is no direct evidence linking
Tafari's conduct to the group's actions, but his leading role cannot be
doubted, because there is no other way to explain the outcome. He
was characteristically working in the shadows, carefully orchestrat-
ing a favorable result. He is said to have prepared the charges accus-
ing Lij Iyasu of apostasy and of conspiring "to exterminate us by
mutual fighting . . . therefore we shall henceforth not submit to
him; we shall not place a Muslim king on the throne of a Christian
king." The indictment for excommunication was so obviously based
on hearsay and malice that Abuna Mattewos requested more precise
information, including Iyasu's responses to the damning allegations.[58]

Nagadras Yigazu yelled out, "We do not ask you for a judgment;
we tell you what it is, and that is sufficient!" Etchege Wolde Giorgis,
the church's executive officer — and Ethiopian, unlike the Egyptian
Mattewos — raged:

Iyasu is a Muslim, you know it, he is no longer a Christian king. You are not
ignorant of the fact that he has married many Muslims, which is not Christian
usage.

Mattewos retorted, "I know only one thing, it is that he has married a
daughter of Abba Jifar [the Muslim ruler of Jima]," and repeated his
call for better evidence. When the crowd hooted down his plea for
reason, he angrily shouted:

If that is the way it is, I am going to declare a general excommunication; I
shall simultaneously excommunicate Sost Lidots [a home-grown group of
heretics who believed in three separate births for Christ], the Catholics, the
Protestants, and the Muslims and declare that I damn all those who might
have betrayed their faith.

The frustrated etchege, obviously party to the conspiracy, erupted:

Iyasu is a Muslim, a true Muslim, he does not deserve to be [considered] a Christian king. He is an enemy of the Christians, he is in the process of betraying our government. I therefore excommunicate as unbelievers Iyasu and all his followers and all those who obey him.

The etchege, of course, did not have the canonical authority to make the declaration, but his words brought a round of loud applause, stilled suddenly when a voice called out, "Why should we do this?," causing a commotion that ended the meeting. As the crowd filed out, some of Iyasu's supporters were molested, but the beating of the huge negarit (war drum) restored order.[59] Creating stability was the work of the main figures who remained behind in the small audience room; Tafari must have been present at this meeting, but he never admitted his participation, preferring instead to portray himself as the choice of the people, not as a politician conniving for office. He would also have liked history to record that the accession of Menilek's daughter as Empress Zawditu I (r. 1916–1930) and his proclamation as "Crown Prince, with the rank of Ras, and Regent of Ethiopia" came during the mass meeting. In fact, the succession was arranged at the smaller gathering, and it was not an easy matter to decide. Tafari was named only because the leadership believed that Zawditu, who would establish policy, needed a weak executive officer, whose authority would also be limited by the Council of Ministers.[60]

In Harer, meanwhile, the coup had gone awry. The order to arrest Iyasu had been delivered by mistake to one of his partisans instead of to Fit. Gabre, one of Tafari's lieutenants. The prince immediately cut communications with the capital, promoted his officers one rank, announced that he would restore land expropriated from the settlers, and called in a dozen priests before whom he confirmed his Christian faith. He then ordered the arrests of those suspected of favoring the new regime (including Geraz. Imru, who safeguarded Tafari's family and interests) and imposed what Jarosseau termed a "system of terrorism" to guarantee the fidelity of his subjects. On 1 October, the missionary was called to Iyasu's palace, guarded closely by Muslims "with very sinister faces under rolls of thick turbans." Abba Andreas sympathetically advised the prince to take courage, to which Iyasu replied that he would never abandon his throne but "he truly repented his errors and had sincerely returned to *the public practise* of Christianity [italics mine]." He attributed his present problems to Tafari, about whom he was paranoid.[61]

He told the priest that he had ordered the newly promoted Dej. Gabre and five thousand troops to march northwestward toward Chercher to counter a government force under Dej. Balcha and had ordered another detachment to Dire Dawa to secure the railway. Jarosseau observed that many of the recently armed Somalis and Afar had fled for security into the adjoining deserts and noted that Iyasu's remaining few hundred bodyguards were demoralized and openly pessimistic. They lost all hope on 8 October, when Harer learned that Dej. Gabre had placed his army under Balcha's command and that the combined force would shortly reach the city's gates. Iyasu and his men quickly retired eastward toward Jijiga, the Muslim police disappeared from Harer's streets, and about two thousand veterans of Tafari's army took over. They immediately began killing Muslims, but the real slaughter began on 9 October, when Balcha's army arrived and began looting the Muslim quarters. The several hundred dead symbolized the failure of Iyasu's reverie of religious and ethnic reconciliation.[62]

Zawditu was now empress; she had a reputation for being stubborn, deeply religious, and conservative. She had arrived in Addis Abeba on 30 September to find Ras Tafari hard at work trying to counter any possible threat from Negus (his rank since 1914) Mikael in Welo. Mikael conceded that his son had erred in carrying out his policies but reasoned that dethronement was an unnecessarily harsh punishment. But not even the prince's appointees agreed with Mikael. By the time Zawditu was formally vested with sovereignty on 2 October 1916, the south and the west had responded loyally to the change, and rases Hailu of Gojam and Wolde Giorgis of Begemdir, the realm's two most powerful provincial rulers, had become, according to Tafari, the new regime's "warmest partisans (they are Mikael's enemies)."[63]

In Welo, the king was slow to respond as he assessed the impact of Iyasu's failure to hold eastern Ethiopia and thereby tie down a considerable number of government troops. Had Mikael moved immediately against Addis Abeba, he would have found it virtually defenseless. On 3 October, only 16,000 men were ready to defend the city against Welo's army of about 100,000 troops, thirteen machine guns, and eleven field pieces. Two weeks later, the situation had changed considerably: about 50,000 men stood by the new regime, of which 35,000, under the command of Fit. Habte Giorgis, were in place along Shewa's northern frontier. By the time Tafari left for the front on 19 October, another 36,000 men had arrived from the south, and more were expected daily.[64] There would be intense fighting before the ras would return in victory to Zawditu's capital.

CHAPTER TWO

Internal Security,
1916-1918

Cast in the role of a leader, Tafari had to command, not an easy chore for a young man of twenty-four who had never directed an army on a major campaign. On 16 October, the ras discussed tactics with the French minister, who advised a war of maneuver and retreat until the government marshaled forces equal to Negus Mikael's. Tafari responded brightly, "That is exactly my idea, and Fit. Habte Giorgis has given appropriate orders." The ras understood the need to assert final authority, commenting that he had "to go to the front, to ensure discipline."[1] He was on the phone daily with Habte Giorgis, who warned that he did not have enough men, supplies, weapons, or munitions to take the full weight of Mikael's army, considered one of the best in Ethiopia. His forebodings became real on 18 October 1916, when Ras Lul Seged's eleven-thousand-man advance force was annihilated in Menz by thirty thousand Welo soldiers, who also captured several thousand modern rifles, five or six cannon, and ten machine guns. When Fit. Habte Giorgis learned of the disaster, he put his men on alert and telephoned Tafari for reinforcements.

Meanwhile, most of Mikael's army moved slowly south, looting the countryside but also allowing the government more time to strengthen its defenses. Early on the morning of 20 October, Habte Giorgis telegraphed Tafari, now en route with a small unit, that sufficient reinforcements had arrived to try a surprise attack. The regent instead ordered "a feint to win time" for him to arrive and take his place on the battlefield. The fitawrari therefore held back and the sluggish Welo army finally was sighted by government outposts shortly after noon on 21 October, a little less than three hours before the ras finally appeared. Nothing happened until the early morning of 22 October, when Mikael sent out patrols to probe the government's defensive lines. By then the government's forces by far outnumbered the enemy, thanks to the enthusiastic response of the men who ruled the conquered southern and western provinces.

Back in Addis Abeba, the empress was out of touch and understandably nervous. Tafari bolstered her spirits by explaining that the government's preponderance in numbers meant victory. Yet he and Habte Giorgis had decided not to attack Mikael, whose forces were in commanding and fortified positions, but to await his decision when his men became desperate for supplies. The relocation of the government's army during the next two days elicited a countermaneuver from Mikael, so that by 26 October, the two camps "spent the night opposite each other at a plain in the Tarra district called Sagale." At 1:00 A.M., 27 October, the negus began to position his army, with himself in the center, "and when the morning dawned, he began opening fire and launched a surprise attack against our gunners who had been spending the night on guard duty."

Tafari took his place at the rear, from where he reported, "The noise of the battle is immense." The ras's position reveals no commanding heights, but he certainly played an honorable part in the battle, staying with the reserves until noon, when it became evident that the government would win. By the time he joined the battle, Mikael's artillery was out of action, his attempt to turn the government's left flank had failed, and he had been forced into a cul-de-sac and surrounded. The negus was still in the center of action atop a small hill called Segele when his machine guns ran out of ammunition. He thereupon sent Abuna Petros, the bishop of Welo, to seek terms, but it was too late to forestall the final government attack—in which Tafari and his Shewans joined — which carried the day. At 3:25 P.M., one of Tafari's officers screamed into the telephone to Addis Abeba: "Hallelujah, hallelujah!! We have won. The negus is our prisoner with his abun; the enemy army is in flight. Ras Tafari and Fitawrari Habte Giorgis are safe and sound. The dead are very numerous on both sides," about three thousand government troops and seven thousand Welo. So complete was the victory that Ras Demissie was able to capture Mikael's camp almost intact, including tons of ammunition and arms stamped with Lij Iyasu's seal.

The materiel had perhaps been awaiting use by the prince and an army that might have given the victory to Mikael. The son, however, had only reached Ankober on the morning of 27 October, where he learned about his father's defeat at Segele. He immediately led his six thousand men toward the lowlands and the relative safety of the desert, from where he could follow the caravan tracks to Dese. Taking a different road to Welo were tens of thousands of Mikael's soldiers, who, thanks to a remarkable act of clemency by Tafari — "we are all Ethiopians" — were permitted to return home after pledging homage to the Addis Abeba government. They lost their weapons, animals, and valuables, but with manhood and life intact, the veterans trudged off, probably worrying about the dangers of the trip home through regions they had looted.[2]

Tafari, meanwhile, was celebrating: on 3 November, he entered Addis Abeba at the head of a victorious army. At the Imperial Parade Grounds (Jan Hoy Meda), fifty thousand participants cheered as twenty-five thousand soldiers individually screamed out their fealty to Zawditu as their units passed the outsized royal tent. Within, surrounded by European diplomats and Ethiopian dignitaries, the empress sat on a portable throne and heard the ovations for the major figures as they dismounted their magnificently decorated mules to bow low in respect for the crown. When the regent appeared, gorgeous in full regalia, he was greeted by great applause and salvos of "Long Live Tafari!" After he made formal obeisance, he entered the tent, standing on Zawditu's left to witness the abject apology that each of the important prisoners prostrated himself to make as he came on foot before the reviewing tent.

The silver-haired, silver-manacled Negus Mikael was permitted to approach Zawditu to make a graceful yet proud bow in personal supplication, after which he was taken to the palace to await the decision about where he was to be imprisoned. Bishop Petros also approached the royal enclosure standing, to make his amends and then to join the imperial party to celebrate a mass of thanksgiving at St. George's Cathedral and later to attend a feast of jubilation.[3] Haile Sellassie apparently forgot most of the details and later characterized this as the day when the empress "and the people of the capital being assembled in full, received us with a great parade, with ululating and joy."[4] The singularity of the remark reveals that Tafari's mind, as always, was on himself and on the personal significance of what was, after all, an event of historic importance for Ethiopia.

At the same moment, Lij Iyasu was still at large, a dangerous threat to the new government and a class traitor. His freedom meant that he continued to broadcast his subversive view of equality of opportunity for all Ethiopians, regardless of race, religion, caste, and way of life. The makwanent had considered this idea so poisonous that, to a man, they had turned against Menilek's heir. The governors of the southern, conquered provinces were especially virulent toward Iyasu, as their economic interests required a servile population. In effect, Tafari acted on their behalf to benefit himself, but probably he did not represent reaction as much as he stood for political orthodoxy. Whatever change he directed or presided over was conditioned by the conventional political wisdom of his own class. In terms of the sweeping economic changes stimulated by the world economy, Tafari and his class would mediate commercial growth, but they would remain conservative and oppressive, qualities that over time would develop into reaction.

Iyasu, in the interim, had crossed the Afar Desert to arrive at Dese on 8 November. He believed himself to be the innocent "victim of intrigues by a few people," the object of vicious Shewan "calumnies." He continued to act as the head of state, futilely making appointments and vowing to one and all that he would never renounce his throne.[5] He sought support among Ethiopia's northern governors, but they merely toyed with him, especially Ras Wolde Giorgis of Begemdir, Menilek's relative and crony. The ras exploited Addis Abeba's fears about Iyasu in exchange for promised new territories and Mikael's now vacant title of king of the north. Satisfied, Wolde Giorgis mobilized his forces and marched south to Dese, while Ras Demissie moved northward to catch the reorganized Welo army in a pincers movement.[6] Iyasu became desperate and turned to Rome for aid, offering unspecified concessions in Tigray.[7] The Italians wisely stayed out, and the pretender fled Dese shortly before one of Wolde Giorgis's lieutenants peacefully entered the town on 10 December, at noon. Iyasu and his father's leading general, Ras Imer, moved southwestward with a small force, only to be blocked, about 26 December, by Ras Demissie's army. Iyasu and a small escort fled to Amba Mekdela, where, on 28 December, from the heights, they watched the defeat of their hapless compatriots.[8]

Iyasu could not even slow down the consolidation of the new government, which celebrated Zawditu's coronation on 11 February 1917. For the first time in Ethiopian history, at Tafari's invitation, European states sent official representatives, albeit the governors of the adjacent colonies, to witness a ceremony that stressed the continuities of an ancient tradition. The usual glittering crowd of nobility gathered in Addis Abeba, and the capital's streets bustled with crowds from all over the empire, gawking at the wide streets, the few triumphal arches, the flags and banners, and the rare stone structures, as if the city were modernity itself. Probably, however, the pageantry was more alluring: about one hundred thousand soldiers from all parts of the empire lined the route that the empress would take from the palace to St. George's Cathedral. The monarch had spent the entire night of 10–11 February in vigil, and at dawn the long ceremony began, "a gorgeous . . . spectacle" of colorfully garbed clerics, chanting and music, and movements heavy with symbolism. In her coronation address, the sovereign — with Tafari immediately behind her right shoulder — referred to the good, old days of her father's time, which she hoped to recreate. She pledged to safeguard her people "without being unjust and without making the poor suffer, respecting the great as my fathers and the small as my brothers." She advised those who suffered injustice to "make it known to my Representative, the heir to the throne Ras Tafari, and I shall set them to right."[9]

The empress's choice of words revealed her intention of taking an active role in government. Yet she was no Hatshepsut and could not even bring herself to emulate Dowager Empress Taitou or her sister, Woizero Yishimabet, married to Ras Wolde Giorgis, both of whom openly sought, grasped, and used political and even military power. She was not at ease with men, and at the feasts following her coronation, Zawditu sat apart with her ladies in waiting, while Tafari presided over the major part of the proceedings with the men. The ras was always the more visible of the ruling duo, especially to Europeans, with whom he could converse without interpreters and formalities. Yet it would be a mistake to consider the empress a strictly honorary ruler. Even had she wanted to opt out of the business of state, her position at the apex of the hierarchical Ethiopian state required arbitrating the claims of competing factions. Zawditu often had the last word, a skill that greatly irritated Tafari but which he respected and tried to manipulate. Though she might be guided to favorable decisions, she was the sovereign, a fact well demonstrated on 18 February when she crowned Wolde Giorgis negus of the north. Significantly, after Abuna Mattewos anointed the crown, he handed it to Zawditu, who placed the symbol of honor on the old man's head. Tafari could not compete with the mystical authority that had come to Zawditu through her coronation, or with the charisma that lingered from her father.[10]

Haile Sellassie's autobiography provides nothing beyond the barest and most confused outline of events from the coup through the coronation. He apparently wanted to hide the weakness of his position, which he lamented every time a European diplomat complained about a border incident or a misadventure involving a foreign national. He sought constantly to obtain modern weapons for his personal forces or favors from foreigners to use in some internal maneuver. He needed leverage to withstand the combined weight of the empress, the minister of war, and the important provincial governors. Tafari had to consult so widely that only the weakest and vaguest policies became law, and he worked from dawn to dusk on the pettiest details of government. Unable to take the time to relax with family and friends, he grew so exhausted that he occasionally suffered depression and melancholia.

His instinct for reform was so thwarted by the political system he inherited that during the times of greatest stress, he threatened to retire to Harerge or speculated aloud and misleadingly about giving the country over to some form of colonial administration. He even considered hiring European advisers and officers as cat's-paws to shock the opponents of change and modernization into confused inaction. This idea, however, was a dream that had to await the weakening of conservative opposition and the development of a progressive coalition. European observers erroneously analyzed continuation of the status quo as a sign of Tafari's irresolution or weakness of character, and not as a temporary situation which could be manipulated and overcome slowly by a wily politician. In fact so wily was Tafari that none remarked on his wiliness.[11] It was a quality that became apparent in retrospect, though there were early signs that he was quietly building a political apparatus favorable to reform.

In 1916–1917, Tafari made a few appointments demonstrating his ability to take the long view. He foresaw the increasing importance of Addis Abeba as the commercial and political center of Ethiopia and began infiltrating his supporters into the city government. Herui Wolde Sellassie (later foreign minister) was appointed the director of the municipality, Tekle Wolde Hawariat (later dejazmach) became the capital's chief clerk with authority over taxation and administration, and Kassa Hailu was named ras and governor of Shewa. The first two men were well educated, progressive, reform-minded, and devoted to Tafari; the conservative Kassa understood the need for administrative and economic change to protect Ethiopia from imperialism, and in this regard he was open to innovation. Other appointees strongly supported Zawditu, but they were assigned to the economically weak northern regions, except for Dej. Balcha, who returned to Sidamo, and Dej. Imru, who took over Harerge. Except for Ras Gugsa of Begemdir and Simen, the empress's exiled husband, who was still in detention, no one was hostile to Tafari, and the new foreign minister, Dej. Mulugeta, cared so little about international relations and work that the heir apparent could be his own foreign minister.[12] So from the very beginning, Tafari outlined the nature of his rule: he would concentrate on Addis Abeba, Shewa, and foreign affairs, around which he would construct a centralized state.

He left the pursuit of Lij Iyasu to others, perhaps an error, because the pretender easily slipped back and forth through the siege lines at Mekdela, won a few victories, and stirred up trouble in the north.[13] In Addis Abeba, Tafari was trying to negotiate Ethiopia's entry into the war against the Central Powers in return for modern weapons and a role in the peace conference. The Allies refused, reasoning that Zawditu's government was too weak to provide effective assistance against the Turks in Arabia. The British in particular feared that an infusion of new rifles would result in the sale of old, surplus weapons to adjacent colonies. The Italians quickly agreed, happy to assist in any weakening of the central Ethiopian government. Rome had been unpleasantly surprised by the heavily armed troops Iyasu had sent close to the Eritrean frontier in 1914 and had subsequently adopted a policy generally designed to subvert Ethiopia's military capacity. Moreover, the Italians clung to the concept of an Italian East Africa, with Ethiopia at the center, flanked by Eritrea and Somalia; indeed, Rome hoped to obtain a protectorate over Ethiopia as part of its postwar settlement and therefore could not admit that Addis Abeba had any role to play in the peace process. The French, of course, were willing to supply weapons for the sake of Djibouti's economic health, but only if Rome and London approved. In the end, Tafari's gambit failed: he obtained no weapons, and he could not even cajole the Allies into donating the use of a few planes and pilots to dislodge his adversary from Mekdela.[14]

No matter. From the heights, Iyasu watched the buildup of government troops and decided to escape on 18 July while the lines and discipline remained loose; he reportedly bought his way out. To add insult to his evasion, when he reached Weldiya he amused himself by placing a call to Addis Abeba, "notably to the Italian legation to announce that he was well and that he had complete confidence in his ultimate success." His small contingents of troops easily outmaneuvered the larger government force, which was encumbered by baggage and animals and could not easily move through the muddy terrain and swollen streams of the rainy season.[15] Iyasu still enjoyed the allegiance of the Welo peasantry, who ambushed government troops, refused to pay taxes, and, on 3 August, attacked Dese, Habte Giorgis's headquarters, only to be driven off after three hours of heavy fighting.[16] It was a Pyrrhic victory for the fitawrari, as the countryside remained under insurgent control, and government troops could no longer forage, forcing Habte Giorgis and his men to leave the town in search of safety and succor. The evacuation had an unsettling effect on Addis Abeba: the pretender's numerous supporters took heart, the most incredible rumors circulated, and during the nights in late August there was looting and shooting.[17]

Government propaganda hastily claimed that Habte Giorgis's retreat from Dese was part of its strategy. Iyasu, however, saw the withdrawal as an opportunity to inflict a humiliating defeat on the government at the moment of its army's greatest weakness, and he ordered an assault along the enemy's line of march. Forewarned by spies in the pretender's army, the defenders prepared a trap; when the Welo struck on 27 August, Habte Giorgis's men pretended to flee in panic, leading their adversaries toward fortified positions from which government soldiers enfiladed Iyasu's troops with machine guns and rifles. The Welo stood and fell, and survivors broke and fled into a nearby swamp, some to escape, others to be shot down by their opponents in pursuit. The government suffered only one hundred dead and about a thousand other casualties, whereas seven hundred Welo died, and thousands were wounded. Many of Iyasu's generals were captured, among them Ras Imer, and many high-ranking officers had fallen.

From the rear, the pretender saw the disaster unfold and, with a few hundred carefully chosen men, again made for the desert. Only a small government force pursued while most of Habte Giorgis's men celebrated their victory by viciously pillaging Welo. The "pacification" was so complete that Iyasu would never again be able to use his home province as a springboard to power, and most observers believed "it . . . impossible that he can recover from the effects of this defeat."[18] Although the prince remained at large another few years, the Ethiopian civil war was over, and it was time for Tafari to assess his position and to plot a strategy.

One fact was clear: the south under its largely Shewan leadership stood fully behind the Zawditu government. As long as Addis Abeba did not threaten the south's political order, there would be nothing to worry about in that direction. Of course, two problems there, slavery and the slave trade, had to be handled gingerly. Ethiopia's international standing required the eradication of slavery, but the time-consuming process needed a strong national government. Strength would also be necessary to break the arms embargo the Europeans imposed on Ethiopia, illegal though it may have been according to the Brussels Act to which Addis Abeba was a signatory. The ban undermined Addis Abeba's sovereignty and independence and made a Roman military adventure more possible, and it was Ethiopian dogma that Italy continued to dream of transforming the Solomonic Empire into a dependency, no matter how vociferous its claims to the contrary.

The danger from Eritrea necessitated a northern unity difficult to forge because of a longstanding struggle for power in Tigray among various descendants of Emperor Yohannes IV (r. 1872–1889). Then, there was the problem of Zawditu's husband, Ras Gugsa Wolie, who would one day be freed to resume his role in Lasta. His ambition of becoming the power behind his wife's throne would be fueled by his strong antagonism to Tafari as his jailer. Ras Hailu of Gojam, however, had no resentments toward the heir apparent; he merely wanted to retain his autonomy and his wealth.

For the time being, Tafari was too weak to move in the north: he was still bound by the Council of Ministers, Zawditu, and Habte Giorgis, one or all of whom could be manipulated to work against him by politicians with national aspirations or by conniving foreigners. To counter the potential threats, Tafari needed to win supporters among the old makwanent, move his own men into strategic positions (a procedure already under way), and enrich himself. Wealth was needed not only to maintain the traditional largess associated with Ethiopian political power but also to modernize both Addis Abeba and the central government as weapons against his internal foes and Ethiopia's external enemies. Tafari's situation was altogether daunting, and his piecemeal approach to problems made him appear weak and vacillating to Ethiopians and especially to the European diplomats. They seemed to delight in forecasting his failure and Ethiopia's ultimate demise as an independent state. The Italians were especially good at this type of prophecy.

In March 1917, Count (Giuseppe di Felizzano) Colli, the longtime Italian minister in Addis Abeba, wrote that although no one doubted Tafari's good intentions, he lacked "the ability and energy necessary to bring the country out of the state of anarchy into which it has fallen." Unable to discern any unity of purpose between empress and heir, Colli concluded that Tafari lacked the authority "to oppose . . . intrigues and the subtle obstacles which the ministers and chiefs put before him." [19] Sir Geoffrey Archer, the commissioner of the British Somaliland Protectorate, succumbing to the evidence seen with his own eyes, deduced that Tafari had neither the physique nor the strength necessary to hold Ethiopia together, and he advised London to prepare immediately for the destruction of the Solomonic state.[20] The French minister, Maurice de Coppet — a master at criticism — believed Tafari so venal and corrupt as to be unable to direct Ethiopia along the righteous paths of reform and fiscal probity. The ras was "grasping," a man who never failed "to profit from any occasion to acquire, whether at the expense of the people's interest or the Treasury, a personal fortune, already considerable." [21]

Tafari's growing personal wealth came at the expense of the greedy Council of Ministers, which sought to cut the youngster down to size. Its members took every opportunity to remind Tafari that he was only heir apparent to the throne and not the regent of Ethiopia; that Zawditu set policy; that he was merely the state's executive officer; and that he should not overstep the bounds of propriety by robbing the empress of ultimate authority.[22] The church believed that Tafari had bent the boundaries of faith by consorting with Roman Catholicism. Other Ethiopians disliked his reformist views of government and administration and the large number of foreign acquaintances Tafari seemed to enjoy. The ras, of course, could relax in their politically anodyne company, and he could quietly associate himself with discreet Europeans and Asians who sought government concessions.[23] The baksheesh he acquired secretly could be used to gain support.[24]

Tafari redistributed much of his wealth to the masses and soldiery of Addis Abeba: "what he takes greedily with one hand he gives out generously with the other . . . and . . . he is thus gaining popularity with the lower classes." [25] He bought an obedient mob whose strength he could manipulate during crises. Tafari made himself a man of the people by cleverly becoming the leader of the urban masses, themselves a new phenomenon in Ethiopian politics.[26] By early 1918, their ranks had been swelled by demobilized soldiers who chose to seek their fortunes in Addis Abeba. The urban economy had suffered from the inability of merchants to transport their goods by sea to war-torn Europe and the Middle East, and construction, transport, and menial work was not available. The unemployed were subsequently joined by the soldiers of an army forming in and around the capital for an expedition to eastern Tigray, where troubles continued. Since the imperial coffers were empty, the troops had not been paid, and the men therefore refused to complete their preparations for the march. They blamed their officers for cheating them out of their salaries and supplies. The officers, in turn, blamed the government, particularly the ministers, for embezzling the funds.[27]

The general urban dissatisfaction provided Tafari with an opportunity to destroy the authority of the Council of Ministers. In this, as in other political crises during his career, he manipulated the situation from behind the scenes; his strategy was obvious, although his tactics may have been obscure. His apparent aloofness and avowals of innocence were sometimes interpreted by his European critics as weakness, vacillation, indecision, even inertia, though Ethiopians understood his self-denial as caginess.[28] Significantly, the movement against the Council of Ministers came to a head just a few days before Tafari was supposed to leave Addis Abeba at the head of an army that refused to budge until its needs were satisfied. In meetings about resolving the impasse, junior officers concluded that the Council of Ministers had to be circumvented. Tafari was fully informed about the deliberations but did not report the intelligence to the government, preferring to see what developed. He recalled the crisis as an uprising of

the people as a whole [who] were very incensed about the ministers' negligence to carry on equitably the business of government and about the gradual deterioration of every aspect of the work [and the people] rose up in league with each other and indicated that the ministers should be changed for the good of the people.

On 20 March 1918, the officers asked for the dismissal of the ministers and the transfer of power to a regency council composed of Zawditu, Habte Giorgis, and Tafari. An executive committee, or derg (the name associated with the present Provisional Military Government of Socialist Ethiopia), went to the abun and asked him to arrange for a prompt resolution of its wishes. On 22 March, after hearing no response, the officers deputized Etchege Wolde Giorgis to deliver to the government a letter demanding the dismissal of the ministers and their exile from the capital, the latter a splendid idea from Tafari's point of view. When the silence remained unbroken, the derg scheduled a mass meeting for the next day. Thousands converged on a field near the palace to hear an officer read an indictment against the ministers and to vote to abolish the Council of Ministers. Copies of the resolution were sent to Zawditu, Tafari, Habte Giorgis, and the abun, and the ministers were placed under house arrest to force a reply.

When the authorities failed to reply, the derg organized another demonstration for 26 March 1918. At 9:00 A.M., eight thousand people met outside the palace grounds to hear spontaneous speeches from the eminent and the ordinary. At about 10:00 A.M., the grand chamberlain of the palace appeared with a letter from the empress, announcing the ministers' suspension. Her offer to meet with the derg to discuss the crisis was immediately seen as a concession insufficient to satisfy the "legitimate claims of the people." One man stood up and delivered a furious speech.

The object of our meeting is very clear; we are indignant at seeing the ministers unabashedly ruining our country and our people. The tone of the Government letter badly conceals its preference for these bandits. . . . The request that we should send a delegation can only have one aim, to escape [making] a decision through subterfuge. If the government wishes in this way to shirk its duty to punish with extreme severity these impudent servants of the state, we shall ourselves seize them, happy if our blood should serve the deliverance of our country, martyred by the claws of these ferocious beasts with human faces.

The speech so electrified the listeners that some began to fear violence. To calm the crowd, Fit. Admassu, a member of the derg, rose and calmly but forcefully asserted, "It would show a deplorable lack of respect for the Queen if we did not acquiesce to her wish, which is just and legitimate." Refusal, "however respectful," would be tantamount to treason and "destroy our holy cause." He saw no reason why the derg should not meet with Zawditu, and if a just outcome could not be achieved, then the soldiers could act with a clear conscience to clean up the government. The crowd agreed to send a delegation to the palace, but continued with increasingly strident and critical speeches against the ministers. Finally, at about 4:00 P.M., Abuna Mattewos, Etchege Wolde Giorgis, and Geraz. Haile, Tafari's private secretary, brought the welcome news that the ministers had been fired, and also an order from the empress to cease "secret" deliberations. She warned that clandestine intrigues had "caused the ruin of Great Russia, whose people, divided into many parts, did not have the unity necessary to repulse the enemy who one day had penetrated into its vast territory." It was nonsense, but the crowd listened quietly, probably not understanding the immense victory it had won for Ethiopia and especially for Tafari Makonnen.

In his autobiography, Haile Sellassie obscured the issue by claiming he opposed the dismissals, because "it had not hitherto been customary for the authority of the people to intervene in the appointment and dismissal of the ministers." He probably was lamenting the demise of the Council of Ministers as an important institution in the central government. He certainly had wanted to replace Menilek's old men and Lij Iyasu's sycophants with his own people. In one of the more vain statements in an autobiography riddled with pomposity, the emperor complained, "Until new ministers could be selected and appointed, the entire work had to be carried out on Our responsibility alone, and this caused great fatigue to Us." If so, he must have reveled in exhaustion, as he was addicted to work and to power. His authority had come a long way since 1916. As one official reported, "Ras Tafari, despite his deficiencies of character and of energy, has been able to concentrate power into his own hands, avoiding conflict with the Empress." [29]

Antagonism rarely surfaced, because Zawditu and her heir had different goals. For example, after Wolde Giorgis's death in March 1918, the queen played personal politics by naming her husband, Ras Gugsa Wolie, and two nephews, Dej. Ayalew and Dej. Admassu, to governments in Begemdir, thus assuaging her feelings about her exiled husband. On his side, Tafari nominated Ato Desta, a palace official, for the directorship of posts and telegraphs and charged him with expanding the number of post offices throughout the country. The postmasters and telegrapher-telephonists would be Tafari's eyes and ears in the provinces, instantly able to communicate with Addis Abeba. Of course, the byproduct of the political project would be better national communications, which would, ipso facto, improve Ethiopia's economy, another of Tafari's concerns.

The ras sought nothing less than functional control over Ethiopia's economy. He named his supporters as nagadrases (the nagadras regulated business and customs) in Addis Abeba, Dire Dawa, Welega,

Wallamo, and Ankober, and designated one of his followers as the empire's treasurer. Because revenue was involved, he tried to introduce modern methods of administration: each of the men was salaried at 250 to 1,000 Maria Theresa dollars (MT$; in 1918, MT$10 = £1) per month, and they were forbidden to take a percentage from every transaction within their jurisdictions as hitherto had been the case. This restriction and the payment of a monthly stipend helped increase the flow of revenues to the central government and led to the salariat, a continuously growing phenomenon in Haile Sellassie's Ethiopia. Finally, Tafari named a foreign-educated young man, Lij Wassanie, to be mayor of Addis Abeba, reporting directly to the heir apparent.[30]

The last appointment signaled the type of "Young Ethiopian" that Tafari intended to use in the construction of the new and modern Ethiopia. Wassanie was about twenty-eight years old, the son of Zamanuel, one of Menilek's intendants, and had been educated at the palace school in English and French, the latter of which he spoke well. He was progressive, and in the first months of his mayoralty, he reformed the city's public works, police, and finance. Lij Wassanie appreciated the need for Ethiopia to reorganize itself and to modernize, but believed it should be done with dignity and prudence. Ethiopians, he believed, must adapt themselves and their traditions to meet current needs, and he did not reject the idea of European advisers during the inevitable transition period.[31] Regrettably, Wassanie's promise was lost during the influenza epidemics that spread through Ethiopia in two waves, first in August and September and then in November and December of 1918.

Tafari was one of the first victims of the epidemics. On 27 August, the heir took to his bed; a few days later, he donated funds to various churches for prayers on his behalf, wrote to Jarosseau to seek his supplications, and, to be on the safe side, called in a European doctor. He badgered the physician to remain by his side, arguing selfishly, "You must stay with me; God will heal the others." Ironically he later attributed his survival to the deity: "But I, after I had fallen gravely ill, was spared from death by God's greatness." On the night of 7–8 September, Tafari's condition was so critical that he received the last rites of the Orthodox church and heart injections of camphor oil and caffeine. After these, luck and youth pulled him through. He began improving on 9 September, and by the twentieth, he was able to receive the diplomatic corps to celebrate the Feast of the Holy Cross and the Ethiopian New Year. Thereafter, he went back to work and showed himself around the town, advertising the end of the epidemic and thereby calming the populace. All was well until 14 November, when, "with a suddenness approaching that of a volcano the epidemic was upon us. . . . The Gibbi was closed and the Government ceased to exist."

Ras Kassa and the abun left town, while others, such as Tafari, barricaded themselves in their villas. Even there, surrounded by guards, the great could not protect themselves. Habte Giorgis became seriously ill, muttering to anyone who would listen, "If I die my country is finished. There is no one, no one," quite a commentary on his colleagues' ability to rule. In fact, the government hardly covered itself in glory throughout the crisis. The police quickly fled or died off, and only one municipal official remained on the job, to facilitate the efforts of the few European doctors. The toll on these physicians was terrible: three died, one became sick, and the survivor almost worked himself into the cemetery. The gravediggers soon went to their own burials, and corpses were left on the streets to be eaten by packs of dogs and hyenas, then and now valuable auxiliaries of Addis Abeba's sanitation department. Out of a population of approximately fifty thousand, probably as many as ten thousand died. Dire Dawa and Harer also suffered considerable loss, and the country as a whole may have had forty thousand dead by early December when the epidemic finally exhausted itself.[32]

By then, the world war had ended, and without Ethiopia's participation. Tafari had failed to barter his country's declaration of war for a role in the peace talks and new weapons. Addis Abeba desperately sought modern arms to defend its sovereignty and to assure internal security—the government needed to be stronger than the most powerful provincial governors, even in combination. Without overwhelming might, the government would be unable to impose nationwide reforms leading to modernization; in the absence of these, Tafari feared that the colonial powers might be able to declare the country a protectorate and impose a rule by European officials. Only France among the European powers seemed concerned about Ethiopia's continued independence. Its minister warned that Rome was determined to let Zawditu's empire "flounder into anarchy . . . by systematically depriving it of arms and . . . to seize the first favourable occasion, or to provoke it . . . [for] the conquest of Abyssinia . . . to make it an African Poland in which they would carve out the largest part for themselves."[33] The Frenchman accurately described Italian intentions, but he underestimated Ethiopia's ability to retain its freedom.

CHAPTER THREE

External Security,
1918-1924

Since the sixteenth century, Europe has been rebuffed in its efforts to recast Ethiopia in its own image. The Solomonic state has always fallen back on its philosophical and religious traditions, and Emperor Menilek, the innovator of the semimodern Ethiopian state, rejected but exploited the materialistic example of Western capitalism by buying weapons to defend his empire against imperialism. As his state waned, European diplomats in Addis Abeba anticipated reforms that would benefit their countries' long-term interests. The British and the Italians sought Ethiopia's disarmament and the end of slave trading and raiding across the frontiers. They cared little, and understood less, about the internal dynamics of Ethiopia's political economy and its government. Whereas Britain was truly concerned about the security of its adjacent colonies, Italy's motive was purely and simply sinister, with a goal of nothing less than Ethiopia's submission as a European dependency. Fortunately, this goal was balanced by France's commitment to Ethiopia as the engine of French Somaliland's prosperity.

The Quai d'Orsay's representative in Addis Abeba invariably advised his host government about how best to strengthen the state or the economy to rebut antagonistic propaganda from London or Rome. To demonstrate the rectitude of keeping Ethiopia weak, officials in those two capitals pointed to various sins of backwardness, in particular, the continued existence of domestic slavery and a flourishing slave trade; an apparently ineffective central government, whose writ appeared to run as far as Addis Abeba's city limits; and an unchecked internal arms trade that seemingly spurred forays across the frontiers.[1] These self-serving views were broadcast in the media, incorporated into the conventional wisdom about Ethiopia, and cited as reasons to keep the Addis Abeba government weak.

Ras Tafari early understood that his country had a serious image problem in Europe. The Ethiopian way of government appeared corrupt and was, in fact, slow to create a consensus; westerners mistook the indirection for misdirection and the languid administrative machinery for inefficiency. Tafari knew that the government needed reform, inevitably a slow process since he did not have enough of a new breed of officials, later dubbed the "Young Ethiopians," who were educated, efficient, modern, and patriotic. Such men might have been relied on to assist in eradicating slavery, regarded by Europeans, if not by most Ethiopians, as anathema, worse indeed than the chaotic internal arms trade. Because solutions to both problems would take years, Tafari chose to temporize with a public relations gambit: on 11 November 1918, he decreed the abolition of the slave trade and the regulation of weapons sales, both necessary if Addis Abeba were to escape the arms embargo of 1916.[2] Part ploy and part wishful prophecy, the new legislation revealed Tafari as a serious man with inchoate modern goals.

From the beginning of his career, Tafari's thinking was shaped by a number of foreign consultants and advisers. In April 1917, the ras received a memorandum on modernization prepared by two long-time foreign residents. It is an interesting document, not only because it pointed out obviously necessary reforms, but also because Tafari began most of them before the second Italo-Ethiopian war. The two Europeans drew immediate attention to the contemptible condition of the Ethiopian Foreign Ministry, "a little hovel composed entirely of one small room, furnished with a table, and a few chairs and a cupboard." They called for quarters that were appropriate to an organization representing Ethiopia to foreigners and that could demonstrate that the country was "capable and worthy of being independent." That goal would also be served by the installation of legations abroad, to endow Ethiopia with the same quality of sovereignty that other nations enjoyed in foreign capitals. The memorandum also recommended the formation of special courts for suits involving Ethiopians and foreigners; the creation of municipalities in Addis Abeba, Harer, and Dire Dawa; the introduction of a uniform national currency; the standardization of weapons in the army; the domestic production of munitions; the establishment of model farms; the improvement of internal and external communications; and the development of education.[3] The recommended programs required considerable capital, which could only be forced from Ethiopia's domestic economy.

Addis Abeba had "energetically rejected" any scheme that required foreign experts to reorganize and administer the country's finances and rarely had taken foreign loans. The Ethiopians feared falling into arrears and being forced to give up a part of their national sovereignty, as they knew had happened in Egypt, Tunisia, and Morocco. When Tafari became head of the government in 1917, Ethiopia's revenues came largely from customs duties and from tributes, which were slowly evolving into taxes. At the local level, there was a kind of feudalism, whereby producers owed customary taxes and services to a political elite, which administered and policed the Ethiopian Empire. It would be impossible to estimate the value of these transfer payments, but it must have been considerable, permitting southern governors in particular to pay relatively heavy tributes to Addis Abeba in gold, Maria Theresa dollars (MT$), salt bars, ivory, hides and skins, and the like. For 1902, tribute revenues amounted to MT$868,942; for 1903, MT$1,274,344; and for 1904, MT$2,255,711. The total probably continued to rise throughout Menilek's active years, but it declined after he became ill in 1909, because provincial officials failed to remit all the revenues due the government and, of course, the extra gifts and honorariums customarily sent to the crown.

During the last two years of Iyasu's rule, the Addis Abeba government was continually strapped for funds. Some of the deficit came
from a reduced volume of trade caused by a shortage of shipping
throughout 1914 and 1915, as the mounting war in the Middle East
required increasingly more of the capacity of the small steamers that
served Red Sea ports. Yet customs revenues were considerable even
for the depressed year of 1916, when the total amounted to
MT$1,953,000, of which MT$1,700,000 was collected in Addis Abeba,
Dire Dawa, and Harer, the main railway or caravan entry points.
The situation began improving in 1917, when revenues grew to
MT$2,803,000, with Dire Dawa accounting for over half of this total.
That year, most of Ethiopia's overseas imports were cotton goods
and various luxury items, taxed at a fixed rate of 10 percent, as were
exports. Ethiopia's most valuable products by far were hides and
coffee, although cereals were significant earners. Total trade in 1917
was valued at approximately £3 million per year, although the
amount was probably greater, as no one knew how many traders
avoided paying customs through bribes or evasion.

Tafari appreciated that any governmental reform of the tariff administration would result in an immediate increase in revenues, and
he had appointed his few Young Ethiopians as nagadrases in strategic
posts such as Harer, Dire Dawa, and Addis Abeba. In the past, these
trade officials had made enormous sums of money by collecting a fee
for each transaction in their jurisdiction. For example, Nag. Ydlibi in
Harer–Dire Dawa annually realized as much as MT$150,000, about
as much as Nag. Haile Giorgis made from Addis Abeba. By providing
monthly salaries ranging from MT$1,000 in the case of Addis Abeba
to MT$250 for smaller posts, the government assumed the "rights" of
the nagadras. The net savings were considerable: in one case, from 16
March to 10 May 1918, the old nagadras of Addis Abeba collected
MT$8,368 for himself and MT$889 for the central government. Under
the new system, bribery and evasion were more difficult, and the
salaried officials remitted an astonishing MT$3,166 just for the pe-
riod between 10 and 30 May 1919. The growth in revenue permitted
Tafari to add to his own income as head of the government. He
directed his new men to collect a personal tax of two piasters on each
sack of grain and cereal exported and four piasters on each sack of
salt imported. So far as the data reveal, the ras used the money not on

personal luxuries but rather to pay unanticipated costs of administration, to finance the education abroad of a number of young Ethiopians, and to subvent charities — activities that inevitably helped him attract supporters. Tafari early showed that he understood the close connection between his well-being and authority and the country's economy.

Over the long run, he also benefited from the shift in the countryside from subsistence to semicommercial agriculture, which produced more revenues and changed feudal lords into profit-conscious oligarchs. The 1920s witnessed the development of cash crops, particularly coffee, a process that Tafari mediated. Not only did he establish his own plantation in Chercher and share in other holdings, but he and others also established the Société Ethiopienne de Commerce et d'Industrie. It was the government's main business agent and facilitated the growth of Ethiopia's economy in the twenties as import-export became Addis Abeba's business. Tafari neither hid nor acknowledged his association with the company, but he decreed that "the Ethiopian Government will favor with all its power the operations of this business without ever becoming responsible financially, if, despite its benevolent aid, the firm loses its commercial or industrial operation." [4] Thus, by adding to revenue collection at a crucial time, by mediating the country's assimilation into the world economy, and by presiding over an umbrella corporation that actively participated in the buying and selling of Ethiopian products, Tafari, the feudal lords who were now suddenly oligarchs, and the Ethiopian government obtained the income necessary to modernize the state if diplomacy could ensure the empire's independence.

Tafari had been pleased by the Allied victory, even if many of his compatriots "would have preferred a result less decisive and less advantageous for the three powers whose possessions surround[ed] their country, particularly for Italy." Immediately after the armistice of November 1918, Zawditu, Ras Kassa, and Tafari deliberated often about Ethiopia's future relations with Europe, and they decided that it would be wise to send missions to congratulate the victors and also to seek Ethiopia's participation in the peace process. In early 1919, after consultations in Addis Abeba with major provincial figures, it was decided that the missions should be ceremonial and preliminary, without authority to undertake serious negotiations, a slap at

Tafari, who had hoped to make Ethiopia a party to the collective security of the League of Nations. He was entirely enthusiastic about President Wilson's notion, which seemed the perfect defense for a backward and poor country like Ethiopia. He bitterly complained that "the priests and the women" kept him in Addis Abeba, sending instead three groups of relatively undistinguished men to carry out the government's first diplomatic foray in Europe.[5]

Shortly thereafter, he confessed to an old American friend that the conservatives in government often blocked needed reforms and thereby ignorantly invited European intervention.[6] Opposition to Tafari's proposals was centered in ad hoc councils of the realm, which had assumed the work of the defunct Council of Ministers. Now, instead of a small group of self-interested men at the center, the ras had to maneuver around varying numbers of more or less self-important provincial lords. These men were easily led by the empress and Fit. Habte Giorgis, both of whom were opposed to foreign alliances and to negotiations in Europe. They believed instead in building a fortress around Ethiopia and in a diplomacy carried out in Addis Abeba under their watchful eyes. They were in total conflict with Tafari's conclusion that national survival depended on policies that extricated Ethiopia from the pull of the tripartite powers and opened it to the other nations of the globe. The difference was so fundamental that the deeply frustrated ras chose once again to evoke the new of Addis Abeba against the old of Menilek's palace. On 4 May 1919, several thousand soldiers, with only a few junior officers, met at the Imperial Race Course and elected a derg (committee) that demanded Fit. Habte Giorgis's dismissal because he opposed the progressive measures the government, "meaning Ras Tafari," wanted to take. The derg declared its disgust with Ethiopia's lack of progress and the government's inability "to work together for the common weal." By now sensitive to the soldiery, Zawditu agreed to work to minimize the differences between the triumvirs; and she sent a conciliatory note that prompted the derg to disperse the mob. She quickly mediated between Tafari and Habte Giorgis,[7] reopening the discussion about entry into the League of Nations as if the Imperial Government had just learned that Ethiopia's independence was "not synonymous with isolation."[8]

Paris believed that an Ethiopian effort to enter the world organization would quickly draw Italian opposition.[9] Rome had entered the fight against the Central Powers only in 1915, upon signing the secret Treaty of London, which promised in article 13 unspecified colonial concessions to Italy after the successful conclusion of the war. Ever ambitious, the Italians dreamed of absorbing British and French Somalilands and taking over the Addis Abeba – Djibouti railway, thus achieving a de facto protectorate over Ethiopia. After the war, however, Paris refused to consider transferring the colony, arguing that possession of Djibouti was vital to the security of communications with Madagascar and Indochina; France would not give up the railroad that ensured the small colony's financial well-being. Once Paris had decided not to yield any of its interests in the Horn to Italy, it logically continued to support Ethiopia's independence, completely disrupting Rome's plans. The British sympathized with the Italians but, for reasons of domestic politics, could not take any public action opposing Tafari's government.[10] London and Rome nonetheless secretly conspired to limit the Ethiopian missions to their declared ceremonial functions and not to permit them to raise real issues about the peace conference or the League of Nations.[11] Even though the two powers would continue to oppose any enhanced international status for Addis Abeba, Tafari was undertaking reforms to impress European critics and help gain Ethiopia's entry into the League.

Habte Giorgis wanted none of it; whatever had been good enough for Menilek was good enough for him. In June 1919, he returned to the struggle against Tafari's newfangled notions with such a vengeance that the two men quarreled openly in public.[12] Haile Sellassie recalled the discomfort of the period: "I spent my time working to the best of my ability, while my own ideas and the people fond of old customs (particularly as the latter had many supporters) squeezed me like wood between two pieces of iron."[13] Street fighting broke out between the partisans of each man, and at night, there was an epidemic of thievery and random shooting.[14] These eruptions masked an economic crisis caused by the deflation of the Maria Theresa dollar, now worth more in silver than as money. Speculators, among them Ras Tafari, were buying up the heavy coins for export to Aden and immense profits. In Addis Abeba, prices went sharply upward, and the ordinary city dweller found it difficult to buy food.[15] The economic crisis permeated the political emergency and created a situation that Tafari could manipulate as easily as he handled the soldiers. Forestalling the ras, the empress intervened, yet again, to work out the conflicts between the progressives and conservatives in her government.

The parlous situation forced her, as Ethiopia's balancer of power, to call a Council of the Realm for early August, even though the rainy season made travel difficult. Among those summoned to the council, there were more conservatives than progressives; the crucial player was Zawditu, who proved a capable leader. Whatever Tafari was, he had a vision of the future, some education, and a program. In sharp contrast, Habte Giorgis had no agenda, and he responded to the future with outdated habits and instincts. However comfortable the empress may have felt with the fitawrari's conservatism, she appreciated that Ethiopia needed foresight and energy as much as it needed the domestic peace that only Tafari seemed capable of achieving. She therefore declared full support for her young colleague, announced that she had transferred her executive power to her "son," and directed the government to look to him for guidance.[16] On Tafari's recommendation, the empress also permitted him to establish and chair a small Council of State composed of five ministers, including Habte Giorgis, to facilitate the government's ordinary activities. Two of the appointees supported Tafari, two were Zawditu's partisans, but only one had ties to Habte Giorgis.[17] The ras had finally achieved the regency he claimed had been his since 1916.

Now in a much stronger position,[18] Tafari began purging officials hostile to reform.[19] The old guard was powerless to intervene because Tafari enjoyed the empress's full support.[20] She even stood aside when her regent went after Habte Giorgis by fomenting an embarrassing mutiny against the commander-in-chief. The military crisis ended only when the fitawrari, now in "a chastened frame of mind," agreed to accept Tafari's authority.[21] The ras imagined himself as the people's champion, their natural leader, which he considered far preferable "to the wave of Bolshevistic feeling which is over-running the rest of the world."[22] He began placing partisans of humble origins in important positions, sending, for example, Sahle Sedalou, a functionary in the Ministry of Foreign Affairs, to Paris for liaison with the Allies and to prepare the way for a high-level mission that would seek Ethiopia's admission into the League.[23] The ras-regent was riding high and seemingly in control when Lij Iyasu re-emerged in the north to threaten the government.

The first alarms were sounded in May 1920 when several officials were arrested and charged with being in contact with the pretender.[24] The government immediately alerted northern officials and asked Ras Seyoum of Tigray to explain rumors that he and Iyasu had met and that the fugitive was under his protection.[25] The poor fellow could not even come up with a plausible story, although he expressed devotion to the central government.[26] When he asked for instructions, he was given the oracular advice "that as a loyal subject he must act as his loyalty prompts him."[27] Because loyalty required detaining Iyasu, ipso facto an admission that the prince had been in southern Tigray, Seyoum arranged for the prince to "escape" to the Afar Desert, to continue his wanderings.[28]

Meanwhile, Zawditu and Tafari decided to mount a major campaign in the north to capture Iyasu. The pretender remained an anathema, and most governors willingly joined the hunt, even Ras Hailu of Gojam, who staunchly defended provincial rights against interference from the central government. In early December, the makwanent gathered in Addis Abeba to plan strategy for the campaign and to commemorate the seventh anniversary of Menilek's death with a final memorial service. This event was of monumental proportions, in scale with the emperor's accomplishments. Throughout December and January, herds of cattle and tons of provisions were shipped into Addis Abeba, and thousands of visitors jammed the city, camping wherever they could. The palace grounds sprouted huge tents in which feasting began on 29 January and ended on 6 February, with a special European-style dinner for diplomats, presided over by Ras Tafari. The next day, Menilek's satisfied spirit responded by delivering up Lij Iyasu in Tigray.[29]

In late January, acting on a tip from one of Iyasu's followers, Ras Gugsa and a small party, including Lij Desta Demtu, Tafari's agent in Adwa, marched to southern Temben, where, on 28 January, they silently surrounded the local church at Seloa and took the heir and a few supporters by surprise. Iyasu surrendered personally to Ras Gugsa, who formally took custody after prostrating himself and kissing the feet of Menilek's grandson. Captive and captor immediately made for Maychew, where they arrived at noon on 31 January.[30] Iyasu was given soap and water, so filthy was he, and provided with new clothes, so tattered was he. Although unbound and detained in comfortable quarters, the pretender voiced fears about his life on the few occasions when Ras Gugsa was able to elude Desta Demtu's close companionship.[31] On orders from Addis Abeba, Iyasu was secretly moved on 10 February 1921 to Ambalage, there to await the government's decision about his future.[32]

The prince's arrest was obviously good news, and Tafari, with Fit. Habte Giorgis and Ras Hailu, immediately took a small army north to arrange custody. On 21 May 1921, in Dese, Ras Gugsa ceremoniously transferred custody of Iyasu to Tafari. The two young men, once friends, now adversaries forever, did not meet; instead, the captive was immediately sent, under heavy escort, north to the fortress-town of Were Ilu. Tafari, Hailu, and Habte Giorgis remained behind, watching the imperial army grow daily until 120,000 troops were available for a campaign against Seyoum. Hapless but not stupid, the ras saw that resistance would be folly, and came to Dese on 11 June, to renew his allegiance to empress and government. An unmollified Tafari removed Seyoum from his governship and ordered him to join the march back to Addis Abeba. Costing only MT$1.5 million, the show of force had avoided civil war cheaply and efficiently, making Tafari's return to Addis Abeba on 20 July a triumph. Although the regent "spoke with diffidence of his political success," his position was strong enough to let him get on with his next task, the suppression of slavery.[33]

Chattel servitude in the Solomonic Empire became internationally notorious when Addis Abeba opened its campaign for membership in the League, and Rome and London began pointing out the candidate's warts and blemishes. With this beginning, the slavery question rapidly became the property of the Anti-Slavery and Aborigines Protection Society, headquartered in London and the plaything of righteous aristocrats and sincere middle-class do-gooders. Although the existence of slavery was one of the cudgels that British diplomats regularly used to beat back Addis Abeba's requests for weapons, they understood the social and political implications of that venerable Ethiopian institution. They privately conceded the enormity of the problems and knew that abolition would take considerable time and effort.

Historically, Ethiopians had owned humans to proclaim wealth and status or to exploit them as domestics or as farm laborers, frequently under gang conditions. As long as Ethiopia was autarkic, the available agricultural surplus could support the mass of slaves. The intrusion of the world economy in the late nineteenth century and the subsequent growth of cash crops in southern Ethiopia transformed the situation. During the 1920s, Ethiopian agriculture became increasingly monetarily profitable, rendering the holding and feeding of slaves uneconomic in terms of opportunity costs. It was sensible to free them and make them participate, as sharecroppers, in Ethiopia's developing market economy.[34] This natural process was taking effect when criticism of Ethiopia's social system was developing overseas. It was difficult for observers in London to appreciate that capitalism in Ethiopia was defeating slavery when they saw an apparently thriving institution. The mounting criticism stung Addis Abeba and prompted a propaganda campaign in response.

As Ethiopia's best public relations man, Tafari told all within hearing that Ethiopia was actively eradicating slavery and that the edict of 1918 abolishing slavery was not a gesture but a turn in the right direction. He pointed to numerous court cases against traders who had been heavily fined and, in some instances, jailed. He patiently explained that final abolition had to be linked to economic growth to absorb the energies and talents of hundreds of thousands, perhaps millions, of freed persons. He was adamant that most of his countrymen did not perceive slavery as a social problem: the institution was historical; the slave-master relationship was normal, even mutually beneficial; and many chiefs profited from the trade.

Nevertheless, in July 1922, Addis Abeba instructed all governors to ban the slave trade in their jurisdictions. Although many Europeans pooh-poohed the effort, the government actually hanged two notorious traders, to the applause of many ordinary Ethiopians; and at least Dej. Nado in Gore and Dej. Bayene in Wallamo strictly applied the order.[35] Owners of large numbers of slaves were of course unhappy, and Fit. Habte Giorgis complained, "What is this? Altayework [his wife] will have to go to the river to collect water and I will have to chop wood."[36] One graybeard of a dejazmach shook his head and lamented that "Abyssinia can no more easily do without slavery than the Europeans could go unshod."[37] So, for the Ethiopians, the government's actions were consequential and important, marking a significant change. The Europeans, however, remained chronically displeased with any action short of total and immediate abolition. They wanted Tafari to cut a new pattern in one piece out of whole cloth, but he understood that he would have to weave a complex tapestry before his design would be complete. He planned slow but steady progress that would not threaten the ruling class, but would guarantee Ethiopia's national survival and his continuation in power.

He constantly sought to enhance his authority and was therefore quick to understand the importance of modern communications, although his enthusiasm for modernity itself was real, vital, and occasionally emotional. It was in Aden, in November 1922, that Tafari began his lifelong love affair with the airplane, instantly understanding how important air power could be in Ethiopia. In Aden the Royal Air Force put on a show for the visiting ras, who had never before seen an aircraft, and he "was unable to control his pleasure at witnessing nose dives, looping the loop, bomb dropping and the skillful manner in which the aeroplanes were controlled." Tafari was so excited that he spontaneously asked if he could go up in one of the biplanes, proclaiming it "very fitting that he, as regent of Abyssinia should be the first Abyssinian to take flight in an aeroplane."[38] Thoroughly exhilarated by the experience, he henceforth championed air communications for Ethiopia, persevering against all advice and the constant European ridicule of his program in a country defined by backwardness and poverty. He was just as persistent when it came to acquiring arms for Ethiopia.

En route to and from Aden, the regent stopped at Djibouti, where, of course, officialdom stood for an arms trade and the restoration of a significant source of transit and transportation fees. As a sign of good will, local administrators informally arranged the purchase and shipment of 1,302 obsolete rifles and 200,000 cartridges of varying quality and caliber.[39] When Rome and London protested, Paris feigned ignorance *ex cathedra* and then sermonized about the Ethiopian government's urgent need for modern weapons to establish its authority nationwide and to end the slave trade.[40] The Quai d'Orsay's litany of support for "the unreserved independence and absolute integrity of the Ethiopian empire" infuriated the Italians.[41] But it nudged Whitehall toward a policy reevaluation, in time perhaps to counter Tafari's allegations that the British fostered anarchy in his country by blocking access to modern weapons and by printing the "most injurious" calumnies about Ethiopia. When one brave soul tried to defend London, the regent ended the conversation abruptly by declaring, "What I have said is unanswerable. There is no reply possible."[42]

Yet the British needed to respond to the ras's charges, since Ethiopia's permission was needed to build a barrage on Lake Tana, where the Blue Nile originated, to facilitate the irrigation of Sudan's Gezira region. The Foreign Office reasoned that intransigence over the arms question would "sooner or later" elicit "positive refusals" for any requests about Tana "we may make of the Abyssinian Government." The Foreign Office was willing, therefore, to concede Ethiopia permission to make modest annual purchases of "say 12,000 rifles" under rigid controls and guarantees.[43] Addis Abeba, of course, insisted on its *right* to import needed weapons as it saw fit. The feckless British minister admitted that the arms question was indeed "complicated" by Ethiopia's adherence to the Brussels Act and by subsequent treaties that recognized that right. He insisted, however, that only France's philo-Ethiopianism blocked interpreting all relevant texts so "as to prohibit totally all imports of arms."[44] For the time being, Paris was unwilling to break Allied unity, preferring instead to await Ethiopia's entry into the League, where international law and comity would prohibit discrimination against a member state.[45]

The first movement toward Ethiopia's application came in July 1923, when the Council of the League went into executive session to consider members' reports about slavery in areas under their jurisdiction. Most delegates were succinct, as their governments had found no incidence of slavery and slave raiding. The French statement was clever, first admitting the existence of slavery in Ethiopia and a slave trade across its colony to Arabia, but then reporting that both had declined sharply since 1916, thanks to the new regime in

Addis Abeba. The French representative conceded that the colonial government could do little to control the small caravans that crossed its loosely administered territory, but promised an enlarged naval patrol to interdict most slave shipments. He stressed the vital role of Ethiopia in destroying the trade and pointed to its need for "arms and munitions . . . to compel [its] inhabitants . . . to respect the orders of the central government." [46] In closing, the Frenchman moved to ask nonmembers, such as Ethiopia, to report their own situations.[47] The Italian delegate strenuously objected, because his government opposed any official Ethiopian activity in the League.

Britain's Lord Robert Cecil insisted that the Italian maneuver rendered discussion "impossible" and impeded any possibility "of finding a means to encourage the Abyssinian Government." Antonio Salandra, in the chair, explained Rome's fear that any League recognition of Ethiopia would lead to membership, whereupon the League's collective security would apply to the country's "independence and the integrity of its territory" under article 10 of the charter. It was an astonishing confession, and Lord Robert was so horrified that he told the French delegate that he now privately favored Ethiopia's immediate admission into the League.[48] The next day, France and Great Britain pushed a resolution through the council, calling on the secretariat to continue its efforts to collect information about slavery and even "to address itself for this purpose to the Governments of non-member States." [49]

The break in Anglo-Italian unity on the Ethiopian question suggested to the Quai d'Orsay that the moment might be right for Addis Abeba to request membership. Haste was required because, to be considered, applications had to be in Geneva at least one month before the annual meeting of the Assembly in September. The French chargé in Addis Abeba, Maurice Boucoiran, raised the matter quietly and confidentially with Ras Tafari, who, after being assured that the League would impose no conditions on Ethiopia's admission, took the question to the empress. On 23 July, during a meeting at the palace with Zawditu, Tafari, and several ministers, the envoy stressed that Paris would brook no attempt to subvert Ethiopia's sovereignty, and he reported France's recent success at Geneva over Italy. After a short discussion, Zawditu assured Boucoiran that, notwithstanding the limited time at its disposal, her government would thoroughly study the question of admission.[50]

For the next six days and nights, there was a continuous meeting of the Council of the Realm at the gibbi, with officials coming and going. So consuming were the deliberations that ordinary government in Addis Abeba was stalled. Boucoiran regarded the process as "the most considerable event I have witnessed during my long stay here." Seventy percent of the participants, he reported, favored entry into the League; even the church's hierarchy was in agreement. Tafari was playing the devil's advocate, raising the greatest number of objections in terms of Ethiopia's internal problems. As it would be the regent's job to ensure that the government discharged the country's obligations to the charter, Tafari not unwisely, and rather deftly, turned the decision into a high-level plebiscite on Ethiopia's modernization.[51]

He "asked for and received from each of the [leading] chiefs, an assurance of his willingness to carry out in his own province any obligations which the Government might incur as a result of admission into the League." Many probably did not comprehend the issues involved in membership, but most viewed the status as charting Ethiopia's continued independence. Progressives hoped that the League connection would prescribe continued reform and yield desperately needed neutral technicians and advisers. Conservatives were attracted to the notion that membership would force Britain and Italy to reconsider the arms embargo, and even the Young Ethiopians believed that procurement of modern weapons was "an indispensable preliminary to the administrative reorganization which must precede reform."[52]

On 1 August 1923, Tafari wrote the League, requesting consideration of Ethiopia's membership during the September meeting of the Assembly. He confirmed that his government was "prepared to accept the conditions contained in Article One of the Covenant, and to carry out all the obligations incumbent on members of the League of Nations." Tafari recorded his country's appreciation of collective security and the League's goals of peace, international unity, truth, and loyalty, "principles . . . excellent above all for a nation which has always remained firmly Christian." Association with the League would therefore permit "this Christian Government . . . to govern its people in peace and tranquility, and to develop its country under prosperous conditions." [53] To make these points to the Assembly, the Imperial Government dispatched to Geneva a delegation headed by Dej. Nado.[54]

The Ethiopian mission did not have an easy time of it, as the British and Italians began by asking embarrassing questions about the "uncontrolled" arms trade.[55] The French countered by raising procedural or substantive objections and by having the Ethiopians offer a statement that bound Addis Abeba to recognize "the system at present established with regard to importation of arms and ammunition"; to conform "to principles set forth in the convention of control of trade in arms and ammunition signed at St. Germain-en-Laye on September 10th, 1919, and in particular article 6 of said convention [establishing Africa as a prohibited zone]";[56] and "notwithstanding provisions contained in any international convention, not to permit the importation into her territory of any arms and ammunition in excess of the amount at present or hereafter agreed upon by limitrophe States." [57] The Italians regarded the declaration as tantamount to continuing tripartite control over the arms trade to Ethiopia, whereas the French and Ethiopian delegations viewed it as a vehicle by which to regain Addis Abeba's complete sovereignty.[58]

Then came an inquisition about slavery led by sanctimonious British and Italian diplomats. Reports of their prejudice caused Tafari to cable their governments, seeking an explanation for the obvious hostility.[59] The simple maneuver was surprisingly effective, for both powers had much to lose from alienating Addis Abeba: Britain might have forfeited Ethiopia's agreement to the Lake Tana scheme; and Italy stood to lose any hope of lulling the Solomonic state into a new Roman Empire. Both governments hastily directed their delegates to shift from resistance to reassurance.[60] Instead of requiring Addis Abeba to present a detailed statement about its plans to abolish slavery and the slave trade, the two European powers asked that the Ethiopian government merely declare that "Abyssinia is and remains ready to furnish the Council with any information it may require, and to take into consideration any recommendation which the Council may make with regard to the fulfilment of these obligations, in which she recognises that the League of Nations is concerned." [61]

Nado recommended adoption of the statements, since their language did not undermine Ethiopia's sovereignty. France, Belgium, Portugal, Venezuela, India, Panama, Liberia, China, and Persia, Ethiopia's friends in Geneva, agreed and added that entry into the League provided not only collective security but also an international arena in which to challenge the arms embargo. After careful examination by the Council of the Realm, Zawditu cabled acceptance of the statements as given, enabling Ethiopia to enter the League by unanimous vote on 28 September 1923.[62] In his acceptance speech, Dej. Nado, as Ethiopia's first delegate to the League, remarked:

While the Empire of Ethiopia may boast of a glorious historic past and a brilliant civilization, it clearly realises that in order to get access to all the advantages of modern organisation, an earnest endeavour on its part is necessary. In order to succeed in all of this, our Government is happy in the thought that it will be able to rely on the solidarity of all the nations of the world.[63]

Back in Addis Abeba there was rejoicing "for no reason other than We thought that the Covenant of the League would protect us from . . . attack." [64]

The country desperately needed peace to mobilize its resources for development. It is hard today to comprehend how backward Ethiopia was in 1924. There were virtually no roads then, and trade followed traditional caravan routes such as the trail south from Gonder and Debre Markos to Addis Abeba. Through Begemdir and Gojam, on the high plateau, the going was easy, but at Dejen, at the rim of the Blue Nile gorge, crowds of men and animals waited their turn to funnel into the canyon, cross through its sweltering heat, and climb up to the cool Shewan highlands on the other side. The track down was "a bad descent at the best of times . . . stony and uneven, with long steps and bad gradients," and it was narrow, with room for only three men to walk abreast. Yet on this track moved traffic in both directions, "a constant stream of thousands of men, mules, and donkeys, untethered, and each with an awkward load," all proceeding at about one mile an hour.[65] This was the passage to and from Addis Abeba, which in the early 1920s was hidden in woods

so extensive and so dense . . . that one seems to enter a forest, and it is only on a near approach to the town that houses begin to stand out amongst the trees, and the rays of the sun sparkling and glittering on the metal roofs and white-washed walls make [one] appreciate that a town, and an extensive one at that is hidden in the foliage.[66]

With a population estimated at between sixty thousand and one hundred thousand, the capital boasted two modern hotels, two cinemas, two hospitals, numerous drinking houses, and approximately twenty-five hundred Europeans, mostly Greeks and Armenians.[67] Their shops were located in the city's commercial center, reached by a main street one traveler classed as the world's worst thoroughfare: "Imagine a street through which a civil war passed, a street of barricades . . . paving stones . . . torn up to form barricades . . . and you have it. It is not a street, it is one long obstacle."[68] From the roadway ran numerous alleys and paths on which were located innumerable small shops and kiosks, constituting the suk, or central market. "The life of the city radiates from the markets where thousands of packed thousands — peasants, merchants . . . hillmen, men-at-arms; women on foot and on donkeys; my lord on a stallion, with squires at his stirrups; my lady closely muffled on a mule — are wedged into a human tapestry."[69]

The economy of the city and the country derived from a prosperous agriculture, which by 1923 had returned to its 1918 level of exports, accounting for about £2,000,000. The high quality of produce surprised an official from the U.S. Department of Agriculture, who remarked on the uniformly "vigorous appearance" of such high-plateau crops as barley, wheat, and broad bean, which looked as good as any seen in Minnesota or in the Bay Area of California; he was equally impressed with the sorghums and durra, which he believed better than those cultivated in Kansas and Oklahoma. He was sure that commercial agriculture in Ethiopia had a great future, once a uniform currency, standard and nationally applied tariffs, modern communications, and other amenities were provided.[70]

The American official had no trouble traveling around Ethiopia with a *laissez-passer*, signed by Tafari, which everywhere elicited the proper respect from provincial officials. He agreed with the English visitor C. F. Rey, who observed that the conventional view that Zawditu's realm comprised "rebellious provinces on the verge of wholesale revolt, and . . . contending factions of the Empress and the Ras only awaiting consignments of arms and ammunition to fly at each other's throats are — well, to put it mildly, 'terminological inexactitudes.' " [71]

In fact, monarch and regent had worked out a good system. She played a significant, perhaps even preponderant, role in the setting of policy, in which Tafari also had a hand, but he was solely responsible for the daily operations of government. He was zealous about his duties, dealing "personally with everything, from the negotiation of a Treaty to the granting of a permit for the import of a revolver." [72] He was also indefatigable, working daily from about 7:00 A.M. to 10:00 P.M.,[73] assisted by Young Ethiopians and trusted, mostly French, advisers.[74] The ras aimed his administration toward progress but within Ethiopia's customs, believing that it would be "a misfortune" for his traditional people to be swamped by change.[75]

Tafari believed that townspeople could adapt to change more easily than rural dwellers, and he therefore concentrated "progress" in Addis Abeba, where a rudimentary educational system was available to help make the transition to modernity. The only government institution was the now venerable Menilek school, staffed by Egyptian Copts. In November 1923, it enrolled 160 students, only 20 percent of whom had been in the school for four years or more. Classes were in English, but entrance was limited to those who could read and write Amharic. Over the years, it had served three thousand boys and youths, many of them now employed "in government service as interpreters, accountants, or secretaries." About fifty young Ethiopian women and girls were among the students at the Francophone Ecole des Soeurs, opened in 1905. The Alliance Française, in operation since 1907, had taught about fourteen hundred boys from all social classes, most of whom had become government clerks. Although another few hundred boys and girls were studying various curricula in the capital's Protestant missionary schools, overall only a minuscule proportion of Addis Abeba's school-age children were being educated.[76] In the provinces, the situation was even worse, but because Tafari considered education directly related to the creation of idealistic and selfless civil servants and to modern and efficient government, he aimed at vast improvements.[77]

Tafari believed that Ethiopia could learn much from Western lore and life, which fascinated him. He was an avid reader, and his study was filled with books in French on all subjects.[78] His recently built modern home contained European furnishings. Its contrast with traditional dwellings could not have been more stark: "The electric light, gold plate, gold-lettered menus wreathed in roses . . . showed our host's appreciation of Europe." As one entered or left the regent's residence, one could not help noticing that the guard saluted smartly in European style, wore a khaki uniform, and was armed with modern weapons.[79] Obviously, Tafari had pretensions, mostly European-inspired. It was now time for him to visit the Continent, to stir people there to assist him in modernizing Ethiopia. Westerners steeped in contemporary racial stereotypes had always found Tafari's features, manners, wit, and intelligence gratifyingly non-African.[80] The ras thus comprised the ingredients for a public relations success in Europe. During his pilgrimage, he would come to personify his country and to symbolize its aspirations, roles he would continue to fulfill throughout a lifetime of service.

CHAPTER FOUR

Europe:
Hospitality and Hostility,
1924 - 1926

In Europe, the regent wanted to test his country's new legitimacy by negotiating an Ethiopian access to the sea, an ambition he made known in January 1924 to the French minister, who hoped that his government would cooperate and retain its economic primacy, and to the Italian plenipotentiary, who dreamed that Rome would yield enough to win an unassailable position in the Solomonic Empire.[1] The empress and the Council of the Realm were tantalized by the possibility of regaining an Ethiopian port and agreed to Tafari's trip to the Occident.[2] Before leaving, the regent sought to ensure successful public relations for his mission by issuing new and comprehensive laws about arms and slavery. Although designed to deflect embarrassing criticism, the new regulations were not window dressing but an agenda for action.[3] The Weapons Control Edict of 9 April 1924 aimed to control and limit arms imports into Ethiopia through increased government oversight and more responsible merchandising. Significantly, the export of weapons and ammunition was "absolutely prohibited." [4] Not so the institution of slavery, as treated in the "Regulations for the Emancipation of Slaves and Their Conditions of Life," issued on 31 March 1924.

The new code guaranteed manumission for slaves seven years after the death of their owners and provided for repatriation of freedmen to their original homelands, government-financed education for some ex-slaves and employment for others, penalties for owners and slave traders who refused to free those qualified for freedom, and a court system to regulate the new legislation. In reporting the reforms to Geneva, Ras Tafari proudly declared that his government had adopted such "energetic and ruthless methods against slave dealers" that it had "succeeded in almost totally suppressing the trade," and that, without resupply, slavery as an institution was doomed. Implementation of the new rules would anticipate the end of slavery by immediately freeing "a large number of persons who are at present slaves . . . and others will be assured of receiving humane treatment." [5]

Claud Russell, the British minister who rarely saw good in anything or anyone Ethiopian, was forced to admit that the measures seemed "reasonably conceived, and in theory calculated to deal gradually with an evil which it would admittedly be difficult to abolish out of hand." [6] Even the notoriously anti-Ethiopian *Westminster Gazette* conceded that the new decree "mark[ed] a notable advance." [7] Louis Gaussen, the French plenipotentiary, was enthusiastic, claiming that the new laws were guided by "great liberalism," shaped by reality, and would "have decisive results in the future." He anticipated that the regulations would transform slaves into an agricultural proletariat, thus effecting "a kind of reorganization of the whole empire." [8] Having begun to unshackle the Ethiopian people, Tafari turned his attention to liberating Ethiopia's international trade by securing for Addis Abeba the freedom of its own port.

On 16 April 1924, the prince-regent boarded a train for Djibouti, accompanied by a large retinue, including rases Hailu and Seyoum, and Blatta Herui Wolde Sellassie, Lij Makonnen Endelkatchew, and Ato Sahle Sedalou, as interpreters, advisers, and functionaries.[9] The party traveled by steamer to Suez, where they disembarked on 24 April, to be whisked by launch to Ismailia, where a "train de luxe" awaited to speed them to Al-Kantara, and thence to Jerusalem, a fitting first stop for the pious Tafari. Upon arrival there, the ras was badly served by Sir Herbert Samuel, whose Jewish sensibilities ought to have armored him against the conventional, even fashionable, British racism of the day. Sir Herbert had decided that Tafari would prefer to stay at the uncomfortable and crowded Ethiopian convent instead of the luxurious Government House, the usual domicile for visiting dignitaries. The regent tactfully turned aside the slight by assuming that he would indeed be the governor's guest at some point during his stay, and after considerable officious consternation and tut-tutting in English, Tafari was installed at the official residence for his last two nights in Jerusalem. By then, he had seen most of the sights, sat through an Easter service at the Church of the Resurrection, and arranged permission for resident Ethiopian priests to say mass at the Greek Orthodox monastery on Mount Golgotha.[10] Having served God first, Tafari was ready to render earthly powers their due.

On 2 May, he entered Cairo, to be welcomed by a much adumbrated pharaoh, King Fuad I, and the potent high priest of British imperialism, Lord Allenby. Tafari was gratified by the "imposing official reception" and the "honour" accorded him. He was wined and dined by the Egyptians and the British alike but was especially pleased by the hospitality of Cairo's large Coptic community. Tafari did his share of sightseeing, recording as "memorable to Us" the pyramids and the Sphinx, the Egyptian Museum, the antiquities at Luxor, the "old churches of early time," and the Valley of the Kings, particularly the recently opened tomb of Tutankhamen.

He was especially interested in hospitals, social institutions, and schools. He was so happy to meet four Ethiopians who soon would complete their secondary educations and return home that he immediately made arrangements to replace them and successfully negotiated additional places in various schools. Wherever he went, he appeared decorous and dignified, and even the briefest exposure to his persona remained memorable. Most people agreed with Lord Allenby's description of Tafari as "agreeable, intelligent, and appreciative of courtesy . . . a person of strikingly refined appearance."[11] The preliminaries were now complete: Tafari had proved his mettle in Palestine as a diplomat and in Egypt as an ambassador. Europe lay ahead as the public relations challenge.

On 9 May, the Ethiopians left Africa behind and sailed for Marseilles, where their arrival on the fourteenth was saluted by various units of the French Mediterranean Squadron in the harbor. After a day in the city, Tafari and his party took a train for Paris, where they arrived at the Gare de Lyon on the morning of 15 May to a grand welcome by president, premier, ministers, mayor, generals, bands, and soldiers.[12] The regent appeared in a "spotless flowing white mantle with the Star and Gold Collar of Ethiopia, and a wide green sash across his right breast, white trousers taken in at the ankle [jodhpurs], and a grey sun helmet." He was serenely unmoved by the pomp of his welcome, though "he smiled from time to time . . . and had the appearance of a deity receiving homage." His delicate mien and "refined features" contrasted with those of his entourage: "Burly and fierce looking, clad in black velvet cloaks, with great pith helmets, they made one realize the force that has kept Ethiopia unconquered throughout the ages."[13]

Tafari and President Alexandre Millerand drove in an open car to the Quai d'Orsay, where "in the Palace of the Foreign Ministry . . . quarters had been prepared for Us."[14] Luxuriating in the gold and blue magnificence of the official guest apartment, Tafari was served a proper French lunch, allowed to rest a bit, and then taken to the Elysée Palace, to be formally received by President Millerand, who thereafter escorted his guest to a reception at the City Hall.[15] That night there was a glittering formal dinner at the Elysée Palace. The toasts were warm and sincere, hinting at the success of Tafari's mission. Millerand referred to France's role in Ethiopia's recent entry into the League of Nations, which he characterized as an event that protected the Solomonic Empire from aggression and guaranteed its political independence. He remarked that France had helped Ethiopia by building the Djibouti – Addis Abeba railway, thus creating a community of economic interests between the two nations that needed to be maintained and strengthened. In reply, Tafari revealed his deep and growing respect for France's activities on Ethiopia's behalf and his conviction that Paris would have an important place in his country's economic development.[16]

His optimism about the port waned quickly, however, when his days were taken up by tourism and social events, with not a word from his hosts about Djibouti. On 20 May, frustration took over, and Tafari voiced his astonishment at the silence about the matter of Ethiopia's access to the sea. Louis Bellefon, undersecretary of the Foreign Ministry's Political Bureau, replied that the question was too important to be hurried, but Tafari pressed on, claiming that Gaussen had committed France to granting part of Djibouti to Ethiopia "en toute propriété." Bellefon rejoined that Gaussen had exceeded his instructions, had failed to mention the promise in his dispatches, and should never have implied that a cession would be easy to arrange. When the undersecretary mentioned that a "free zone" at Djibouti could be managed, the regent countered that his government would look elsewhere, perhaps to Italy. The unruffled Bellefon was skeptical that Tafari would be successful in Rome and simply asked if Addis Abeba really wanted to have an Italian-controlled railway traversing northern Ethiopia.

"With a certain impatience," Tafari retorted that Great Britain would exchange a dam on Lake Tana for Zeila on the Somali coast. When the Frenchman ridiculed the idea as impractical and dangerous for Ethiopia's sovereignty, the ras simply expressed his regret that France was unable to negotiate seriously, as leasing provided neither the security nor the rights that his country wished to exercise over its *débouché*. Bellefon commented rhetorically that France's offer gave Ethiopia what it really needed, even if Tafari had to abandon part of his dream about the country's future. The undersecretary expressed hope that the ras would prove sensible and directed his staff to work up a draft agreement while Tafari visited Belgium and Luxembourg, 22–31 May 1924.[17]

Meanwhile, the undersecretary convened two meetings of the interministerial committee overseeing the negotiations about Djibouti. Its members agreed that an Ethiopian port at Zeila or Mitsiwa would devastate Djibouti's economy and decided to offer Tafari a free zone, which incidentally would yield the colony a high annual rent and costly haulage fees.[18] Tafari found the plan too expensive and contrary to his instructions to obtain a site "en toute propriété," in which the Ethiopian government would "be master."[19] The impasse remained unbroken while the ras took a side trip to Sweden and had hardened by 16 June, when he departed Paris for Rome.

The magnificent hospitality shown Tafari on arrival in Italy on 17 June led him to believe that the Italians would be forthcoming on Aseb. He had been met at the frontier by the royal train, which splendidly conveyed him to Rome, where he was greeted on 18 June by a gaggle of grandly dressed officials, King Victor Emmanuel, and Mussolini. The monarch escorted the ras to his quarters at the Quirinal Palace, the royal residence, where, from the balcony, both men greeted the crowd below.[20] Haile Sellassie recollected that the people cheered "with one voice joyfully: 'Long live Italy! Long live Ethiopia! Long live H.H. Crown Prince Tafari!' "[21]

At a state dinner that evening, Victor Emmanuel toasted his guest: "It is my sincere wish that the government, which God by his desire has given into your hands, may continue to prosper. . . . Your visit to Italy now will, I believe, progressively strengthen the friendship and mutual benefit between the two governments. . . . I pray that God's blessings may descend upon Ethiopia." The regent was romantic enough about monarchs to trust the sentiments so expressed: "We Ethiopians consider the speech of a king of a great country to be like a pledge given under oath, and the words spoken by H.M. the King of Italy . . . seemed to Us to augur a stable peace and amity between the two governments; and it did not appear to Us a matter of deceit." Tafari responded positively, promising to strengthen Italo-Ethiopian peace and friendship.[22]

He got down to cases the next day with Mussolini, whom he found physically impressive: "His powerful face, his enormous eyes, his projecting jaw, his voice with its always changing inflections [demanded attention]; he took advantage of everything. He was theatrical." As had his king, il duce voiced only peaceful sentiments toward Ethiopia, whose independence he claimed to cherish. He listened carefully to the request for a port, asked intelligent questions, and smilingly undertook to make a quick decision.[23] A strategy had already been decided; and the next day Count Colli presented Tafari with a draft treaty that superficially attempted to meet Addis Abeba's needs but was in fact a blueprint for transforming Ethiopia into an economic dependency.

The Italians offered a ninety-nine year lease for a sovereign "access point" to the sea at Aseb and a territorial connection to the frontier upon which a railway could be built. In return, Ethiopia was to permit the formation of an Italian-manned but jointly held firm to construct the port, the rail link, and feeder roads to Gonder, Adwa, Mekele, and other points, and favor joint or Italian companies for any economic development programs it might undertake.[24] Had Tafari accepted the package, it would have institutionalized Rome's economic supremacy over Zawditu's realm.

Given the obvious Italian goal, it is hard to believe that Fascist policy makers would have permitted the "access point" to be used for weapons imports. Furthermore, Tafari likely understood the real meaning of the Italian offer, as Ethiopian statesmen had learned the hard way to read important documents for every nuance and inference. He nevertheless diplomatically conceded that the proposals should be considered in Addis Abeba, knowing well that his government would reject them. In terms of the later conflict between the two countries, it might have been wise to have accepted the Italian offer as a basis for discussion and then negotiated programs that strengthened Ethiopia's infrastructure and its national identity. In 1924, however, none could have foreseen that the consistent frustration of peaceful Italian efforts to transform Ethiopia into an economic dependency would lead to a colonial war. While Addis Abeba was making short shrift of Rome's scheme, Tafari returned to Paris to see if he could use the offer to force French concessions.

He could not. The Quai d'Orsay found a myriad of excuses for inaction: governmental crises, the need for further study, the absence of key officials or documents, and the like.[25] The studied indifference grew from the realization that Italy had yielded nothing and the conviction that neither would London.[26] The more Tafari pressed, the more languid Bellefon became, until, finally, the Ethiopian was left with one more card to play, the British trump. The sceptered isle represented only slight hope, however, so rampant was British racism. On 17 June, the *Manchester Guardian* commented that during one of Tafari's outings in France, "his hosts gave the black monarch what no northern rival for his favours could attempt, a kiss from little [six-year-old] Marcelle Colin. . . . A kiss for a Negro king is more than all the wealth of England can afford."[27]

Nor did King George V (r. 1910–1936) especially want to embrace his royal brother. He apparently did not like Africans, except in menial and servile situations, and the Foreign Office had to apply unremitting, if loyal, pressure to convince the monarch to break bread with Tafari. The diplomats sketched out the Sudan's need for a barrage on Lake Tana and then appealed to the monarch's vanity: "If the King could see His way to invite Ras Taffari to spend two nights at Buckingham Palace and give a banquet in his honour, it is most likely that the impression upon His Highness would be so indelible that his earlier experience at Rome, Paris, and Brussels would be completely eclipsed." [28] Although such a dubious equation was more an arrogance than a reality, King George would agree only to fete Tafari at a luncheon on 21 June, but regretted that he could not "invite him to stay for the night," because race week at Ascot and its many social events had priority. [29] A scandalized Foreign Office viewed the royal response as an artifact from 1824, "when . . . Abyssinia was not known at the Court of St. James." [30]

The king remained aloof, if not hostile, even when a changed schedule brought Tafari to London during a relatively quiet time. George could not even trouble himself to greet Tafari on 7 July at Victoria Station, not very far from Buckingham Palace; nor could the Prince of Wales, later Edward VIII (r. 1936), pull himself away from the Olympic Games in Paris to welcome his crown princely peer, a responsibility that he characteristically passed to the second son, the shy Duke of York, the future George VI (r. 1936–1952). The best the king could muster was a formal welcome at the palace on 8 July and a visit that afternoon to the ras's residence in nearby Albert Gate. The two royals would meet again at a luncheon at the palace on 9 July and at a farewell audience at noon on the twelfth. [31] Tafari's treatment was shoddy compared to the lavish hospitality he had experienced elsewhere, and his humiliation might have turned to mortification had he known about the well-modulated hubbub in the establishment about awarding him the Grand Cross of the Order of Bath. It was the highest honor available for European royalty and other very important individuals; "it is undesirable that it should be cheapened by being conferred on someone who, after all, is only the heir apparent to the throne of an uncivilized and primitive country." [32] King George naturally agreed but saw no other possibility, as Tafari had received the Grand Cross of the Order of St. Michael and St. George in 1917, upon Zawditu's accession. [33]

If the establishment preferred to ignore or demean its Ethiopian guest, the press and the public were fascinated by his appearance, although there were touches of ridicule. The *Daily Express* reported inevitably that Tafari wore "shiny elastic-sided black boots of a peculiar make"; that during his visit to the Tower of London, the ras-regent had "carefully examined" the execution block, a headsman's ax, and a model of a woman on the rack; and that "the instruments of torture and weapons pleased the chiefs most," casting them and their leader in a barbaric and bloodthirsty light.[34] Mostly, however, the press was open-mouthed, gentle, and respectful about the exotic ruler in their midst. Tafari was portrayed as a man with an "extraordinarily handsome face, next door to black, with high standing curly hair, a crisp black beard, a fine hawkish nose, and large, gleaming eyes."[35] *The Times* applauded the ras's devotion to modernization: "The tremendous rupture with the past which his journey . . . involves shows the boldness, the resolution, and the enlightenment of the Prince's character."[36] *The Observer* alluded to Tafari's policy of sending Ethiopian youths abroad for secondary and higher education: "from among these on their return will be nominated the staff of the administrative and educational departments designed to carry out his progressive policy."[37] But the accolades changed no official minds.

The government continued to believe that Tafari was a native princeling who had come to Europe to confirm the grandeur of the British Empire. Its rulers were unused to treating men of color as equals: the problems faced by such men were unimportant in the face of the larger needs of imperial policy, even if London wanted something from them, as they did from the Ethiopians. On 11 July 1924, Prime Minister Ramsay MacDonald met with Tafari and opened the discussion undiplomatically by referring to cross-border raiding into British-administered territory. The regent calmly responded that his government moved quickly against all miscreants, was working hard to ensure tranquillity along the frontiers, and that the problems would be finally solved when the borders were delimited properly enough to be respected by both sides. Ignoring the riposte, MacDonald bumbled forward to mention the administration of justice in Ethiopia but was quickly turned aside by the regent's explanation that he had established a special court in 1922 to deal with cases between foreigners and nationals, that he had recently improved the court's procedures, and that he currently was seeking to employ a European judge.[38] The meeting was over before any other business could be raised.

The next encounter, on 16 July at 10 Downing Street, vividly demonstrated official Britain's disdain for Ethiopia. Tafari raised the matter of his country's access to the sea in terms of Britain's cooperation in Ethiopia's modernization plans, artfully connecting London's desire for a Tana barrage with Addis Abeba's need for a port. MacDonald had not been briefed adequately on the complexities of the arrangement and begged off from any discussion. Tafari was so astounded that he "did not press the proposal and passed on to a request for arms," which MacDonald turned aside by claiming that Britain no longer supplied weapons to foreign powers. Turning to Lake Tana, Tafari explained that his government could not understand how Ethiopia would benefit from the dam's construction and therefore had decided to have an American firm undertake a feasibility study. MacDonald agreed with the decision, and Tafari quickly commented that it was also Ethiopia's sovereign right "to carry out the work and be entirely responsible for it."[39] The declaration elicited no response, and the ras's subtle demand for mutual respect and reciprocity was lost in a welter of arrogance, racism, and downright incompetence.

Tafari was dejected by the "lack of warmth" encountered during his official visit in London. The Prince of Wales's absence at Victoria Station rankled, as did King George's failure to lodge him at Buckingham Palace or even to honor him there at a state dinner. The ras was also distressed by the evasiveness of functionaries who treated him with "superior politeness . . . and official caution," underestimating their Ethiopian guest, himself a master at prevarication, politesse, and prudence.[40] Still, Tafari was able to put aside his disappointments to enjoy the private part of his stay. London fascinated him; he enjoyed its orderliness, the solidity of its monuments and institutions, and the scale of its famous shops. He spent over £1,000 at Harrod's, "buying with excellent judgement and with little of that love of the ornate and curious which eastern potentates so often display." He liked the clarity, sincerity, honesty, and courtesy of transacting business and making purchases in London.

He was enraptured by the British aristocracy's apparent voluntarism and sense of duty, and he longed "for men among my chieftains who would serve their country without thought of reward." He attributed the public service ethic to the country's elite schools and universities, and he was especially pleased with the honorary doctorate granted him by Cambridge University on 18 July. Its award recognized his efforts at bringing education to Ethiopia and acknowledged the importance of his plans to establish British-style schools to train "young men . . . in the path of service. The young men are our hope — if we can set them on the right road." [41] Throughout his life, Haile Sellassie would voice his admiration for the "innate character" of the British people while privately criticizing the London government's colonial mentality.[42] He was content therefore to return to the more respectful ambiance of Paris on 21 July.

While Tafari had been across the channel, the Ministry of Colonies finally bowed to increasing patriotic pressure not to give up a centimeter of Djibouti. Although the Quai d'Orsay was fully aware that neither the Italians nor the British had offered the Ethiopians very much, the French Foreign Ministry worried about alienating Tafari and convinced the cabinet to concede at least a rented "concession," over which both the French and Ethiopian flags would fly.[43] A draft convention was drawn up to provide Ethiopia "an emplacement . . . reserved for its use and . . . under its own customs regime." [44] But the draft never got to Tafari because a governmental crisis intervened. Instead, he received a letter from the Foreign Ministry, explaining that the negotiations were suspended until the new prime minister and his government could study the matter fully.[45] The Ethiopian government inevitably would have rejected the French offer, but Tafari gave the possibility, though unseen, the best possible interpretation: "We were glad when We read this letter, for its wording gave hope that an accord would be concluded within the near future." [46]

It was enough to permit Tafari to record his appreciation of the Quai d'Orsay's "affability" and hospitality, his regard for Paris as the most beautiful city in Europe, and his respect for France as a citadel of modernity. He told a reporter that he had learned much in Europe and was eager to return home to begin the many projects he had in mind. Development in Ethiopia, the ras advised, would take time, because "progress is not achieved simply by decrees, but through

adapting tradition to change and by eliminating ignorance and superstition." The journalist commented: " 'Time is needed' is his favorite expression. He does not mean by this to wait—waiting is
unproductive—but not to rush people or things. Do each thing in its
own time but fill each hour." [47] This impression conformed beautifully with the notion expressed by a contemporary English writer:
"Not the least striking characteristic of the Prince Regent is his genius for hastening slowly. He has been content to consolidate his
position gradually, refraining from the more spectacular methods,
which make attractive reading, but inevitably play into the hands of
opponents." [48] Tafari now slowly made his way back to them and to
Ethiopia, leaving Marseilles on 15 August for Greece.

    In Athens, the future emperor was lionized for the sake of the large
Greek colony in Ethiopia. Visitors and hosts lavished fulsome praise
on the antiquity and glorious history of Ethiopia and Hellas, transforming mythology, fact, and fancy into a functional relationship.
The African country sought skilled technicians and professionals,
and Greece needed to settle its surplus population abroad. In fact,
some emigrants embarked for Addis Abeba a few days later, on the
same ship that carried the Ethiopians home via Djibouti, where they
arrived on 31 August. Awaiting Tafari were two imperial emissaries
carrying a strange letter from the empress, who, ignorant of geography, believed that her second-in-command had been touring the
tropics: "While I was distressed about your toiling in strange and hot
countries, when you were thinking only of our country's freedom,
respect, and honour, I am now pleased about your safe return." [49]

    The ras was not surprised therefore by the excellent welcome he
received upon his arrival in Addis Abeba on 4 September. Awaiting
him were Fit. Habte Giorgis, Abuna Mattewos and the church hierarchy, leading military and civil officers, the diplomatic corps, and
thousands of Addis Abebans and soldiers. The throng escorted Tafari's carriage to the palace, where the ras renewed his fealty to the
empress and reported that he had honored her name throughout
Europe. In reply, Zawditu praised Tafari, who "had endured the turbulence of the sea and the heat of the sun" to carry out the plan
"which we had devised for the prosperity of our country and the good
fortune of our people." That night palace revelers feasted, not in the
shadowy light of candles and lanterns, but in a large palace hall well
lit by electricity, a "symbol . . . of a new age." [50]

The political situation, however, was less clear and certainly old-fashioned. Tafari's governmental colleagues considered his trip a failure.[51] The Council of the Realm regarded the Italian offer of a free port and the limited French undertakings unsatisfactory, demeaning, and dangerous and directed Tafari to abandon all negotiations concerning Ethiopia's access to the sea.[52] Of the nineteen members of the council in 1925, only nine could be classified as Tafari's partisans, giving Zawditu and Habte Giorgis a majority on most issues. In cases of major importance, as in the case of membership in the League, certain provincial personalities and nongovernmental figures were consulted, but these men were invariably conservative, if not reactionary, in outlook.[53] Tafari therefore suspended his quest for a port, a failure that in the next year nonetheless helped erode the arms embargo.

Paris was uneasy about its rejection of Ethiopia's plans for Djibouti and reasoned that French prestige in Addis Abeba could be restored by assisting the Solomonic government "to recover more freedom of action than they presently have concerning arms and munitions." Resumption of weapons sales would also help Djibouti and perhaps reduce Addis Abeba's insistence on "having a more independent access to the sea."[54] In March 1925, Paris therefore strongly supported Tafari's initiatives in the League of Nations to break the arms embargo by appealing for equal treatment as a member state. The Ethiopian government requested that an imminent League conference on arms control "examine with special care the situation of Abyssinia in the matter of her right to import arms, munitions, and implements of war necessary for her legitimate requirements."[55]

During the conference of May 1925, the British and the Italians argued obstinately that Ethiopia had agreed, upon joining the League, that Africa was a "prohibited zone."[56] France interpreted their stubbornness as a flagrant interference in the internal affairs of a member state, in Africa, to be sure, but not part of the colonial prohibited zone. The Quai d'Orsay pursued the logic of this distinction to the flat assertion that Ethiopia, as a sovereign state, enjoyed absolute freedom of arms importation, a stance supported by many small states that considered any great power limitation on access to arms as subverting the concept of sovereignty.[57] The Anglo-Italian position therefore "commanded the support of the Turk only. Others were neutral or hostile."[58] In the voting for the "Convention for the

Control of the International Traffic in Arms, Munitions, and Implements of War," Ethiopia was removed from the prohibited zone.

The Belgian government, in an obviously prearranged move, immediately asked the tripartite powers to permit the sale to Ethiopia of one hundred machine guns, each with one hundred thousand rounds, before ratification of the new accord, since "the destination was 'perfectly honourable', viz., the police and armed forces of the Abyssinian Government." [59] An unhappy commentator in London remarked that the request showed that Ethiopia had broken "the ring which we and the Italians were trying to construct around her in order to prohibit that unlimited importation of arms." [60] Abruptly, the British changed their tactics, suddenly asking for the establishment of a transit permit system "although purchases would not necessarily be vetoed, delivery could always be prevented." [61] Such a mechanism would take time to arrange, and meanwhile Ethiopia freely purchased arms from Switzerland and Czechoslovakia, giving Tafari a notable success.

He also began to import European experts to assist in modernization programs. Immediately after World War I, Tafari had employed tens of low-cost White Russian émigrés as technicians, [62] but the new men were attached to the ministries as advisers and planners. In 1924–1925, Tafari hired two Belgian mining engineers, a Swiss hydrologist to survey Lake Tana, two Swiss legal advisers for the Special Court and the new Court of Appeals, and two French teachers. [63] He also planned to obtain a commercial adviser, several English teachers, and a few road-building engineers. [64] He was particularly interested in American expertise and capital and invited the U.S. consul in Aden to visit Addis Abeba, as a prelude to restoring diplomatic ties, suspended when Washington had closed the American legation during World War I. [65] Tafari also repaired relations with the Soviet Union, which appointed a diplomat of the old school to represent its revolutionary interest in a country ruled by a traditional regime. [66]

Yet the ras also aimed to change Ethiopia through the creation of a more knowledgeable and open society. In 1921–1922, he imported two printing presses and undertook the publication of Amharic-language books and tracts. In 1924–1925, he established the important weekly newspaper *Berhanena Selam*, which provided news, homilies, sermons, propaganda, and the like for an increasingly aware urban population.[67] Another important innovation in 1925 was the establishment of the Tafari Makonnen School, a quasi-secondary school, which the regent—a title he had recently begun to use in correspondence[68]—operated at his own expense. The school had cost £12,000 to build and equip, and its annual maintenance was calculated at about £3,000. The school's capacity was estimated at fifty boarders and the same number of day students, all boys, although by year's end, it had enrolled 160 pupils, ranging in age from nine to twenty-five; some were even married.[69] At the school's inauguration on 2 May 1925, Tafari advised the students that "the time was past . . . for mere lip service to their country. The crying need of the people was education, without which they could not sustain their independence."[70]

Not everyone believed that newfangled ideas would save Ethiopia, especially some low-ranking or minor figures who felt abandoned by an aristocracy more interested in import-export than in fiefs and dues. Tafari, as Ethiopia's leading merchant-prince, was the inevitable magnet for their dissatisfaction. Citing their hatred of his programs and policies, they plotted his assassination. Fortunately, an informer reported the conspiracy; a dozen people were jailed and tried for treason; and death sentences were pronounced but subsequently commuted to prison terms.[71]

An embittered and dejected ras wallowed in self-pity: the people did not want modernization; the empress did not care about anything except the church; and the aristocracy thought only about wealth, status, and intrigue. Rumors circulated that he was a Roman Catholic, that he had embezzled state funds, and that his only objective in Europe was to display himself as a "modern" statesman, not to improve Ethiopia's international standing and certainly not to negotiate access to the sea. The ras was outraged; abroad and at home, he had worked long hours and responsibly implemented policies to safeguard Ethiopia's independence.[72] At the end of 1925, his strategies were tested by an attack on Ethiopia's sovereignty.

On 14 December 1925, Ambassador Ronald Graham in Rome wrote Mussolini that in exchange for Italian support to build a dam on Lake Tana, Great Britain would recognize Italy's right to construct a railway from Somalia to Eritrea, acknowledge Rome's "exclusive economic influence in the west of Ethiopia," and recom-

mend that all Ethiopian government concessions in the area be given
to Italians. Graham pointed out that the undertakings were con-
gruent with the provisions of the Tripartite Treaty of 1906, which
defined French, British, and Italian zones of interest should Ethiopia
break up.[73] In reply, Mussolini agreed that nothing in Graham's letter
contradicted the 1906 treaty, and he confirmed his government's
acceptance of the views presented about the Tana dam, the Italian
railway, and Italy's economic primacy in western Ethiopia.[74] In London, the Foreign Office was sensitive, almost embarrassed, about
negotiating with a third party about another's territory, but it justified
the exchange of letters as a specification of the conditions under
which Britain would "support the Italians in attaining a position
which they do not in fact at present possess."[75] Rome, of course, was
keenly aware of its feckless incumbency in the Horn of Africa, was
eager to obtain even modest recognition of its primacy in Ethiopia,
and was delighted to negotiate with London as if the Addis Abeba
government did not exist.

The discussions leading to the exchange of letters demonstrated
that both countries had been influenced by the conventional opinion
that there was no government in Ethiopia; that the central administration could not control the provinces; and that the country would
soon dissolve into anarchy. The Foreign Office had listened too
closely to the vitriol of Claud Russell, its man in Addis Abeba, who
disliked all blacks, especially those who held power and refused to
defer to whites. Ethiopia, in his opinion, needed European rule for
the sake of progress, a position also held strongly by Count Colli, the
durable Italian legate, who considered the Solomonic Empire a chi-
mera, merely a name on a map, without any kind of sovereign legitimacy. Neither European was attentive to the traditional excellence
of Ethiopian diplomacy or to France's need to restore its prestige in
Addis Abeba.

When notified of the Anglo-Italian initiative, Ethiopia reserved its
right as a sovereign state to reply on receipt of the full text.[76] A
jubilant French government immediately concluded, however, that
the accord "has the drawback . . . of scarcely respecting the international situation of Ethiopia, [and] of violating its territorial and
sovereign rights, presently under the safeguard of the League of
Nations."[77] The Quai d'Orsay offered its regrets to the Foreign Office

that such an agreement had been negotiated with the Italians, who now enjoyed "a *free hand* in their sphere of influence in Abyssinia [italics mine]." The accord, in the view of Paris, "implied a sharp alteration of the political and territorial status of Abyssinia" little short of "partition of a member state of the League of Nations." The Quai sympathized with Britain's need to guarantee its rights to Lake Tana's surplus waters but stressed its inability to accept an exclusive Italian economic zone in Ethiopia's west: "This was the real stumbling block of the whole business. . . . It was in Rome, not in London, that territorial ambitions in Abyssinia were harboured and designs to undermine her independence were being matured."[78] The French unabashedly advised Tafari of the same, influencing London to ask Rome to soften the language used in the original letters.[79]

Mussolini claimed to be flexible "so long as the substance of the agreement was maintained," but he conceded no changes,[80] spurring the French to charge that Italy's ultimate goal was the destruction of the Ethiopian state or at least its "Moroccanisation."[81] The Ethiopians agreed: the usually reserved and noncommittal Ras Kassa publicly expressed his outrage, vowing that Ethiopia would never "take orders from Italy."[82] Charles Bentinck, the new British minister, gloomily forecast a diplomatic defeat. His French colleague was advising "point blank" rejection of the letters and an appeal to the League, "in which case we would look rather foolish."[83] He was nonetheless instructed to officially transmit the accords to the Addis Abeba government on 10 June 1926.

The Italians, meanwhile, were trying to explain away the growing crisis. Count Colli fictionalized the Anglo-Italian stipulations as "exclusively economic," respectful of "the sovereign rights of the Ethiopian Government," and "new proof of the friendly intentions of Italy and England toward the Ethiopian Empire, which remained absolutely free to accept or reject any requests of an economic nature that might be made by either of the two governments."[84] On 15 June, at breakneck speed for the Addis Abeba government, Tafari rejected Colli's humbug by formally advising Rome and London that Ethiopia regarded the Anglo-Italian accords as an infringement of sovereignty, a matter that he would refer to the League of Nations.[85] In indictment, he charged that the Anglo-Italian initiative derogated the sovereign equality of a League member, whereas the charter pre-

sumed "that the independence of all [adherents] would be respected." The wording of the Anglo-Italian accords was "incompatible with Our country's independence, in particular when it is stated
that a part of Our possessions is to be given over to the economic
influence of a certain Great Power . . . [and was therefore] incompatible with the basic idea of the League of Nations." [86]

In Addis Abeba, the government undertook a propaganda campaign against Italy, which became an immediate target of suspicion,
resentment, and hatred.[87] The newly educated Young Ethiopians
were especially vociferous in their denunciations as published in
the pages of *Berhanena Selam*.[88] In Rome, the brouhaha alarmed
responsible officials, "especially the colonial authorities,"[89] who
watched "cordiality between Italian and Ethiopian frontier officials
[along the Eritrean border] drop . . . to a low, and even trade . . .
suffer[ed]." [90] Indeed, the situation appeared so ominous in Italy that
the chief of the general staff, Pietro Badoglio, who would direct
Ethiopia's invasion in 1935, asked for a thorough study of Eritrea's
defenses, including the possible use of poison gas, either through
aerial bombing or through shelling.[91] Before the situation deteriorated further, Rome concluded that there was nothing to gain from
holding stubbornly to the letter of the Anglo-Italian accords and
agreed with London's longstanding request for moderating the language, though not the spirit, of the arrangement.[92] Conciliatory and
explanatory letters were sent to Geneva.

The British Foreign Office regretted that the Anglo-Italian arrangements "should have been misconstrued and intentions attributed to the British and Italian Governments which they have never
entertained." [93] Rome grieved that Addis Abeba had "not clearly understood the letter and spirit of the agreements reached between the
Italian and British Governments." The two had merely coordinated
"certain economic issues"; the consequent harmony "in actual
practice would naturally be subject to the decision of the Abyssinian
Government and the latter's recognition that those interests were in
keeping with those of Abyssinia and would be beneficial to the country's economic and civil progress." The Italian explanation closed, as
had the British note, by stating that nothing in the accords could
"detract from the right of the Abyssinian Government to take such
decisions as it may think fit, or limit the possible action of third

parties."[94] A satisfied Ethiopian government considered the mildness of the statements "as a withdrawal through fear of public opinion, from the original intention of the two Governments to arrange a 'partition' of Abyssinia."[95] Addis Abeba subsequently advised the League that it appreciated the friendly intentions of the British and the Italians, who had admitted Ethiopia's "full and complete freedom to decide any requests which may be made to it, and [its] perfect right to judge what is in the interest of Abyssinia."[96]

Ethiopia's decision to join the League had been vindicated; the success of Tafari's appeal for justice "seemed to demonstrate in a striking way how a weak state could use the international organization as protection against the machinations of great powers."[97] The crisis also underlined the importance of French diplomatic support,[98] a truth overlooked during the next few years as Ethiopia became involved in expanding its international relations and developing a centralized state. The new period was prefaced by the deaths in December 1926 of Abuna Mattewos and Fit. Habte Giorgis, two men who represented the old Ethiopia.

CHAPTER FIVE

From Regent to Royal,
1926-1930

With Fit. Habte Giorgis gone, the empress lost an important ally, the government its strong man, and southern Ethiopia its longtime overlord. For Tafari, the political opportunities were immense, especially in the south, which protocapitalism had made into Ethiopia's richest region. There, during the previous quarter century, the position of overlord (neftenya) had changed to landlord, transforming the traditional agriculturalists into sharecroppers or rural proletarians. The process had begun before World War I, when land was measured and classified as fertile, semifertile, or poor depending on the availability of a settled population from which labor could be drawn.[1] By the late twenties, the metamorphosis was so complete that the south constituted "for the Ethiopia Government . . . a large colony of exploitation — meant in the most rigorous sense of the term."[2] Cash crops as such and money came to dominate Ethiopia's political economy, and control over appointments in the populous south, and therefore its armies, added greatly to Tafari's wealth and power. The ras quickly let it be known that Habte Giorgis's holdings would be divided among cooperative partisans, whom he would directly oversee to assure trade and tranquillity along Ethiopia's southern frontiers.[3]

Believing he was at a personal "crossroads,"[4] the regent immediately recruited the fitawrari's personal force of fifteen thousand well-armed men and then assumed Habte Giorgis's governmental responsibilities, learning to his dismay "what a great amount of work the fituarari had taken off his shoulders."[5] As he considered nominees for the War Ministry, he was heard to complain that "there is not a man in the country that can be trusted completely to take charge of a department of government without using his power for his own ends to the detriment of the country as a whole."[6] Sensitive to potential competitors, Tafari decided to divide the fitawrari's functions in the central government. He created a new position, chief of staff of the armed forces, and cleverly filled it with Ligaba Wodajo, Zawditu's master of ceremonies. He named as minister of war Dej. Mulugeta, the current minister of finance, a survivor from Menilek's regime and a good friend of the empress but "incapable of wielding the enormous influence attributed to his predecessor in the War Ministry" because of the presence of the new chief of staff.[7] Finally, in a brilliant stroke, Tafari appointed his trusted henchman, Nag. Zelleka, to the Ministry of Finance, where he could manipulate the Imperial Exchequer to benefit his master.[8]

Most money revenues came from taxes on trade. From the provinces to Addis Abeba came "droves of donkeys laden with products of farm and forest, long strings of pack-mules, interminable files of camels," each animal contributing its load to Ethiopia's gross national product.[9] The produce was shipped either from towns that had evolved since Menilek's period or from strategic posts placed at or near customary trading sites or at new centers built near coffee-growing areas.[10] Population and demand for produce grew apace, permitting several types of transactions and far greater returns than could be obtained from the usual two-party exchanges made in small traditional markets. In the south, therefore, there emerged enough substantial centers of demand to stimulate regional production, transforming such subsistence commodities as grain, ensete, and meat animals into semi-cash crops.[11]

In Harerge, which contained the increasingly important railhead at Dire Dawa and Harer City, together comprising a large market, Tafari, Princess Menen, Imru, and others facilitated commercial agriculture from which they derived great profits. The princess governed the Chercher region of Deder, where coffee was king. In Deder town, fourteen hours by mule from Dire Dawa, ten firms shared the coffee trade, which in 1925 accounted for an export of forty thousand bags. Each dealer paid Menen a one-time fee of MT$100 for a permit to do business, and thereafter MT$25 annually for each trading post and MT$50 for each coffee scale. The princess also traded in coffee grown on her own lands by sharecroppers,[12] as did Tafari, who worked an experimental farm six miles from the Erer train station on the rail line. The ras had irrigated a thousand hectares, which were planted in citrus, grapes, nuts, sugar cane, and kapok as well as coffee. At the suggestion of his Italian manager, Tafari permitted impoverished local Oromos to work the land as sharecroppers.[13] In this way, and in hundreds of other plantations and farms, some of Ethiopia's rural poor participated in the economic growth of the twenties.

So did Addis Abeba's masses, who found paid work in the town's many businesses or as day laborers moving the coffee, hides, and grains from warehouses to the railway station, for export to Aden and Djibouti for shipment elsewhere. Available economic data for 1926–1928 reveal a doubling of exports and imports, a sharp increase in the circulation and number of Maria Theresa dollars, an upward surge in commercial litigations, and the increasing willingness of Ethiopia's aristocracy to invest in commerce and in real estate in the capital, where property values soared.[14] The workers spent their money on low-cost Indian and Japanese textiles, forsaking expensive, locally made cottons. The richer among them, including an emergent bureaucratic bourgeoisie, put on shoes and airs, abandoning round, wattle-and-daub thatched homes for "stone-walled, tin-roofed," square houses, and locally crafted furnishings for imported household goods.[15] The wealthy—this category includes foreign merchants and some shopkeepers—purchased automobiles, some three hundred of which circulated in the city in 1927,[16] symbolizing Ethiopia's growing involvement in the world economy.

Most of the profit, however, accrued to an oligarchy increasingly composed of individuals who sought power for the sake of making money and who, in exchange for appointments and other prefer- ments, contributed to the princely purse. They were mostly the partners of and expediters for the Greek, Indian, and Arab merchants who worked in their provinces. In Gore, for example, Ras Nado built and secured roads, improved the town, and stabilized the region to facilitate commerce and to sustain the growing coffee trade and his percentage of the profits.[17] The wealthier the governing class be- came, the more it wanted a strong central government to protect its interests in the face of the postwar consolidation of imperialism.[18]

As heir to Amhara-Tigray nationalism, personified by his father and Emperor Menilek, Tafari was sensitive to challenges to Ethio- pia's sovereignty wherever and whenever they were made. He con- sistently and correctly refused to permit Europeans capitulary rights, in part because the country had its own hoary legal traditions but mostly because he wanted to protect the proceeds of the modern economy, which made wealth and reform possible. He sought also to safeguard Ethiopia's periphery and peoples from encroachment by adjacent colonial governments, though the difficulties of communi- cations made for slow and often incomplete responses.

In 1925–1926, Addis Abeba made a serious effort to improve secu- rity along the country's frontiers. At the Kenya border, Fit. Ayella was able to move around enough men to control the anarchic hunters and poachers who operated in loosely administered zones. He also disciplined or replaced administrators who had been overtaxing the Oromo and underpaying the central government.[19] Along the border with the British Somaliland Protectorate, the newly appointed gov- ernor of Jijiga, the energetic Kenyaz. Gadla Giorgis, came into con- flict with European officials, in October and November 1925, when he established a customs post apparently within the confines of the colony.[20] Upon protest, Addis Abeba closed the station and withdrew its few troops to Milmil, but the incident served to point out the need to demarcate Ethiopia's eastern frontiers.[21]

The Italians had long sought to stabilize the Ogaden line in order to eliminate raiding, but unrequited diplomatic efforts after 1916 led to Rome's frustration and unilateral action.[22] In October 1925, Gover- nor de Vecchi di Val Cismon acted to secure the territory that ran from the Wabe Shebele to the Gulf of Aden. He therefore took control over a line of water holes defined by the settlements of Geregube, Welwel, Warder, and Geladi, which, the Italians later argued, "constituted the natural, legitimate and ancient frontiers of the Sultanate of Obbia with the Ogaden."[23]

In October 1926, after the regularity of Italian patrols from these places had become obvious, Tafari verbally protested that Somalia had "occupied with its troops . . . localities which the Ethiopian Government deems within its territory" and had compromised the local population, "whose interests were gravely prejudiced by the fact that these localities [are] the only ones that have water." Count Colli questioned the accuracy of Tafari's *note verbale* and asserted that Geladi was definitely within the Italian frontier and had long been occupied by Mogadishu. The count stressed his government's desire for friendship with Ethiopia, its willingness to settle any differences over the frontier, and advised that Addis Abeba could easily avoid border problems by establishing order over its Somali subjects.[24] Ras Tafari took the advice to heart, and his riposte was a strong assertion of Ethiopia's sovereignty and independence.

On 6 June 1927, the Italian resident at Belet Uen received an official letter from Gadla Giorgis, advising that he was nearby with a large army, that he knew Mogadishu had occupied "our territory outside the Italian frontier," and that the European and his askaris had ten days to evacuate their station. The Ethiopian was bluffing: he had neither sufficient force nor authority to eject the Italians. His threat, however, attracted local reinforcements,[25] a reaction sufficient to contradict later Italian assertions that Addis Abeba never made "any kind of protest" against Mogadishu's unilateral assimilation of Ethiopian territory.[26]

Ras Tafari, however, refrained from further action because of a possibility that Italy might finally concede an Ethiopian port at Aseb. The matter surfaced again in May 1927, during the visit to Ethiopia of the royal Duke of Abruzzi, who headed a high-level mission including Iacopo Gasparini, the governor of Eritrea, and Raffaele Guariglia, a ranking Foreign Ministry official, both of whom had been charged to repair the damage done by the Anglo-Italian accords of 1925.[27] The timing was right; Tafari was frustrated by his inability to obtain a port, and he was greatly upset with the French, who "kept us waiting for about two years without giving a firm decision." [28] Moreover, the ras could now negotiate without worrying about Habte Giorgis and his influence on the empress and the conservatives on the Council of the Realm. The Italian mission was thus an important opportunity for Tafari, and he decided to impress the visitors with his authority.

On 18 May 1927, the ras-regent and his government effusively welcomed the Italian party to Addis Abeba. To an ovation of ululations, the duke and ras, escorted by a mounted guard of honor in red, white, and blue uniforms and Tafari's men in khaki, headed a procession from the lower town to the gibbi's commanding heights, where Zawditu formally greeted her royal guest. In reply, d'Abruzzi emphasized Italy's great sympathy for Ethiopia and Rome's conviction that friendship was the "essential condition" for developing mutual interests. Platitudes finished, the Italian party retired to Tafari's estate, where a newly built and furnished villa offered comfortable accommodations and a convenient location from which to visit nearby schools, hospitals, government buildings, and even Menilek's tomb.

At 8:00 A.M., on Saturday, 21 May, the duke and his entourage took the salute at a military review of troops from Sidamo, Harerge, and Shewa. By 1:00 P.M., "the parade showed no signs of ending," and first the visitors, then the diplomats, and finally Tafari withdrew to the Italian legation for lunch. The parade finally ended at 4:30 P.M., after eighty thousand men had marched past a reviewing stand that by the end held only a few stalwarts, among them Captain L. Ornati, the duke's hungry naval aide, who decided that the event had effectively demonstrated Ethiopia's unity and discipline and its determination to safeguard its independence. He noted, however, that only Tafari's army wore standard uniforms, marched in unison, and were armed with modern weapons, to which d'Abruzzi added an obsolescent tank, a gift that nonetheless delighted the ras.[29]

To even a trained observer's eye, the Italians spent their visit in a round of sightseeing, luncheons, dinners, entertainments, and ceremonials.[30] Behind the scenes, a different tableau was being developed: Guiliano Cora, Count Colli's successor, Guariglia, d'Abruzzi, and Tafari were shaping the outlines of a major agreement conceding Ethiopia a free zone at Aseb and a road connection to the frontier[31] and providing for a twenty-year treaty of friendship.[32] With the main points worked out, a satisfied Italian mission left Ethiopia to complete details in Rome with Mussolini and others. Guariglia was especially keen to see the negotiations succeed, so that Somalia and Eritrea might associate themselves with Ethiopia's obvious economic growth and modernization.

Without a vital hinterland, the two colonies lacked economic importance. In a memorandum dated 1 January 1928, Guariglia pointed out that the dependencies had been acquired with the larger objective of Ethiopia in mind and that the accord outlined in Addis Abeba might bring Ethiopia into Rome's orbit and thereby give vitality to the coastal holdings.[33] Quickly appreciating the possibilities, Mussolini personally directed Cora's detailed negotiations in Addis Abeba. These negotiations were not easy, as important Ethiopians, among them the empress, had reservations about building a road from Aseb to Dese, which many envisioned as the main invasion route from Eritrea.

These worries were somewhat assuaged when the Italians quickly agreed to include a statement of "bon voisinage" in the agreement. In March 1928, the Ethiopians offered a draft treaty of five articles, one of which called for conciliation and arbitration by the League of Nations in case of any dispute. An exultant Cora cabled that acceptance of this stipulation would allow Tafari "to follow, without fear of opposition, his amicable policy towards us, putting reality into the accords and providing for the development and deepening of commercial contacts and communications with the adjacent Italian colonies."[34] Mussolini agreed, although a number of details remained to be worked out, at least one of which was significant in terms of the subsequent war of 1935–1936.

On 26 March 1928, il duce directed Cora to avoid all textual references to delimitation of the frontiers between Somalia and Ethiopia.[35] Although specific designation was relatively simple to avoid, Tafari clung to the language of article 4, which specified recourse to the League to resolve conflicts "originating from questions of the delimitation of frontiers, of commerce, or of an analogous nature and not to resolve them by force of arms."[36] The net effect of the stipulations, the minister of colonies argued, would place Italy under the League's jurisdiction in each and every case of frontier delimitation between Ethiopia and Somalia.[37] Mussolini was annoyed that the Ethiopians apparently were making the League "the court of last resort [for] the whole gamut of human conflict," and he confided to

Cora, "Your excellency is not unaware of the delicacy and importance of the question of our frontiers and in a completely special way
that of the Somali-Ethiopian boundary. *In fact, we have no interest in
hurrying to resolve it and it is for this reason that . . . I have excluded
it from the present negotiations* [italics mine]." He suggested that the
minister obscure the frontier issue by explaining to Tafari that the
proposed treaty removed Ethiopia "from any danger that eventual
controversies concerning the borders might degenerate into armed
conflict."[38]

To obtain the language he preferred, Mussolini was willing to
make a number of apparently significant, but actually meaningless,
concessions. He agreed to give the Ethiopians a 150-year lease to
thirty thousand square meters of property on the Aseb coast, docking
rights for non-Italian vessels, and participation in all companies established to further the goals of the new agreement.[39] In return,
Tafari acquiesced to more general language about the settlement of
disputes, and given his new political power, he forced a skeptical
sovereign and Crown Council to approve the Treaty of Friendship
and Arbitration,[40] finally signed on 2 August 1928. Article 2, its most
important provision, committed Rome and Addis Abeba "to submit
to a procedure of conciliation and arbitration, without having recourse to force of arms, on questions which may arise between them
and which they have not been able to settle by normal diplomatic
means." In addition, Tafari and Cora formalized a Road Agreement
and Lease for a Free Zone in Aseb, which also permitted, according
to article 4, "rights of passage from the docks to the warehouses and
from there to the frontier on the motor road."[41]

The Italians believed that the treaties had given much to Ethiopia.
Guariglia wrote, "With a policy of sincere friendship towards Italy
and with a real will to collaborate with us, the Ethiopian Government
could have had at Assab an access to the sea in more favorable
conditions than at Jibuti or Zeila."[42] Eritrean officials were even
more enthusiastic and immediately surveyed Aseb and its environs,
deciding that thirty thousand square meters was "absolutely insufficient" for even a modest free zone. Corrado Zoli, the governor, was
willing to provide one hundred thousand square meters in a good
location, a move seconded by Cora and a syndicate composed of
FIAT and Credito Italiano.[43] Although Tafari professed his "every

intention" of fulfilling the promise of the treaties,[44] he probably signed them to obtain Italy's formal pledge of peace and friendship and agreement to a mechanism of conciliation and arbitration. He never intended Italy to gain important influence in Ethiopia, and, in fact, his policy sought to reduce the country's dependence on Europe by widening its international relations to conform to Ethiopia's economic reality.

By 1927, the major European powers no longer monopolized Ethiopia's trade; France, for example, only retained 4 percent of the import market, mostly by selling luxury perfumes and liquors, though the Djibouti railway remained a potent interest.[45] India and Japan accounted for most of Ethiopia's imports, and the United States took most of the nation's hides and coffee. In 1927–1928, the new economic order stimulated Washington to reopen its legation in Addis Abeba; and Austria and the Netherlands signed commercial treaties with Ethiopia, as did Japan, which also established a legation.[46] The French reacted by reviewing their role in Ethiopia, and in January 1928, the Quai d'Orsay circulated a memorandum entitled "About Franco-Italian Relations in Ethiopia," which established the rationale leading directly to Laval's offer to Mussolini, on 7 January 1935, of a "free hand" in Ethiopia.

The document bitterly described France's diminished economic role in Ethiopia and claimed that the Anglo-Italian accords of 1925, concluded without Paris's consent, had compromised the provisions of the Tripartite Treaty of 1906. Only timely Ethiopian action at Geneva, supported by France, had blocked Italy and Great Britain from obtaining the "special rights" enunciated in their agreement. If Paris decided to withdraw its de facto protection from Ethiopia, Italy might be willing to abandon its nationals' special privileges in Tunisia and make concessions in Europe. For the right price, then, the Quai d'Orsay might offer a "free hand" in the west of Ethiopia, making it clear to Italy, however, that any accord should expressly stipulate a commitment to maintaining Ethiopia's integrity and independence. Such a statement would suffice to discharge France's responsibility toward its one-time client.[47] Although the archives do not preserve any internal responses to the memo, its appearance augured badly for Ethiopia's international position.

France's alienation was perhaps inevitable, given Ethiopia's economic developments, but astute diplomacy might have salvaged the relationship. Tafari's policies seem to have been motivated, however, by strictly local concerns, which often blocked appreciation of the country's long-term interests in a world of imperialism and racism. The myopia was also present in negotiations with London about the Tana dam.

Logic demanded that Britain develop enough interests in independent Ethiopia to want to protect both its interests and Addis Abeba's sovereignty. Yet Tafari refused Britain special rights in the Tana area, blaming the restriction on the xenophobic "people around the lake." He also reasoned that Addis Abeba could raise the capital for the project by borrowing against the revenues projected from the sale of surplus water to Sudan and Egypt[48] and that, "in view of local prejudice," any concession should go to a private company, in which Ethiopians might be able to invest.[49] After long consideration of possible strategies, Tafari concluded that it would be best to do business with an American firm, not only to ensure high technical standards for the project but also to involve Washington in the country's future.[50] Although London would have preferred British control over the planning and execution of the projected dam — and such involvement might have worked to Ethiopia's benefit — Addis Abeba's approach was considered reasonable, and it was therefore accepted in principle.[51]

Dr. Workneh Martin, a British-educated physician, traveled to New York and negotiated a $20 million contract with the J. G. White Engineering Company to construct the Tana dam.[52] The American press was fascinated by the arrangement with exotic Ethiopia. The *New York Times* printed an interview with an eminent scholar who explained, "There is naturally a feeling in Addis Ababa that America, by virtue of its remoteness, offers no threat, . . . that American enterprise has the least 'political taint' and that it threatens no infringement of Abyssinian independence."[53] Reporting from London, the *New York Herald Tribune* characterized Ras Tafari's interest in the United States as a " 'gesture' with a two-fold purpose — administering a snub to the British and at the same time drawing the attention of American capitalists in dramatic fashion to his country as a possible field for commercial exploitation."[54] The *San Francisco Chronicle*, situated at the continental frontier of America's manifest destiny, commented that in Ethiopia "we are . . . asserting once more the American doctrine of the open door for trade and investment." The *Chronicle* pridefully assured its readers that the inchoate relationship with Ethiopia "is but part of a policy we have been pursuing quietly since we began to feel that America has become a world power and must have a world field for its activities."[55] The *New York World*, a major black newspaper, welcomed Addis Abeba's invitation to the New World to invest in Africa and hailed Dr. Martin's invitation to Harlem's artisans to emigrate to Ethiopia as an antidote to the popular view that the Solomonic state was disinterested in Afro-America.[56] Although the hoopla repelled the staid men of the London Foreign Office, they decided to accept the American-built dam.[57] It was a victory for Tafari, although the unforeseen long-term implications again revealed that in international relations, his hand then lacked the deftness so obvious in domestic politics.

Throughout the 1920s, the wealth and power of Ethiopia's central city and government eroded the administrative authority of provincial leaders, especially those who had adapted to the modern economy but who did not make generous contributions to Tafari.[58] The tightfisted Dej. Balcha of Sidamo made an obvious target: he and his lieutenants had greatly improved provincial transportation, and they had cooperated with Indian traders to establish a relatively efficient marketing and credit system. "Balcha was no mere incorrigible relic of the old order defying the Regent's authority, but . . . an obstacle to Tafari's control of [a] rich province."[59] Moreover, as the coffee business and revenues had boomed, the old dejazmach grew to detest the regent's rules and regulations.

Balcha and other provincial lords were now accountable for tax revenues reckoned through the issuance of numbered receipts to payees, and they were responsible for capricious and arbitrary acts against their subjects. If too many peasants complained about exploitation and cheating, offending governors were called to Addis Abeba to explain their behavior, an infuriating and insulting procedure, for, according to Tafari, Addis Abeba "meted out impartial justice . . . without paying heed to . . . high station."[60] The old guard could no longer look to the empress for relief; her power had dissipated with the death of Habte Giorgis, and, in any case, she was ailing, suffering from progressively worsening diabetes with liver complications.[61] Zawditu's impotence might have transformed Balcha's sense of grievance into neurosis, leading him to a futile challenge of the new political economy.[62]

After receiving numerous peasant complaints, Tafari recalled the dejazmach for explanation and consultation. In high dudgeon,[63] Balcha turned up in the capital on 11 February 1928, escorted by five thousand troops, "with the characteristics more of brigands than of soldiers."[64] As the old man approached the gibbi, he directed that his drum of office sound his presence, a distinct breach of etiquette for one who did not rule in Addis Abeba.[65] Once inside the palace to render homage, Balcha eccentrically declined, on the grounds of illness, to embrace Tafari or to accept Zawditu's kiss. He pointedly looked around the reception hall and asked if Lij Iyasu were still alive; upon receiving the expected reply, he loudly asked why Tafari was at the empress's side. He then refused to participate in the feast prepared in his honor and was generally insolent and threatening in conversation. All in all, it was a striking performance, given the usual restrained and reserved deportment of the Ethiopian aristocracy. So alarmed were his lieutenants that they secretly met with Tafari to testify that neither they nor their soldiers intended to be killed because of "a rash act of an old crazy man."[66]

Never one to miss an opportunity, Tafari convened his colleagues on the small Crown Council, Zawditu, Ras Kassa, who motored in from Fiche after being summoned by telephone, and Chief Secretary Wolde Maskal, each of whom voted to remove Balcha from Sidamo and to confiscate his property and wealth. On 18 February, twenty-three hundred police surrounded Balcha's camp on the outskirts of the capital, and Kantiba Nasibu, Addis Abeba's mayor, delivered the council's written judgment to the dejazmach. His soldiers quickly deserted, and on 19 February, the old man and a small bodyguard capitulated without a shot being fired. On 21 February, Balcha shouldered a stone of penance from the central post office, through Addis Abeba's commercial sector, to Tafari's villa. He subsequently was sent as a prisoner to Gurage country and, after a time, was pardoned and permitted to retire to Sidamo with some of his personal property restored.[67]

Given the limited data, the episode is difficult to analyze. Balcha clearly hoped for Zawditu's support and perhaps for the assistance of the old guard. They remained aloof because the confrontation was couched in reactionary terms now unpopular in the capital. After Habte Giorgis's death, Tafari had transformed the governmental Council of State into a liberal organization by mostly replacing its conservative members with progressives and protégés.[68] By 1928, it appeared that "the Government of Ethiopia is for practical purposes the Prince Regent, Tafari Makonnen,"[69] a fact made more obvious when he transferred Dej. Balcha's property to loyalists, among them his son-in-law Fit. Desta Demtu.[70] The heir's power was obvious also to the empress, who made a final, and bizarrely untimely, attempt to resurrect her own authority. She should have acted in February in concert with Balcha; instead she dallied and, without obvious allies, chose to confront Tafari over the issue of ratifying the Italo-Ethiopian treaty.

In August she insinuated that the regent had gone too far by agreeing to the Italian-built road from Aseb to Dese, thereby destroying Ethiopia's natural defenses.[71] Then, during a meeting on 5 September 1928, she directly accused Tafari of ignoring her early criticisms of the treaty and consequently undermining her authority. She told Tafari that members of her retinue believed that he wanted her off the throne, stupidly naming Dej. Beru and Ligaba Beyene, both of whom commanded palace troops. When a furious regent ordered the two men arrested, the dejazmach and a number of soldiers withdrew, with unintended symbolism, to Menilek's mausoleum on the palace grounds, which Tafari and members of his army surrounded, only themselves to be encircled by Ligaba Beyene and his command. After an uneasy night, dawn revealed the entire palace area ringed by the regent's khaki-clad guard, well armed with modern rifles, machine guns, small cannon, and, ironically, the Italian tank.[72] "Later on [Dej. Beru] sent as intermediaries the Etchage and some priests, lest We should impose the death penalty upon him, and then he surrendered" at 1:00 P.M. on 6 September.[73]

This strange incident is best explained as an episode in the struggle between the conservatives, who wished Ethiopia to remain a self-reliant, isolated fortress, and the progressives, who believed that the country could survive as an independent state only through contact with the world economy and Western technology. Tafari's use of the tank showed his preference, and Addison Southard, the new American minister—his presence another example of the regent's inter-nationalism—foresaw a glorious future for Ethiopia's strong man: "He is . . . exceptional and . . . will in time rank among the great characters of history in the cleverness and strength which he has displayed in the climb to almost supreme power in Ethiopia."[74] Tafari now wanted formal recognition of his political primacy and turned again to his network of minor officers—now grown to three hundred or so—who commanded units in the capital.[75] They dutifully organized a derg to present certain demands to the empress.

On 19 September 1928, at a meeting on the palace grounds, a small group of military men read a manifesto extolling the regent's work on behalf of Ethiopia and asking the empress to make him king with full powers. Zawditu temporized, arguing that as king, Tafari would have to reside in his realm, necessitating nomination of another regent, since two monarchs could not be domiciled in one capital. The logic escaped the derg, which formally requested a quick decision, suspecting that the empress was merely playing for time "in order to issue a refusal after consultation with her friends who follow her way of thinking and who do not like modern conditions." After more imperial silence, during which Zawditu failed to win over Ras Kassa, the military insisted that Tafari be named negus immediately "to preserve peace so that the people's blood does not flow." The empress had no other option, and on 22 September she decreed a new royalty, "His Majesty King Tafari Makonnan, Heir to the Throne of Ethiopia and Regent Plenipotentiary." A jubilant derg wanted the new monarch crowned immediately, but Tafari, always the publicist, convinced his ardent supporters to delay so that representatives of adjacent governments "might come and take part in our joy"[76] and legitimate the political change. Meanwhile, at the celebrations of the Feast of the Holy Cross a few days later, the ras entertained Addis Abebans by mounting a grand review of twelve thousand soldiers, including the few thousand modern troops that had helped him win a kingdom.[77]

On 6 October 1928, the mayor of Addis Abeba, a company of well-trained troops, and a band met a special train carrying the governors of Eritrea, British Somaliland, and Djibouti. The "impressive" scene flabbergasted the resident European diplomats, who were unprepared "for a display of such efficiency." Their surprise "was the first of many surprises" as the Ethiopians proceeded to mount excellent ceremonies, full of decorum, pomp and circumstance, and superb hospitality, capped, of course, by Tafari's elevation to the kingship on the morning of 7 October. At 6:30 A.M., in an outsized tent on the palace grounds, the European visitors, accredited diplomats, and high Ethiopian officials and dignitaries witnessed "the most gorgeous and the most imposing spectacle of a day of spectacles. It was a scene of splendour, and, although the rites performed were Christian rites, the impression left on the spectator was that of a coronation such as he would have imagined happening at some period covered by the Old Testament." [78] After Zawditu placed the crown on Tafari's head, she remarked:

My beloved son! When God almighty graced me in placing me upon the throne of my August Father, Menelik II, he well willed that you be my support. In execution of this divine wish, I today confer upon you this crown. I pray that the Divine Creator also permits you to ascend to the Imperial Crown one day. May God help you in your labours.

It is recorded that the king responded, "Amen." [79]

Tafari's new role did not elicit universal approval; Ras Gugsa Wolie of Begemdir and Ras Hailu of Gojam, scions of old and aristocratic families, were jealous and hostile. Hailu characterized himself as "Ras of Gojam . . . son of the King" (referring to Tekle Haymanot, king of Gojam, b. 1847, r. 1870 – 1901),[80] an interesting declaration of hereditary autonomy and a distinction that irritated Tafari as much as the Gojami's avoidance of paying taxes to the central government. Hailu was also an arrogant snob who publicly scorned the regent's personal appointees to the central government as "people from nothing who were only simple stablemen during Menelik's time." [81] He was smart enough, however, to understand the economic forces changing the land, and he became, in Ethiopian terms, the quintessential modern oligarch, ready to do anything to acquire cash. As governor of Gojam, Hailu introduced money taxes, sold offices to the highest bidder, levied his own customs fees, and required corvée on his large farms that grew cash crops.[82] With his profits, he modernized Debre Markos, his capital, but mostly he invested in Addis Abeba, where he owned a fleet of taxicabs and considerable rental property.[83] He abhored anyone who impeded Gojam's

lucrative commerce, especially his northern rival, Ras Gugsa of Begemdir, who refused to permit his neighbor duty-free transit for
items destined for trade in Eritrea.

Gugsa was an old-fashioned governor, interested in his province's
revenues and trade but not personally involved in the evolving national economy. He stayed put in Gonder and Debre Tabor, living in
traditional state but aloof from and resentful of the central government, which had caused his separation from Zawditu and had
banned his presence in Addis Abeba. Embittered and isolated, Gugsa
was not a party to the great changes sweeping the empire.[84] He was
completely out of step with Tafari's progressivism and scorned the
Young Ethiopians running the government. Not only did he belittle
their Western educations (mostly in Roman Catholic schools) as
un-Ethiopian, but he also found them personally unpalatable: "They
are mainly from families not included in the aristocracy of the country from which heretofore most aides and assistants have come." The
ras was equally unhappy about Tafari's use of foreign experts and
advisers, because their presence revealed the inability of the old
ruling classes to administer an increasingly complex Ethiopia.[85]

In 1928–1929, the north suffered from drought and locusts. Especially hard hit were arid and semiarid regions, largely inhabited by
Muslim pastoralists, whose herds were sharply reduced. Although
they and farmers in the transition zones in Tigray and Welo soon
were starving, provincial and local governments insisted on payment of taxes, sparking a popular and spontaneous eruption that
quickly took on class, religious, and ethnic overtones: rich and poor
struggled for resources, Muslims and Christians fought, and Oromo,
Afar, and Somali turned on each other at water holes and at scarce
pasturage, to settle old scores and to create new blood debts. Thus,
insensitivity and greed combined with ecology to create a major
political crisis.[86]

By early 1928, Addis Abeba was concerned that the Italians were
using the widespread social unrest[87] as a cover to continue infiltrating the Ogaden. They established a post at Warandab, on the Fafen
River, about one hundred kilometers from the frontier, laid out motorable roads to Somalia, and began air patrols as far north as Ginir.[88]
The international situation thus demanded an end to the domestic
crisis, and the government directed Ras Gugsa to reestablish order in

Raya country. When several of his skirmishing parties were defeated in a series of bloody battles in October and November 1929, the ras held secret talks with enemy leaders. Some type of bargain was struck because raiding adjacent to the Eritrean frontier was ended, Gugsa and his army withdrew to Debre Tabor, and Addis Abeba celebrated his success.[89]

But as the insurrection continued to grow, Tafari became anxious, and then uneasy when Gugsa refused to travel to Dese for a meeting to plan a more successful strategy against the rebels. Gugsa thought that he had been found out and that now his enemies expected self-immolation. As he considered his misfortune, he focused his ire on King Tafari, in whose absence he might now be in Addis Abeba by his wife's side, perhaps even the most powerful man in Ethiopia. He pondered the present, disagreeable though it was, and the future, nasty as it was likely to become, and drank himself into melancholia, depression, self-pity, and, finally, a rebellion born of despair. He made Tafari his primary enemy, charged him with apostasy to Roman Catholicism and treasonous cooperation with Italy, raised the flag of tradition against change, and joined the rebels.[90]

The king easily met the ideological challenge. He immediately condemned Gugsa's cooperation with the peasant-pastoralist dissidents. When many of Ethiopia's leaders agreed, among them the vociferous Ras Hailu, Zawditu was unable to challenge plans for a general mobilization against the northern rebels.[91] Dej. Mulugeta was ordered to gather forces for a major campaign, while local forces would immediately attack Maychew and the surrounding region, Korem and Alamata, and Raya country. The preliminary offensives began on 11–12 February, while troops from southern Ethiopia passed through Addis Abeba en route north, once again to show the empire where real power resided. On 28 February, after a priestly effort at conciliation had failed, letters bearing the signatures of the empress, king, and abun were sent from Dese to government and church officials in Begemdir and Yeju, reporting the ostracism and excommunication of the rebel Gugsa Wolie and releasing his soldiers from their vow of allegiance. Shortly thereafter, Zawditu presided over a council — her last — which ordered the immediate pursuit of the war against her husband.[92]

In late February, Dej. Mulugeta's well-equipped army arrived in

Dese. The appearance of such a force and the effects of the pacification already accomplished had a noticeably chilling effect on the peasant-pastoralist uprising and on Ras Gugsa's soldiers. They grew skeptical of their leader's chances and scornful of charges that Tafari was an apostate and a traitor. Gugsa, however, remained defiant, although he was completely isolated in a hopeless situation. For a time, however, Mulugeta attended to the complete eradication of Oromo and Afar resistance, a campaign that ended successfully in mid-March. His victorious army then marched on Debre Tabor and unleashed its secret weapon, aircraft equipped with French-made bombs.[93] King Tafari had introduced aviation in August 1929, mostly to improve governmental communications but also to police the country more efficiently. Tafari had won a crown by using a modern tank; the airplane would confirm his kingship.

The central government's biplanes followed rebel troop movements and permitted Mulugeta the luxury of perfect defensive emplacements. The machines also terrorized Gugsa's soldiers: on the morning of 31 March, near Debre Tabor, the Imperial Ethiopian Air Force, in the form of one plane piloted by a Frenchman, made three bombing runs over an enemy force of ten thousand men, who broke and abandoned the battlefield to the government. To this day, many still believe that one of the bombs fell directly on Gugsa, astride a white charger, as he heroically led his forces forward. The truth is simpler and less generous. The ras was, in fact, at the head of troops scattered by the air attack; left unprotected, Gugsa drew fire, was shot several times, and killed. Tafari's faith in foreign technology and experts had been vindicated, and he had "shown his ability to conduct a war without the traditional leadership of troops."[94]

Zawditu never heard the salutes fired from the gibbi on 1 April to announce the king's great victory and her husband's death. During the previous fortnight, she had suffered from paratyphoid fever, complicated by her diabetes and the stringent Ethiopian Lenten diet. She refused to accept the regimen recommended by her European doctors and relied, as she usually did, on faith alone for succor. The Christian science failed, just as the empress had foiled the Western science, but her priests prescribed emergency dunking in Holy Water as a last resort.[95] Its efficacy was debunked by an almost immediate coma and death between 1:00 and 2:00 P.M. on 2 April, with a grief-stricken King Tafari at the bedside during her long passing. Given the proximity of Gugsa's death, however, Addis Abeba was awash with rumors that Tafari had poisoned the empress. The facts ridicule such views: "The King long had demonstrated his patience in waiting for his natural turn to take the throne. His Majesty had carefully prepared [and] it would seem impossible for him to have considered treachery." [96]

Following Orthodox traditions, the abun conducted Zawditu's ob-sequies during the night of 2 April, in Menilek's mausoleum, where she was interred. Early the next day, Tafari convened but did not participate in a Council of State that unanimously named him em-peror. In an easily accessible nearby room, he modestly consented to the elevation when formally asked by the abun, who thereupon led him to the throne room and blessed his imperial person. The new sovereign addressed the council from his seat of power, quoting in full the Orthodox Bible's 151st Psalm, which treats the choice of David as King of Israel in preference to his older brothers and after his victory over Goliath.[97] After this clear message to competitors and enemies, Tafari issued the following statement:

The passing of Her Majesty, the Empress, is a cause of sorrow to me and to the whole of Ethiopia. But because it is our custom that when the shepherd of the people dies a King succeeds, I have ascended the Throne of David, to which I was betrothed. By the mercy of God I will protect you. Therefore let the trader carry on his trade; let the farmer plow; for I will keep you accord-ing to the law of succession which has come down to us from our fore-fathers.[98]

CHAPTER SIX

From Royal to Imperial,
1930-1932

In his autobiography, Tafari failed to record his emotions upon assuming the imperial throne as Haile Sellassie I.[1] He believed that
such feelings were allowed lesser men but not monarchs. Never a
fount of intimacy and spontaneity, Haile Sellassie as sovereign came
to embody tradition and ritualized decorum. Indeed, after 1930, he
submerged his personality into the emperorship by making himself
into an aloof and distant symbol, surrounded by a deep moat of
ceremony, for whom the form, not the substance, was paramount.[2]
Even his posture became straight and stiff, especially when seated on
the throne. The new monarch was eager to assume "the trappings of
imperial glory,"[3] and he packaged himself as an emperor. With ap-
praising eyes directed toward Europe and its modern sovereigns,
Haile Sellassie chose to deport himself not only as an Ethiopian
prince but also, he hoped, in the fashion of his Western counterparts.
Although he took to wearing European-style uniforms and clothing,

and his court was regulated by the heavy, formal, and stylized Swedish royal protocol, he never forgot that he was before all else an Ethiopian politician.[4]

Haile Sellassie's business was power, a métier curiously derided by his detractors, who have forgotten that the having and holding of authority is the preoccupation of most public men. Its assiduous pursuit hardly made the emperor a dangerous megalomaniac, unless all politicians are similarly afflicted. Yet Haile Sellassie never admitted that he was a politician, calling himself instead a statesman. He believed that the overt quest for power contradicted his majesty as emperor. He attributed his public success to destiny or to God's will, even as he manipulated men and situations to his advantage. Besides aiming to confirm his power, the emperor sought also to build a renewed and modern Ethiopia. The construction of a centralized government, a modern professional army, an efficient system of communications, and prominent public works in Addis Abeba not only demonstrated power but also projected imperial grandeur. The practical needs of authority and the carefully cherished notions of majesty thus coincided. Put another way, the ideal and the real matched, helping to stimulate the progress so obvious in Ethiopia between 1930 and 1935.

An ambitious road-building program was undertaken to link the capital to every economically important province and to tie important commercial centers into a national grid.[5] Each project put money into the national treasury through its original sale as a concession, an annual payment, and a percentage of any profits from tolls and other transport charges; and it also put money into the pockets of the oligarchs who financed the mostly Asian and European concessionaires with whom they joined in establishing trucking firms to exploit the growing economy. The British *Morning Post* reckoned that Tafari had been more successful than Amantula of Afghanistan in modernizing his country, thanks to the new roads, which facilitated trade and brought the enlightened administration of the central government to outlying areas. It editorialized, "We may yet see the last of the independent African empires giving the lie to the fairly generally accepted theory that the African cannot govern himself on modern and progressive lines."[6]

The newspaper also commented favorably on education, attributing Ethiopia's several thousand students to Tafari's determination, "held in his heart," to modernize his land. In the thirties, most schools were placed in Addis Abeba, where the emperor actively oversaw their activities. He liked to have his monuments nearby, and education was in fact one of the creative monuments of his reign.[7] Given his limited resources and the many expenses that the state shouldered, Haile Sellassie accomplished much for education, even if some found it "curious to see so much of this good thing concentrated in one place, whilst whole provinces in the interior are without a single modern school."[8] The new monarch proudly proclaimed his great faith in Ethiopia's youth "as intelligent, patriotic [and] full of desire [to work] one day in the service of their country." Their European teachers were full of praise for their quickness in assimilating information but acknowledged that national pride or prejudice often impeded its application. When their students discussed Ethiopia's military prowess, they asserted, "Ah! We are strong! Our warriors are brave! No European army can defeat ours! Adwa has proved it!" They discounted the importance of air power: "Oh, planes don't frighten us. Our priests know certain words; they say them, and the planes will crash."[9] Such patriotic stupidity aside, the newly educated knew enough about modern life to become enlightened members of the growing central government.[10]

Financial administration, for example, took many of the Young Ethiopians because of their relative efficiency, honesty, and, above all, their loyalty to Tafari. The country's customs houses returned "big revenues to the State," and Tafari early developed the policies of suppressing all internal tariffs and nationalizing frontier posts, thereby eliminating "restraints upon the development of agriculture" and garnering new monies for his government.[11] He used educated staffers in the Ministry of Finance to inaugurate a standard process of revenue collection by field agents in place of the often arbitrary and capricious formulas of local and provincial officials. For example, in 1928 Ilubabor sent only MT$140,000 in taxes to Addis Abeba, "but of course much more was collected and disappeared."[12] The central government's increasing ability to capture such funds permitted Haile Sellassie to marshal, even during the nadir of the

Great Depression, sufficient resources to pay for such expensive national programs as rearmament, acquisition of the Bank of Abyssinia, and establishment of a diplomatic corps.[13]

Early in 1927, Tafari, nominally Ethiopia's foreign minister, appointed Blatta Herui Wolde Sellassie (1878–1938) as director general of foreign affairs. A commoner with no important connections, he was completely dependent on the regent's patronage. Herui was nonetheless a widely respected man of letters who had enjoyed an advanced Church education and some secular training in French, which he spoke well, and English, which he read and understood. Over the years, Tafari gave Herui a number of delicate jobs dealing with foreigners: in 1916, he became director of the municipality of Addis Abeba; in 1921, head of the Special Court; in 1924, secretary to the delegation Tafari led to Europe; in 1925–1926, one of Ethiopia's representatives to the League of Nations; and in 1926–1927, special councilor for foreign affairs. By then, he had published some romances and novels in Amharic, using a "simple, sober, English-like style in harmony with the simplicity of his concepts." Though Herui was vain about his intellectual attainments, he was above all Tafari's man and a patriotic nationalist who could be expected to fight stubbornly for his country's best interests.[14] To assist him, Tafari provided capable directors in charge of British, Italian, and French relations, and they, in turn, supervised the Ethiopian plenipotentiaries accredited to Paris, Rome, and London in 1929–1930.

The Ethiopian diplomats spent much of their time interviewing candidates for government jobs. In a rush toward reform, Tafari had decided to place advisers in ministries and other branches of government. He sought experts whose nationality was consonant with the goals of his administration and tended therefore to hire individuals from Europe's small powers or Americans, whose government was not apparently in the business of African colonialism. Tafari was smart enough, however, to hire an Englishman in the Ministry of the Interior, to supervise the antislavery campaign and to plan manumission programs, thus endearing himself to Britain's influential antislavery zealots; and he placed a Frenchman in the Ministry of Posts, Telegraphs, and Telephones, an organization long associated with French training and techniques. By the time of Tafari's coronation as emperor in 1930, there were two French advisers, one Englishman, one American (with two others under consideration), one German, one Greek, two Swiss, but *no* Italians.[15] The Ethiopian government also hired foreigners, as needed, for short-term and specific jobs. For example, Gaston Jèze, a Swiss expert in international law, expertly guided the Ethiopian minister in Paris toward the signature of an agreement recognizing Addis Abeba's right to purchase arms relatively freely.

By 1929, London was sufficiently impressed with the revival of the Ethiopian central government to conclude that a minimal infusion of modern weaponry into the Solomonic Empire might help Tafari control cross-frontier raiding.[16] When it voiced its policy change at a four-power meeting in Paris in mid-November 1929, the French responded enthusiastically, but Italy continued its refusal to consider any arms trade for Ethiopia.[17] In order to appease Rome, the British and French agreed that prior to any new arms treaty, Ethiopia would have to provide detailed information about its weapons needs over an agreed-upon period.[18] The proposal rankled the Ethiopian delegation and M. Jèze, who argued during a plenary meeting that the Addis Abeba government had neither army nor arms in the modern sense and that it awaited emancipation from foreign control to develop its forces.[19] After the session, the Swiss lawyer confided informally that Ethiopia planned to import only modern armaments, that procurement would be limited sharply by lack of money, and that no ammunition would be purchased for the country's store of obsolete weapons, "thus to proceed to a policy of gradual [internal] disarmament."[20]

The negotiations were interrupted by the rebellion in the north, the death of the empress, and Tafari's succession, as well as by a diplomatic shell game that failed to entice Washington into an arms trade with Ethiopia, no questions asked.[21] On 22 May 1930, the Ethiopian delegation finally delivered a memorandum explaining that Ethiopia's great size and sparse population made security dependent on widespread garrisons and "greater military forces than those countries which are well furnished with means of communication." Nevertheless, any program of rearmament was limited by Ethiopia's chronic shortage of cash, especially since so much was being expended on economic development. The emperor had decided therefore to allocate, over the next few years, £300,000 to £400,000 (MT$3

million to MT$4 million) annually for weapons "to provide the po-
lice and army the material means to assure . . . the tranquility indispensable for the economic development of the empire." These
included a modest number of rifles, rapid-fire weapons, light field
pieces, and armored vehicles "to assure the maintenance of order
and the energetic repression of troubles," but no offensive items
such as heavy artillery.[22]

The Italians remained obdurate until London bluntly advised that
Ethiopia had earned a right to purchase modern weapons, even if
£300,000 to £400,000, 12 to 16 percent of the country's estimated
£2,500,000 export trade, was an inordinately high annual cost for a
country as poor as Ethiopia.[23] To obtain a shift in Rome's policy,
Whitehall sought to reduce the sum considerably, but the French
rejected the logic of relating arms needs to trade figures, though the
Quai d'Orsay was willing to advise the Ethiopians to make modest
concessions in procurements.[24] The British were sufficiently satisfied to insist that the Italians adhere to a new arms agreement or
watch its signature without them.[25] Such isolation would have revealed the hypocrisy of Rome's profession of friendship for Ethiopia,
and the Italians caved in.[26] At the meeting of 31 July 1930, the French
delegation gently asked the Ethiopians if they could provide a rationale for the £300,000 to £400,000 figure.[27]

M. Jèze replied that the sum was "a maximum which in all probability would never be attained," because it allowed for price inflation
and for unforeseen requirements in cases of civil strife or war. Arms
acquisitions, he clarified, would depend on "circumstances" and the
need for "political stability," without which "no economic development [was] possible."[28] It was a sensible answer, but it gave no
satisfaction to his listeners, who feebly decided to note officially that
the amount was a maximum, "which in all probability would never
be reached," and that only £100,000 could be used to acquire rifles
and small arms, which all three delegations continued to believe
were peddled by the Ethiopians to adjacent colonies. Begrudgingly,
the tripartite powers also conceded that Ethiopia might encounter
difficulties in providing detailed information about long-term plans
for weapons procurement and therefore agreed to accept an annual
figure, to be supplied on 1 December, for the coming year only.[29]

The new arms treaty, signed on 21 August 1930, was a victory for

Addis Abeba; its preamble described the agreement as completing and supplementing the 1925 Geneva Convention, which treated Ethiopia as a sovereign state freely exercising its powers to ensure security within its territory. Toward this end, the tripartite powers undertook to assist Ethiopia "to obtain the arms and munitions necessary for the defense of its territory against all outside aggression and for the maintenance of internal public order." Articles 1 through 8 enumerated the type of weapons available for purchase, the form and order of delivery, the submission of reports, and the measures the Ethiopian government would take to secure the new arms. Article 9 guaranteed Ethiopia the right to transfer the arms through adjacent colonial territories, although "if the troubled posture or situation of Ethiopia menaces peace or public tranquility, transit authorization would have to be refused by authorities in the limitrophe states, until this threat had ceased to exist." [30] This stipulation was later used against Addis Abeba, but for now the treaty was an important victory for the new emperor, removing yet another limit on Ethiopia's freedom of action. He was similarly successful in pursuing policies leading to the establishment of a truly autocephalous Ethiopian church.

A mistranslation of the fourteenth-century *Fetha Negast* (The law of the kings), which many authoritative Ethiopians regarded as a kind of constitution, denied the Orthodox church the right to name its own patriarch, a responsibility given over to the See of St. Mark in Alexandria. During Ethiopia's resurgence in the late nineteenth century, the government was able to force the Alexandrian authorities to consecrate several bishops for provincial posts, but no further advances toward autonomy were made during the long tenure of Abuna Mattewos (1881–1926). During the last decade of his episcopacy, the Young Ethiopians classed his preeminent position as an example of "Coptic imperialism," and the Orthodox clergy began grumbling about a foreigner holding the best ecclesiastical job in the realm. The oligarchy was also distressed that the church was becoming rich from the sales of coffee and other commodities grown on its large landholdings. Tafari in particular wanted to tap the church's treasury and to neutralize the patriarch's political importance. "Pressure for . . . Ethiopianization became very strong. As long as the *abun* had no power, his nationality [had been] irrelevant." [31]

After Mattewos died, Patriarch Kerelos V of Alexandria refused

Addis Abeba's request for a locally elected archbishop,[32] quickly causing Tafari to decree that the etchege would henceforth, as an officer of the imperial court, exercise sole financial and executive powers in the church, leaving the abun only the powers of ordination and consecration.[33] Kerelos was so insulted that he refused to nominate anyone for the Ethiopian post,[34] and the stalemate was complete until Tafari became king and a new patriarch, Yohannes, succeeded to the See of St. Mark.

Both men had reasons to compromise. As king, Tafari anticipated becoming emperor, an elevation that required the services of an abun. In Alexandria, Yohannes needed Ethiopian recognition of his position, and he therefore offered to consecrate some suffragan bishops if Addis Abeba would accept a Coptic abun. On 3 April 1929, Tafari forced his clerical subjects, meeting in church assembly, to accept the offer, although they wanted to hold out for an Ethiopian archbishop.[35] The delegation that left Addis Abeba for Cairo on 10 May 1929 included four out of five future prelates (one was ailing).[36] They and their compatriots participated in the selection of a new patriarch for Ethiopia, a monk named Sidarow Antoni: "He is practically unknown and is said to be devoid of both secular and religious learning . . . appointment of such an inadequate Abuna will tend to weaken the ecclesiastical connection between Egypt and Abyssinia." The archbishop designate took the name Kerillos, and he and his suffragans were consecrated by Patriarch Yohannes on 2 June 1929.[37]

The Ethiopian church now had a weak Egyptian archbishop assisted by strong Ethiopian prelates firmly under the control of the central government through the etchege. Tafari crowed to an old friend that "for hundreds of years, his predecessors had conformed to the rule of the Fetha Negast . . . that no Ethiopian priest could be consecrated bishop. He had succeeded in securing the virtual abolition of the rule, and Ethiopia would now have Ethiopian bishops." While he thanked God for permitting appointees "chosen from among Ethiopia's own savants," he also savored the implicit certainty that the country's five primates would one day compose a synod to elect its own leader.[38] In recognition of having a virtually autocephalous church, Ethiopia enjoyed the spectacle of a visit, in early 1930, by Patriarch Yohannes, the first ever to the Solomonic Empire by an incumbent of the See of St. Mark.[39]

During this period, Tafari also sought national control over Ethiopia's money. In 1929, the economy suffered as the value of the Maria Theresa dollar dropped in response to the decline in the international price of silver. Ethiopia had too long been dependent on a specie that had an intrinsic value often different from its face value. When silver prices were high, exporters tended to treat the dollar as a commodity and to export large amounts to the Middle East. As money went out of circulation, commercial activity declined, as did the collection of customs duties and transaction taxes. When silver prices fell, imports became excessively expensive, merchants refrained from ordering, and whole categories of goods ran out. Demonetization of the Maria Theresa dollar would lead to a stable money supply, but it required a national bank that could impose a national currency.[40]

Tafari decided to transform the Bank of Abyssinia, a government-chartered, private organization, into a central state bank.[41] By 1930, the old bank had run down its capital and was essentially moribund, but its holding company, the National Bank of Egypt, held out for a selling price of £190,000, including £40,000 for cancellation of Menilek's concession of 1905, and £25,000 for its buildings and equipment.[42] Government coffers were empty, but as Tafari and the state were then identical, he closed out his personal account at the National City Bank of New York and in July 1930 transmitted £125,000 ($320,000) to the National Bank of Egypt in partial payment.[43] An expensive coronation intervened, the Great Depression deepened, and the government had to postpone discharge of the remaining £65,000 when it fell due on 31 January 1931.[44] Subsequently the exchequer was swept clean of its "gold dust, ivory, coffee, and silver dollars [which] were sold for sterling and the proceeds remitted to Cairo" on 1 July 1931. Although the government was now strapped for funds to attempt an immediate currency reform,[45] the new Bank of Ethiopia opened for business on 12 October 1931, another example of national resurgence and a further assertion of sovereignty.

The same motive led to official attempts to regulate European activities. In January 1929, the government began to require entry visas for all visitors, in order to reduce the flow of undesirable characters into Addis Abeba. A month later, the minister of commerce ordered the registration of all commercial firms operating in Ethiopia, a reasonable requirement for national and foreigner alike. Yet the various European legations advised their nationals not to comply, and the diplomats worked assiduously to retain jurisdiction over their subjects in legal cases between Ethiopians and foreigners.[46] They based their stance on a mistranslation of article 7 of the Franco-Ethiopian (Klobukowski) Commercial Treaty of 1908, a version always rejected by the Ethiopians. The Addis Abeba government, however, permitted consular courts to settle cases between foreigners and established a special court to handle mixed cases. To ensure efficiency, its administrator ordered the registration of all lawyers appearing before it and asked them to explain their qualifications and credentials. Although the tribunal always sought to accommodate its European clientele, it operated unabashedly as an Ethiopian institution, to the considerable distress of the prideful legations, whose racist members delighted in terming the government's law savage, primitive, and antiquated.[47]

The emperor did not blanch in the face of such criticism. He sought, as did the young nationalists he fostered, to retain total control over all things Ethiopian,[48] but shortages of technicians, bureaucrats, and money inevitably delayed, disrupted, and dissipated programs and plans. The Italians, who eagerly anticipated the Aseb-Dese road, ascribed its continual postponement to official Ethiopian policy. Although there is no evidence that procrastination was Addis Abeba's strategy, the government never hired Italian advisers; it reduced the importance of trade with Eritrea and Italy; and it ignored Rome's offers of technical assistance and loans.[49] Italian efforts were in fact frustrated, if not through government machinations and the deeply ingrained suspicions of the Ethiopian people, then as a consequence of a general shift away from dependency on Europe's great powers to a reliance on the world market to supply the country's needs. While laissez faire was a reasonable approach to diversifying Ethiopia's suppliers, it fanned Rome's fears about its future in the Horn of Africa.

Britain already had shown itself willing to permit Italy economic primacy in northern Ethiopia. Addis Abeba's insistence upon using the J. G. White Engineering Company of New York to build the Tana dam further alienated the British and also delayed the project until the Depression killed the market for cotton and any chance for the project's capitalization.[50] Had Tafari been more forthcoming about the dam, had he been less punctilious about ensuring that every detail offered no insult to Ethiopia, had he been willing to move ahead with frankness about his own internal political complications, then an agreement with London might have been signed as early as 1925 or 1926. The Anglo-Italian agreement would not have happened and Great Britain would have obtained a stake in Ethiopia's continued independence. As it turned out, London became estranged from Addis Abeba, both sides falling victim to Ethiopia's lack of technicians, bureaucrats, and money.

Tafari spent the country's revenues on modern armaments and programs of reform. He believed in the intrinsic worth "of schools, hospitals, maternity clinics, orphanages, teachers, veterinary doctors, agronomists, and the like." He planned and began the beautification of the capital and spurred the construction of roads and communications connecting the political center with the provincial peripheries. He advanced on all fronts at once rather heroically, though never having enough resources to carry out all his plans. In the financial shortfall, the Italians saw an opportunity for economic subversion. Ostensibly full of admiration for Ethiopia's efforts, Rome offered a loan under conditions that would favor Italian capital investments and technicians.[51] Addis Abeba diplomatically refused, knowing full well that the Fascists scornfully believed that "the Central Government is more a name than a substance" and that the emperor "is today more than ever a prisoner of the Rases."[52]

Nothing was further from the truth. The firepower mustered by Tafari's forces had changed the Ethiopian balance of power for all time. The appearance and impact of aircraft in the war against Ras Gugsa made a profound impression, convincing some dissidents that the "invincible" machine rendered struggle against the emperor futile.[53] The signing of the arms agreement meant that only the central government would receive a steady supply of modern weapons. Perhaps, however, the most important military factor was the arrival in early February 1930 of a cadre of six Belgian officers to train the Imperial Bodyguard. By August 1930, they were hard at work drilling thirteen hundred of the country's best men, carefully selected by the emperor and Major André Polet, the head of the mission.

Haile Sellassie subsequently shifted two Swiss soldiers, an officer and a sergeant, to Jijiga, there to train troops for service on the Somaliland frontier,[54] where the Italian infiltration into Ethiopia continued. Mogadishu made no effort to mask its activities, and from Korahe messages were sent to all clan leaders, "stating that Italy now controls the southern Ogaden and will soon be taking over Daga-bur."[55] Given Roman policy and the Ethiopian response, an official in London foresaw that hostilities would be possible "in the compar-atively near future."[56] For the British, at least, the Ethiopian central government was therefore more a substance than a name, a fact also readily discernible in its exercise of internal authority.

Ras Kassa's appointment to Begemdir heralded a new relation-ship between the sovereign and his agents because Tafari named central government officials as mayor and as head of merchants for Gonder. Their responsibilities over social and economic life consid-erably reduced the autonomy of the office of the governor, even if, in Kassa's case, his commission yielded extraordinary powers to re-store law and order. The ras's acceptance of a mandate that explicitly denied him full control over his province's finances demonstrated his conviction — no less than Tafari's — that Ethiopian officialdom should place Addis Abeba's needs before their own personal ambi-tions,[57] as only then would it be possible to build a modern state.

Haile Sellassie's coronation in November 1930 advertised his in-tentions to reign in a manner both innovative and reformist. Having brought Ethiopia into the League of Nations and established diplo-matic relations with a number of countries, the new emperor deter-mined to make the event a coming-out party for the revitalized and renewed state he headed. This decision, made at a time of economic crisis, when most of the government's programs remained incom-plete or unstarted, reflected the emperor's pride and faith in himself and in the ability of Ethiopians "to get things done somehow."[58] Ever mindful of Ethiopia's historical isolation and the lack of foreign par-ticipation at dynastic events,[59] Haile Sellassie set his heart on royal representation at his coronation and was ready to consider "a refusal a deliberate slight."[60] Invitations went to seven monarchs and five presidents, each of whom agreed to designate an appropriate envoy; to representatives of the world press; and to every important Ethio-pian and foreign resident.

Aiming to create a "favorable impression" of his country and

Emperor Menilek II, ca. 1905.
Reprinted from Gen. Eric Virgin, *The Abyssinia I Knew* (London:
Macmillan, 1936).

Tafari Makonnen in 1895, age three, wearing Father Jarosseau's pectoral cross. Reprinted from Haile Sellassie I, *My Life and Ethiopia's Progress*, vol. 1 (Addis Abeba: Berhanena Selam Press, 1973).

Left to right: Tafari Belew, later kenyazmach; Tafari Makonnen; Beru, the children's attendant; Imru Haile Sellassie, later ras; ca. 1900–1901.
Reprinted from Haile Sellassie I, *My Life and Ethiopia's Progress*, vol. 1
(Addis Abeba: Berhanena Selam Press, 1973).

Tafari with Ras Makonnen,
ca. 1903–1904.
Reprinted from Christine
Sandford, *The Lion of Judah
Hath Prevailed* (New York:
Macmillan, 1955).

Dej. Tafari, Lij Iyasu, Dej. Beru (later minister of war), ca. 1911–1914.
Reprinted from Stuart Bergsma, *Rainbow Empire* (Grand Rapids, Mich.:
Wm. B. Eerdmans, 1936); photo by Mody Studio, Addis Abeba.

Dej. Tafari, ca. 1915–1916.
Reprinted from Haile Sellassie I, *My Life and Ethiopia's Progress*, vol. 1
(Addis Abeba: Berhanena Selam Press, 1973).

Empress Menen as a young woman, probably before her marriage to Tafari. Reprinted from Angenore Frangipani, *L'Equivoco Abissino* (Milan: Ulrico Hoepli, 1936).

Empress Zawditu at her coronation, 11 February 1917.
Reprinted from Stuart Bergsma, *Rainbow Empire* (Grand Rapids, Mich.: Wm. B. Eerdmans, 1936); photo by Mody Studio, Addis Abeba.

Ras Tafari and Empress Zawditu, ca. 1923.
Reprinted from Rosita Forbes, *From Red Sea to Blue Nile* (New York: Macauly, 1925).

Ras Gugsa Wolie, Zawditu's
husband, ca. 1927–1928.
Reprinted from Angenore
Frangipani, *L'Equivoco Abissino*
(Milan: Ulrico Hoepli, 1936).

Ras Tafari, ca. 1926–1927.
Reprinted from Haile Sellassie I, *My Life and Ethiopia's Progress*, vol. 1
(Addis Abeba: Berhanena Selam Press, 1973).

Dejaz. Balcha, ca. 1935.
Reprinted from Ladislas Farago, *Abyssinia on the Eve* (London: Putnam, 1935).

Tafari at his coronation as king (negus), 7 October 1928. Reprinted from Haile Sellassie I, *My Life and Ethiopia's Progress*, vol. 1 (Addis Abeba: Berhanena Selam Press, 1973).

Left to right: Rases Seyoum, Hailu, and Desta, probably at the coronation of the emperor in November 1930.
Reprinted from Gen. Eric Virgin, *The Abyssinia I Knew* (London: Macmillan, 1936).

The imperial couple at their coronation, 2 November 1930. Reprinted from Gen. Eric Virgin, *The Abyssinia I Knew* (London: Macmillan, 1936).

Empress Menen, Crown Prince Asfa Wossen, Haile Sellassie, and Prince Makonnen (later the duke of Harer), during coronation festivities, 1–10 November 1930. Reprinted from Gen. Eric Virgin, *The Abyssinia I Knew* (London: Macmillan, 1936).

The emperor opening
parliament in 1934.
Reprinted from Gen. Eric
Virgin, *The Abyssinia I Knew*
(London: Macmillan, 1936).

Ethiopia's soldiers.
Reprinted from Addison Southard, "Modern Ethiopia," *National Geographic* 59
(1931); photo by W. Robert Moore, © 1931 National Geographic Society.

An officer in ceremonial uniform.
Reprinted from Addison Southard, "Modern Ethiopia," *National Geographic* 59 (1931); photo by W. Robert Moore, © 1931 National Geographic Society.

Dejaz. Nasibu, ca. 1935.
Reprinted from Ladislas Farago, *Abyssinia on the Eve* (London: Putnam, 1935).

Emperor Haile Sellassie I reviewing troops in 1935.
Reprinted from William J. Makin, *War over Ethiopia* (London: Jarrolds, 1935).

The emperor manning the Oerlikon antiaircraft gun near his Dese headquarters, early 1936.
Reprinted from Haile Sellassie I, *My Life and Ethiopia's Progress*, vol. 1 (Addis Abeba: Berhanena Selam Press, 1973).

"King" coffee at a drying and storage warehouse in Addis Abeba, 1930.
Reprinted from W. Robert Moore, "Coronation Days in Addis Ababa," *National Geographic* 59 (1931); photo by Addison Southard.

capital, the emperor took charge of Addis Abeba's renovation, making a daily round of the city to ensure that ordered public works were being carried out. Haile Sellassie dryly recorded that "arrangements were made for the principal streets . . . and the houses along each street to be repaired as well as for electric light to be installed along the main streets and in all the houses by which the guests would pass." When not acting as a foreman, the emperor supervised the creation of coronation vestments and such symbols as the imperial crown, orb, sword, ring, "and all similar things . . . specially made of gold and diamonds." He even oversaw the design of new and gorgeous uniforms and other paraphernalia for the royal family and the Ethiopian aristocracy. The emperor also spent considerable time squeezing merchant, official, prelate, and nobleman for contributions amounting to much of the estimated MT$3 million that the week-long extravaganza cost.[61]

Yet it was not until the months of September and October that people became fully conscious that in November the world would visit Ethiopia. "Suddenly hectic and frantic preparations were made." Paint appeared everywhere as the town was tidied up, and what could not be refurbished was hidden behind whitewashed fences. Beggars and lepers were banned from the capital, soldiers drilled everywhere, and, on the city's streets, the eight newly purchased Austrian horses rehearsed their task of pulling the recently bought ceremonial coach of the ex-emperor of Germany. By the fortnight before the great event, thousands were at work in Addis Abeba: steamrollers chugged day and night, and "men, camels, donkeys and mules were to be seen staggering beneath huge blocks of stone and other building materials." Meanwhile, boxcars of imported food and drink were unloaded and sent to stock the just-completed guest houses. "It was difficult to recognize the old town in this transformation and unusual activity." Most astonishing was the metamorphosis of the city police and the Imperial Bodyguard, who shucked off their tatters and appeared in smart new khaki uniforms from Belgium.[62] Miracles were everywhere: triumphal arches went up, electric lines were laid, telephones installed, streets graded and paved, and even sidewalks were provided. Often the work was completed in the nick of time; two days before the arrival of the Maréchal Franchet d'Espérey, his quarters lacked a kitchen, piped water, and electricity, all of which were in place when he crossed the threshold of the front door.[63] To Evelyn Waugh, Addis Abeba seemed a new town, "so new, indeed, that not a single piece of it appeared to be really finished." [64]

During the fortnight of frenetic activity, Addis Abeba "filled to overcrowding with black, yellow, brown, and white men from the ends of the earth." At the new rail station, the emperor and the crown prince greeted foreign envoys and escorted them to their various residences.[65] Reporters and tourists were met by taxi drivers who charged such high fares to get from the lower to the upper part of the city, where the two European-style hotels were located, that the emperor had to decree reasonable maximum charges. He did nothing, however, about the exorbitant prices charged for room and board in hotels or makeshift inns. Yet, visitor or inhabitant, the entire population was in a good mood, and any inconvenience was more than balanced by the colorful street scenes, the official tableaux, the feasting, and the magnificent hospitality leading up to the coronation.[66]

Shortly after dawn on 2 November, Ethiopian dignitaries called at various legations and residences to escort foreign envoys to the event at St. George's Cathedral. Ras Gugsa Araya of Tigray, grandson of Emperor Yohannes IV, appeared at the modest U.S. residency in resplendent uniform: "His trousers were red velvet, with a rich gold band around the bottom, his coat was of purple velvet embroidered in gold, and his cape of velvet likewise embroidered." On his shoulders were epaulets of gold lace "with lions' mane trimmings"; one side of his chest was draped in a broad green sash and the other decorated with the gold star of the Order of Solomon; on his head perched a golden coronet, lined with velvet and studded with jewels; and at his side curved a large saber with a mother of pearl handle and a gold, richly ornamented scabbard. Next to the ras, the American delegation in morning dress appeared drab, even severe.

Addis Abeba's streets were colorful with the empire's peoples in traditional dress and with patriotic decorations of green, yellow, and red. The national colors were prominently displayed on the cathedral and were also worn by troops who guarded the city's main avenues. Attached to the edifice's left portal was a large temporary structure "decorated very gaily with the Ethiopian colors, flags, oriental rugs, and red curtains . . . [presenting] a very fine appearance, very suitable for the occasion, and very imposing in effect." At its front, nearest the door, there was an open space where two large golden thrones, a smaller one, and a variety of chairs had been placed for the sovereigns, the crown prince, the royal family, and various lords and ladies in waiting. Behind them, there were wide steps occupied by visiting choirboys from Alexandria, "all dressed in white, wearing white caps," who seemed to be guarding a table full of coronation garments and symbols of state. At the sides, gilded chairs had been arranged to accommodate gorgeously attired Ethiopian dignitaries, who alternated with foreign diplomats, mostly "in the fullest uniforms." Arrayed around the doorway into the church were Abuna Kerillos, his suffragan bishops, and the imperial confessors, all of them in simple and dignified hooded white capes.[67]

They waited until 8:00 A.M., when all the guests were seated, before they entered the church to fetch the imperial couple, who had kept a prayer vigil within during the night. Chanting and praying, the clerics led the imperial couple to their thrones, and the ceremonies began. The churchmen made the most of the occasion: "Psalms, canticles, and prayers succeeded each other, long passages of scriptures were read . . . candles were lit one by one; the coronation oaths were proposed and sworn."[68] Shortly after 10:00 A.M., "the emperor was anointed copiously with sacred oil . . . clad in his purple and gold robe, and then crowned by the Abuna with a magnificent gold crown studded with jewels." Then, for the first time in Ethiopian history, a crown prince was installed, followed by the empress and the royal family, broadcasting Haile Sellassie's — Tafari's baptismal, now regnal, name — clear intention to create a dynasty. Finally, the emperor and his consort retired with the clergy into the cathedral for a ninety-minute mass, during which the bored audience only caught "the hum of prayers and the chanting."[69]

When the couple reappeared, a visiting British naval band played the newly composed national anthem, a 101-gun salute was fired, and Ethiopia's great men made formal obeisance. Then, the emperor and empress, in full regalia, made their way through the throng in the churchyard and climbed into the state coach for a two-mile journey through Addis Abeba to show themselves to the broad masses. Following them were automobiles carrying the crown prince, the royal family, the special envoys, and the diplomatic corps. The city streets were lined with people whose culture eschewed most public displays of emotion. "No sound greeted the procession at any time, except occasionally 'you-yous' [ululations] were heard. . . . No cheering, handclapping, or other demonstrations were heard." On arrival at the gibbi, Haile Sellassie and Menen received their foreign guests briefly in the throne room, before all parties retired for a well-deserved rest before festivities were renewed.[70]

That evening the emperor and empress gave a large dinner party for ranking Ethiopians, visiting foreigners, and resident diplomats. The 114 guests were easily accommodated in the palace's great reception hall, where an elaborately laid, U-shaped table of sterling plates and gold cutlery gleamed in the reflected light of silver candelabra. The imperial couple headed the table, flanked on either side by guests according to rank. The menu consisted mostly of European food and drink, although there were a few Ethiopian stews and some honey wine, reflecting perhaps the paucity of Ethiopian wives and the predominance of European women present at the party. The evening ended with a fireworks display that was meant also to entertain the city's population. The show began simply with showering rockets and roman candles, but then the inexperienced soldiers managed "to set off the entire stock, causing a tremendous display but not one that had been expected."[71]

Mostly the day had gone very well, even if it had been in general devoted to the ruling classes. Evelyn Waugh correctly recalled that only a few Ethiopians were present at the coronation, but among those hundreds were the country's leaders. The people nonetheless were a palpable presence, a remote, if "dense . . . rabble that was constantly held at bay by the police."[72] Yet they had to be humored, and on 4 November Haile Sellassie and Menen, in full coronation garb and without uncomfortable crowns, progressed from church to church, to pray in each, to receive the blessing of the ordinary clergy, and to distribute alms. But mostly, in the fashion of monarchs, they sought to display their majesty to a rapt public. They were preceded by officers in colorful silk tunics and lion-mane headdresses, carrying gleaming spears and gilt-edged rhinoceros shields, and riding richly caparisoned mules; mounted, red-clad drummers beating out a victory march; companies of soldiers in traditional attire; a battalion of modern, khaki-clad infantry; and, just before the royal car, a troop of modern cavalry. Following behind came the vehicles of cabinet ministers and other officials, followed by a chaos of soldiery, "forming all in all a magnificent procession upward of a mile in length." [73] The extraordinary activity attracted huge crowds, who seemed to enjoy the pageantry as much as they would enjoy the military review on 7 December, at the Imperial Parade Grounds (Jan Hoy Meda).

There, at the summit of a hillock, a large pavilion had been erected to accommodate the imperial party and special guests. The emperor, dressed in a scarlet and gold military uniform, with a tall, lion-mane busby on his head, "presented a magnificent appearance, as he sat on his red throne . . . attended on each side by the diplomatic group and the high dignitaries in full military dress." [74] As far as his eye could see were masses of soldiers—"densely packed . . . forming around the entire field a living wall of men . . . in excellent order" —awaiting the ceremonial march past, which many of them would never make, given their vast numbers. From time to time, an officer would rush up to the emperor and shout out or pantomime, as was the custom, his feats of bravery against wild beast and enemy, all the time declaiming his fealty to the crown. So realistic were some of the performances that the foreign guests "feared that some attack had been premeditated against the person of the emperor himself." The self-praise was in Amharic, which was fortunate for the Prince of Udine, Rome's envoy, because several of the older officers recounted how many Italians they had killed during the war of 1894–1896.

The parade began with the emperor's personal army of eight thousand uniformed troops, marching in the fine order they had learned from Swiss instructors and former noncommissioned officers from neighboring colonial forces. Then came units from every province in the empire, and by late afternoon, perhaps one hundred thousand men had saluted their sovereign. He, however, was more interested in the final unit he reviewed, an oversized battalion of his fledgling regular army, consisting of infantry and a few squadrons of cavalry. Armed with up-to-date rifles, light machine guns, and mountain howitzers, they and their smart uniforms signaled the emperor's commitment to change.[75]

Thus the coronation was much more than a public relations campaign. The ceremonies and events had been unabashedly modern, although Ethiopian in execution, symbolizing the amalgam that the emperor sought to refine through his administration. That Ethiopians could mount such a complex celebration, "with a surprising absence of chaos,"[76] demonstrated the government's ability to mobilize and organize its population and resources. The Addis Abeba regime became credible to the Europeans, whose presence at the coronation was evidence enough for Ethiopians that the world recognized their nation's sovereignty and independence, confirming thereby the correctness of Haile Sellassie's foreign policy since 1916. By the time most Europeans left for home on 10 and 11 November, the city "had already shed almost all of the colorful petals of the coronation festivities, but within the calyx of the blossom [were] seeds of progress and enlightenment."[77]

The emperor was quick to prepare his land for growth by reforming his government. In 1930, Makonnen Habte Wolde was appointed director general in a Ministry of Finance led by Bit. Getachew Abate, not especially reactionary, but a profligate "devoted to wine, women, and song." In the latter's place, Haile Sellassie named Bejirond Tekle Wolde Hawariat, later to become a political gadfly in and out of favor and jail. Through 1930, however, Tekle had been a devoted member of Tafari's cabal of young and educated advisers. In previous positions in the municipality and in the Ministry of the Interior, the bejirond had diverted funds to Tafari's use for liberal and progressive projects. Haile Sellassie believed that he had a perfect team at the exchequer: the idealistic but flexible Tekle and Makonnen Habte Wolde, "a taciturn, canny individual, with an eye that seems to view this world of men as an interesting if rather dubious lot."[78]

The same could be said of Dej. Nasibu Zamanuel, whom many courtiers attacked as un-Ethiopian because he was a mission-educated Catholic, spoke Italian and French, and wore modish European clothes and uniforms. Haile Sellassie, however, valued Nasibu's isolation from the mainstream as much as his commitment to progress and his ability to inspire and lead men. After 1926, Nasibu had transformed the gendarmerie of Addis Abeba into the strong and disciplined unit that proved its dedication to the regent during the crisis of 1928. Tafari never forgot the dejazmach's efficiency and devotion and appointed him director in the Ministry of War on 22

January 1931, shortly after the minister, the powerful Dej. Mulugeta, had been elevated to ras and given responsibilities elsewhere.

In Mulugeta's place, Haile Sellassie made a weak appointment, Fit. Biru Menilek, a youngish man with antiquated ideas. He had been born out of wedlock in the old emperor's palace, his father a minor court functionary and his mother a serving girl. For sentimental reasons, Menilek—whose own mother had been a servant at court—became the boy's guardian, permitted him his name, saw to his education, raised him as an aristocrat, and started him on a successful career in government. Biru's appointment would give the War Ministry a titular leader important enough to impress many traditionalists and to balance Dej. Nasibu's reformist zeal.[79] At the Foreign Ministry, however, Herui Wolde Sellassie became minister without a deputy. He had always been assiduously loyal to the emperor, had given him many years of devoted service, and, significantly, did not head an organization directly concerned with internal politics. Moreover, he was unfailingly grateful when Haile Sellassie intervened in the flow of diplomacy and he meekly accepted the counsel of the excellent Swedish adviser, Johannes Kolmodin, hired in March 1931.[80]

Ethiopia's more complex foreign relations demanded that the troublesome issue of slavery be resolved. Part of Ras Mulugeta's domains included the anarchic province of Gamo Gofa, along the Kenya border, and he was instructed to stop slaving and cross-frontier forays. Dej. Mengesha Yilma, the emperor's nephew, was appointed to the newly formed administration of Maji and Goldiya, adjacent to both Kenya and Sudan. The fierce slave raiding in the area had spilled across the frontiers and had antagonized a generation of colonial officialdom, whose matter-of-fact racism attributed the entire problem to the innate inefficiency and barbarity of the Ethiopian government. In the late 1920s, they had ignored the sharp decreases in raiding as the Addis Abeba government's anti–slave-trade programs were applied in the nation's more remote areas. By selecting his nephew as governor, Haile Sellassie sought to catch the attention of British frontier officials and to dramatize the renewal of Ethiopian authority in the borderlands.[81]

His appointment of a nagadras for Jima startled the city-state's officials.[82] Although the act augured badly for the future of the hitherto autonomous province, it was part of a larger program that assigned imperial directors of customs for Adwa, Mekele, and Dese, with orders to collect taxes and duties independently and to send the proceeds directly to Addis Abeba.[83] The governor of Welo was quick to agree to the change in Dese; since February 1931, he had been Asfa Wossen, the crown prince, who was also given the title of meridazmach (prince) and his own personal household, but who remained under the authority of Dej. Imru and a personal tutor.[84] The two Tigrayan lords had no other option but to accept the imperial fiat: since the coronation, they had remained in Addis Abeba, along with Ras Hailu, the "honored guests" of the emperor. Ostensibly they were in the capital to advise the emperor on the organization of his new government, and they were, in fact, directly involved in the creation of the Ethiopian Constitution announced on 16 July 1931, another assertion of central authority and the dynastic principle.

Haile Sellassie later recorded that he long had contemplated "the promulgation of a constitution for Our reign, to bequeath to our heirs a rule that is based on law and to bring Our people into partnership in the work of government." He had asked Zawditu to proclaim a constitution, but the project had been blocked "by some of the great nobles," who feared an erosion of her "authority and dignity." Soon after his coronation, the emperor decided to issue a constitution, and by December 1930, rumors were circulating in Addis Abeba about his intentions. The leaks came from members of a committee commanded by the emperor "to select and extract, from the constitutions of foreign countries, what was appropriate for the Ethiopian people—and then to submit recommendations to Us." The prime movers here seem to have been Messrs. Jèze and Kolmodin and Bej. Tekle Hawariat, who sent their recommendations to a large working group for criticism and decision.

Ministers and other official members, among them the Young Ethiopians, broadly supported constitutional concepts that strengthened the central government and legitimated a civil service based on education and experience, whereas nobles generally favored a charter that perpetuated the hereditary principle and imposed a kind of feudal federalism. When the matter went to the emperor for decision, he "explained to the nobles, it was no longer proper that, since We were aware that feudal rule had ceased in the world, We should now once again re-affirm it." [85] The constitution's final drafting was therefore guided by the principle "that all power emanated from the Emperor and could be enjoyed by others only in the form of temporary and revocable delegation by him." [86] The document's ultimate approval by the large committee legitimated the emperor's longstanding efforts "to establish more strongly the power of the central government over what has heretofore been a loosely joined group of provincial governments." [87]

At 10:00 A.M., on 16 July 1931, Haile Sellassie presided over an impressive ceremony to celebrate the installation of the new, fifty-five-article constitution. After he had signed the document, representatives of each of Ethiopia's ruling classes appended their endorsements. Never before had a monarch achieved such a broad national consensus; in this way, the constitution was a statement of national unity, a theme the emperor mentioned in his speech inaugurating the constitution. Invariably paternalistic, Haile Sellassie declared Ethiopia's need as a family to be "controlled by one law and governed by one Emperor." The rule of law and the people's participation in government through parliament were nevertheless vital to forging a united community. Yet the crown retained the upper hand always; only when "approved by His Majesty the Emperor" would parliamentary decisions be implemented by ministers. The emperor emphasized that the concepts embodied in the constitution were "not just idle fiction or discordant with the country's customs," but the product of "Our nobles and Our officials and of other Ethiopian subjects," repeating the theme of national consensus. If the imperial remarks stressed unity, fraternity, and popular participation in government, the decree that made the constitution law asserted the legitimacy of Haile Sellassie's succession through God's grace and "the unanimous voice of his people," and his right, "of Our own free will," to legislate laws for his people. [88]

The emperor's supremacy was the constitution's point. Article 3 provided that "the Imperial Rank shall remain perpetually in the line of His Majesty Haile Selassie . . . whose lineage continues unbroken from the dynasty of Menelek I, son of King Solomon . . . and the Queen of Sheba." Article 5 made "the person of the Emperor . . . sacred, His dignity inviolate and His power incontestable," and article 6 simply declared that "within the Ethiopian Empire the Emperor holds the supreme power." Articles 7, 8, and 9 concerned the Senate and the Chamber of Deputies, but even here the emperor was supreme. "The Laws drafted by these chambers will become effective by His promulgation." Article 46 empowered the monarch to reconcile disagreements between the Senate and the Chamber of Deputies and gave him the right, in the face of continued legislative conflict, "to choose and promulgate the conclusion of either one or the other, or to postpone the question."

Article 12 made the emperor the sole arbiter of war and peace, article 13 proclaimed him commander-in-chief of the armed forces, and article 20 stipulated that all soldiers owed "absolute allegiance and obedience to the emperor according to the provisions of the law." Articles 48 through 54 were studiously vague about the rights and powers of ministers and judges, but seemed to affirm their dependency on the crown as its servants.[89] With all its problems and assertions, the constitution was a progressive document that established a framework within which modern government could develop, an innovation that would have been supported by even the most vehement of Haile Sellassie's later critics "if they were born then."[90]

On 3 November 1931, the anniversary of the coronation according to the Ethiopian calendar, Haile Sellassie presided over the rushed, formal opening of the new parliament. He hoped that the new institution would stimulate nationalism and unity and that its members would popularize sociopolitical change in the provinces. He appointed senators from among the high aristocracy and ranking officials (article 31) and deputies from the lesser nobility and middling bureaucrats "until . . . the people are in a position to elect these themselves" (article 32). In 1931, Ethiopia's broad masses had limited political awareness, and to achieve reform, the government had to obtain the cooperation of the ruling elites.[91]

In his inaugural speech to the senators, the emperor stressed the necessity of their participation in government to promote "Our Imperial Constitution [whose] fundamental principle is that the progress to be effected in governmental methods be closely associated with the Imperial conception of the State." The emperor pledged to respect the "due reward" and "honors" owing to the senators as descendants of those who had "served Ethiopia," although he advised that they would work more efficiently for "the benefit of the public . . . by renouncing voluntarily the prerogatives to which your nobleness, your fortune, or services rendered, give you right." Finally, Haile Sellassie admonished them to guide their colleagues in the lower house so that they might "advance and acquire higher conceptions," especially national unity, the theme of his message to the lower house.

He wanted the deputies to put nation before province, to eschew "narrow individualism," and to appreciate

that other provinces exist near the provinces where you were born; that there exist besides your native towns, other towns; that a nation is composed of the total of these towns and provinces; and that the inhabitants of this Nation are the children of the whole of Ethiopia. . . . Learn that there exists a collective union composed of a community of interests.

Parliamentarians should carry home the message of unity symbolized by the monarch and his parliament, for national amalgamation was the key to Ethiopia's future success and the only vehicle for the eradication of "injustice, iniquity, malice, and bad faith." [92]

Now that the country's ruling elite had sanctioned the modern centralizing state, Haile Sellassie moved to eliminate Ethiopia's two outstanding anachronisms, Abba Jifar of Jima and Ras Hailu of Gojam. The latter was in a dangerously exposed position in Addis Abeba; only he, among the rases, was not permitted to leave after the formalization of the constitution and the inauguration of parliament. Tax evasion was his major sin: over the years, Hailu had exploited his autonomy as a hereditary prince and remitted little in the way of taxes to the government.[93] Other great rases, among them Kassa and Seyoum, had earlier conceded imperial control over customs and revenue collection in their provinces. Hailu also embarrassed the crown by openly seeking favors from the American and British legations, insinuating that otherwise he would block their access to Lake Tana and the Blue Nile.[94] Worst sin of all, he negotiated with the Italians, who regarded him as the stereotypical Ethiopian lord: independent, avaricious, treacherous, and subject to blandishment and bribe. Rome was always willing to weaken the national government, and Haile Sellassie increasingly came to regard Hailu as a security risk and, ipso facto, an enemy of the central state.[95]

The Depression provided the immediate background to Hailu's destruction. Gojam was an inevitable target for an administration short of funds, and Hailu an obvious victim, since his penny-pinching ways had made him many enemies. The central government therefore had little trouble in finding complainants wishing to charge Hailu with crimes. Immediately after the coronation a trickle of Gojamis made their way across the Blue Nile to the emperor, acting as the court of last resort, to plead for justice. Not surprisingly, Haile Sellassie consistently sided with the plaintiffs: "even cases over ten years' old have been reopened and on one pretext or another [Hailu] has been mulcted of sums amounting to over 80,000 dollars." The ras quickly concluded that Haile Sellassie was determined to destroy him but could do little to counter: he and his son were hostages in Addis Abeba, much of his property was there and vulnerable to confiscation, and the government enjoyed overwhelming military superiority.[96] Moreover, he was not a popular figure in Gojam,[97] and during his enforced stay in the capital, his government's authority had broken down, leading to increased banditry and small insurrections, some doubtlessly arranged by imperial *agents provocateurs*.[98]

The anti-Hailu campaign leapt forward on 14 April 1932, when the ras again went before the emperor's court to hear the complaints of yet another Gojami delegation. Haile Sellassie listened for a time and then commented that the province had indeed been misgoverned by Hailu, "notwithstanding the good advice that I never ceased giving him . . . [he] neither wanted to listen to my counsel nor to your complaints." The emperor's denunciation immediately led to formal allegations of maladministration and lese majesty against Hailu and to a quick verdict of guilty as charged.[99] Haile Sellassie levied a fine of MT$300,000, divested Hailu of Agew Midir, Wembera, and Beleya— virtually half of Gojam—placed customs and taxes under imperial jurisdiction, and formally detained the ras in Addis Abeba. Hailu uttered not a word in his defense and bowed low to the emperor in obedience.[100] The emperor stonily looked beyond his humbled subject to the anachronism of Jima, the next sacrifice to the logic of centralization.

In 1884, in return for an annual tribute and allegiance, Menilek had agreed to Jima's autonomy under Sultan Abba Jifar and his successors. By mid-1932, however, the arrangement had become a reactionary obstruction to an Ethiopian government intent on modernization, development, and fiscal reform. Haile Sellassie certainly would have preferred to await the aged sultan's death before annexing Jima, but the Depression forced his hand.[101] On 5 May 1932, *Berhanena Selam* editorialized that Menilek's arrangement had enriched Jima, the sultan, and Ethiopia. Now, however, the sultanate's good fortune was at risk because Abba Jifar had been "overtaken by old age and illness," and Abba Jobir, his grandson, was no longer cooperating with the Addis Abeba government. Jobir had correctly concluded that Haile Sellassie coveted his patrimony, and he decided to resist by building up a national army, a policy the newspaper considered a *casus belli*.[102]

On 12 May, the paper reported that three hundred soldiers from nearby Limu had been sent to Jima, where they had been joined by a planeload of officials from Addis Abeba, who were to oversee the sultanate's government. *Berhanena Selam* advised its readers not to pity Jima, which had invited its own dénouement, but to "lament its bad luck" in being poorly governed.[103] The truth was more complex: Jima's autonomy had been undermined by the declining world economy, the deteriorating health of its ruler, the road that slowly advanced from Addis Abeba, the advent of air power, and the transcendent needs of modern, centralized power. Both Abba Jifar and Ras Hailu suffered from becoming obsolete, indeed reactionary, in terms of Ethiopia's changing political economy. Just as had Lij Iyasu, they would fall to the new order.

Like Banquo's ghost, the prince had been invoked, or had been heard rattling his chains, from offstage since his capture and subsequent incarceration in 1921. As the years passed, he had become less threatening to the state, although imaginative diplomats and Ethiopian gossips, usually in direct proportion to their frustration with Tafari, imagined that he might again regain power. Such thinking was at worst sophistry, at best whimsy, but with a frustration born of his desperate position, Ras Hailu decided to manipulate Iyasu to regain the emperor's favor.[104] The ras plotted to free the prince and then to betray him to Haile Sellassie, who would gratefully permit the Gojami to return home. Had Hailu's position not been so hopeless, he would have seen that the scheme was foolhardy and unworkable. Moreover, from its inception, it was a botched job.

True enough, bribery bought Iyasu's escape from his jail in Fiche on 15 May, during the absence of most of Ras Kassa's family. The dropsical and fat fugitive did manage two days later to get to Ginderbert, to meet one hundred of his old followers, equipped with arms and ammunition supplied by Hailu. Iyasu announced his success in a letter dated 19 May, which Hailu received on 26 May; the next morning, the ras obtained an immediate audience with the emperor, to whom he showed the letter as, so he said, a sign of loyalty. Haile Sellassie immediately called in Ras Kassa, gave him the surprising news, and both men turned to Hailu and asked him to produce the messenger, whom he had undoubtedly detained. When the Gojami equivocated, Kassa suspected his complicity in a plot and said as much, but the emperor refused publicly to consider the charge until he could find corroborating evidence. Instead, he ordered Dej. Aberra, Kassa's son, to pursue and capture Iyasu, asked Kassa and Hailu to remain for an 11:00 A.M. meeting of the Council of Ministers, and confidentially instructed trusted men to enter and search Hailu's villa.

When incriminating letters were found, the Gojami was arrested, placed under house arrest, and shackled with the silver chains of respect accorded high nobles. Meanwhile, on 30 May, Dej. Aberra reached the Ginderbert area, only to find that Iyasu had escaped across the Blue Nile into Gojam, where on 11 June he was captured by Fit. Gessesse Belaw, Hailu's nephew. After telephoning the good news to Addis Abeba, he turned the prince over to Desta Demtu, the emperor's son-in-law, who had reached Gojam with crack imperial forces. On 18 June, Iyasu was flown to the capital, to be moved at 8:00 P.M., by special train, to Dire Dawa, where he arrived on the evening of 19 June. Under the tightest security, he was quickly transferred by car to Gara Muleta, to be imprisoned under the watchful eyes of Haile Sellassie's faithful officer, Dej. Abbashaul.[105]

By then, Ras Hailu had been taken from the comfort of house arrest and placed in the palace's dungeons, where his bonds of silver were exchanged for iron shackles. On 27 June, he was tried before the emperor, the Council of Ministers, various dignitaries, and leading churchmen. He was quickly convicted of treason and condemned to death, but on clerical intercession, his sentence was commuted to confiscation of all property and life imprisonment. In an

extensive article recapitulating the hearing and its outcome, *Berhanena Selam* railed against Hailu: "He had been poisoned . . . by cu-
pidity. His only thought was to accumulate money at any cost, without consideration for the affliction of the poor." He had wrecked
Gojam and had "brooded over plans which would cause the ruin of
the whole of Ethiopia and widespread bloodshed." [106] Left unstated
was the newspaper's implicit argument that no individual, however
powerful, could block Ethiopia's progress.

CHAPTER SEVEN

Domestic Concerns,
1932-1934

Haile Sellassie moved quickly to consolidate the central government's gains. In July 1932, he made Desta Demtu ras and added Jima
to his domains, although he permitted Abba Jifar to retain titular
authority. The new ras was one of Ethiopia's modern administrators,
as eager for progress as for profit. While governor of Kefa, he had
dutifully remitted taxes to Addis Abeba, simultaneously enriching
himself by skimming off a percentage of his province's coffee revenue. He understood that his wealth and the nation's strength depended on the development of infrastructure, and he had improved
trails and roads, opened telephone and post offices, built schools,
and imposed a uniform code of law and order on his subjects. As
master of Jima, he was expected to spur the completion of the road to
Addis Abeba and to foster commercial agriculture. No one expected
Desta Demtu to be loved by the Jimans, as he was likely to make them
"work much longer and harder" to pay his personal levies and the
hitherto exempted imperial taxes.[1]

Imru Haile Sellassie, another newly elevated ras, was directed to integrate Gojam into the modern state. His new charges were irate that the emperor had sent officials and planes to Debre Markos to sell off Hailu's property, to confiscate his wealth, and to transport all money, jewels, gold, and silver to the imperial exchequer.[2] In late 1932, before Imru even appeared on the scene, the discontent led to an insurrection by Fit. Admassu, one of Hailu's natural sons, who was distressed by the obvious loss of his birthright and those of his brothers and sisters. He based his disobedience on a decree of 24 October 1928, which declared that the property of those "found guilty against the King or Government . . . shall at once legally pass to his children."[3] On 30 September, Admassu and a small force entered Debre Markos, ejected the few central government officials found there, and took the little that remained in Hailu's warehouses. The challenge was purely symbolic, and before too long the fitawrari sent emissaries to Haile Sellassie asking his pardon.[4] On Imru's recommendation, the emperor granted clemency and even restored some of Hailu's children to government posts.[5] Paradoxically, the accommodations won no friends, nor did Imru's liberal reforms, which enriched producers and traders[6] and increased the flow of revenues to Addis Abeba. Imru was invariably viewed as an outsider, the emperor's agent, and, unable to rule by consensus, he governed by force. He once remarked that "the province . . . exhausted his energy."[7]

Popularity was not so important as power, and intimacy with Haile Sellassie provided Imru with sufficient authority and legitimacy. By 1932, the emperor enjoyed unchallenged ascendancy in Ethiopia, even if he was not especially popular. He had constructed a central government apparatus totally reliant on the crown for policy and direction, and his men in the provinces guaranteed imperial writ there. The aristocracy was with him, appreciating that he would guarantee their prosperity through nation building, but his reserve put them off, and their loyalty lacked the "cordial warmth of friendship." The distance between monarch and minions placed Haile Sellassie in "a more independent position than if he had won their friendly affection with resulting and sometimes embarrassing obligations for reciprocity in kind."

The emperor relished aloofness, apparently imitating the remoteness of the Japanese monarch, whose "attitude of exclusiveness," in Haile Sellassie's opinion, created "an imperial dignity lacking in Ethiopia." He had consequently made himself less available to aristocrat and diplomat and had fashioned "a wire pulling arrangement to be operated through a chosen few." [8] Though he selected his operatives carefully, many critics believed that the emperor's success depended on "a marvelous amount of luck and most of what might be called the breaks." Others concluded that he added "unbounded energy" and supreme intelligence to a "sense of humor that probably saves his life ten times a day." Not a few were persuaded that Haile Sellassie was a clever "humbug who merely plays up to the Foreign Legations and the League of Nations, while all he cares for is absolute despotism and as much wealth as he can collect." That conclusion was contradicted by the emperor's obvious dedication to education, progress, and good order while simultaneously undermining the status quo. The constitution of 1931 was a good example of putting "the cart of a constitution before the horse of education, but so long as the cart stays in status quo the horse will probably be led into the shafts in time," thereby changing Ethiopia forever.[9]

Nevertheless, the recent crisis over Lij Iyasu had revealed the inchoate nature of modern government in Ethiopia. The emperor had not used the central administration, preferring instead to be guided by "a very efficient system of collecting private information, for he knew almost hourly the moves of the fugitive." He never revealed his intelligence sources, and he confided in no one, especially his ministers, "probably because in a matter where his own sovereignty and life were concerned he could not trust them all." Indeed, his behavior here epitomized Haile Sellassie's political tactics throughout his reign: he collected information from all sources, and he could control any situation by withholding news, by manipulating reports, or by distorting reality. He also sought advice widely, especially from foreign advisers, whom ministers regarded as imperial agents. He tried always to create factions, the more easily to respond to a barrage of competition, here choosing one side, there the other, creating and dissolving a shifting series of coalitions. Throughout, Haile Sellassie maintained himself as Ethiopia's sole source of authority.[10]

The Italians also regarded the emperor as the source of all change in Ethiopia. They concluded that his impressive programs of national rejuvenation "demonstrate [that there] exists a will to lead Ethiopia through a phase of rapid evolution, to form a country different from the traditional Abyssinia to which we have up to now been accustomed to refer." [11] From Eritrea, Riccardo Astuto, the newly appointed governor and an ardent Fascist, signaled his preference for a feudal Ethiopia by advising the subversion of Addis Abeba's effort at centralization and modernization, especially at the limits of Haile Sellassie's authority. He recommended bribing provincial leaders with money and the masses with schools, hospitals, and clinics. The governor considered his "peripheral policy . . . a limited action, modest, anonymous . . . [where] Italians would work in silence and in obscurity . . . for the future." [12]

During 1932, however, without abandoning Astuto's strategy, the Italians also undertook a more active policy. Mussolini was warned that progress had made the Solomonic state into "a threat, today only potential, tomorrow perhaps real, to our East African colonies, territories which are considered by the Ethiopians as *terrae irredentae*" and had eliminated the possibility of transforming Ethiopia into an economic dependency and then into a protectorate. [13] At every turn, Italian efforts were thwarted, probably not so much as a matter of policy but because suspicion of Rome was an Ethiopian birthright. The prevailing attitude was "anybody but the Italians," rendering the 1928 treaty a failure. [14] In August 1932, Marchese Gaetano Paterno, minister in Addis Abeba since 1930, advised that only strong measures would reverse the weak Italian position in Ethiopia.

Strong action necessarily presupposes the preparation of an Italo-Ethiopian diplomatic situation such as to permit us at the right time to create or provoke the *casus* which might allow us also to confront the Abyssinian question internationally. . . . A program which presupposes a strong policy, while today essentially a political program, inevitably becomes in its execution an essentially military program. [15]

The arch-imperialist Raffaele Guariglia, undersecretary in the Foreign Ministry, agreed; he fancied that all great nations needed colonies, " and one cannot expect them to fall from the sky as manna. If it is true that nothing great can be accomplished in this world without bloodying your hands, it is indisputably true in the history of colonization."[16] Developing his ideas, the undersecretary stressed that Ethiopia was being "civilized, armed, and united through the exceptional ability of the present emperor" and therefore represented "an increasingly grave obstacle and a threat to our colonies."[17] He advised that Somalia and Eritrea be strengthened militarily, especially in air power, to guard against a future in which Ethiopia might be "an aggressive danger to our two colonies." Meanwhile, he recommended that his government negotiate a "free hand" in Ethiopia in return for abandonment of Italian rights in Tunisia.[18] Such an arrangement had been sounded in Paris in 1928[19] but only became a possibility three years later.

On 28 March 1931, the Ethiopian authorities had sensibly raised import duties in order to acquire the additional funds needed to complete the purchase of the Bank of Abyssinia and to introduce a national currency backed by gold.[20] A hefty 30 percent sales tax was levied on luxury goods, most of which were shipped from France. Paris's plenipotentiary, Serchère de Reffye, reasoned that the consequent drop in French imports would cause the Quai d'Orsay to reconsider its Ethiopian policy. He even foresaw that Paris and Rome would come together to fight the new levies on the basis of article 3 of the Franco-Ethiopian (Klobukowski) Treaty of 1908, which stipulated a flat 10 percent ad valorem duty on most imports.[21] In response to Italo-French protests, the Ethiopian government explained that it had merely imposed taxes in order to pay for nation building, "a difficult task, not only from the social and political point of view but especially difficult on the financial side."[22] The decision to tax nonessential imports was, as Washington and London agreed, an act of sovereignty, in the face of which Italy and France backed down. The victory was, however, won at a high cost, for it jeopardized relations with France. Reffye hoped that Haile Sellassie could be taught, before it was too late, that Ethiopia was not "the center of the world, that it only plays a peripheral role in the relations between great powers and that it is above all France which up to now has been the principal safeguarder of its independence."[23]

Significantly, the memorandum of 1928, which first raised the possibility of bargaining with Italy over Ethiopia, surfaced again, this time masquerading as a "Note pour le ministre."[24] On 20 April 1931, the Quai sent a copy to its ambassador in Rome, seeking his advice on the Ethiopian question. Count Beaumarchais, who knew of Ethiopia only through the highly prejudiced Italian media, reported his skepticism that Haile Sellassie would be able, by himself and using only national resources, to develop the country to the point of "civilization." He therefore considered it logical to involve the Italians, who had deep feelings about the Horn of Africa, in the work of building a modern Ethiopia. Besides, the task was so monumental that it would dissipate Italy's nationalistic energies harmlessly and distract Mussolini from the intrigues and uncertainties of European great-power politics. In view of these vital consequences, Ethiopia's continued independence was unimportant, and Beaumarchais therefore advised Paris to be ready, if necessary, to "disinterest ourselves in Ethiopia's future." Although abandonment of Ethiopia would inevitably upset public opinion, the ambassador believed that Rome's friendship was "worth a sacrifice and . . . Ethiopia . . . would be the least costly [sacrifice] as much for our self-respect as for our European interests." He cautioned patience, to wait for the Italians to "ask us to let them have a *free hand* in Abyssinia [italics mine]" in order to make the best deal.[25]

In July 1931, subtle hints were delivered during conversations in Paris between the foreign ministers Dino Grandi and Pierre Laval, persuading Guariglia that the Quai d'Orsay was leaning toward the idea of permitting Rome a "free hand" over most of Ethiopia.[26] In early 1932, after further meetings between French and Italian officials on a variety of issues — none of them concerning Ethiopia — Guariglia concluded that Paris would not interfere with "our future expeditions in Ethiopia" and would renounce some of the "special rights based on the accord of 1906." The quid pro quo for Italy was abandonment of extraterritorial jurisdiction over its nationals in Tunisia, a concession easily made because, according to Guariglia, Rome's prerogative there would be regained after "our victorious conflict with France."[27] Six months later, after another series of subtle signals, Guariglia advised Mussolini that the Quai d'Orsay was already framing policy permitting Italy a "free hand" over most of Ethiopia.[28]

In Addis Abeba, M. Reffye fought against the policy change and for a continuation of French paramountcy.[29] He tended therefore to respond enthusiastically to every Ethiopian attempt to restore the old and intimate relationship and consequently misled the emperor by welcoming an Ethiopian effort in early 1932 to open negotiations leading to a formal Franco-Ethiopian treaty of alliance.[30] Paris spurned the offer, instructing its minister to explain that France had abandoned alliances in favor of arbitration and conciliation pacts under the auspices of the League of Nations. Reffye was admonished confidentially that French policy in Ethiopia would not be permitted to disrupt "the equilibrium of our general policies and disturb England and Italy." Nor did Paris seek another entangling alliance, especially with a country governed "so capriciously by a self-serving oligarchy."[31] When Reffye subsequently requested a loan for Ethiopia to purchase weapons and to finance roads, he was turned down flatly. Finally, when the emperor desperately sought, in mid-1932, a secret treaty guaranteeing Ethiopia's independence, the Quai d'Orsay refused unreservedly.[32] Thus, the French sources confirm Italian perceptions that Paris really abandoned Ethiopia to Rome in mid-1932, just when Haile Sellassie was moving men and resources into the Ogaden to counter infiltration from Somalia.

The advance had been considerable: in August and September 1931, Englishmen motoring from British Somaliland to Kenya discovered that, according to War Office maps, a portion of the new Italian-built road, especially the section from Danot to Geladi, seemed to be in Ethiopian territory. Repeated questions brought the invariable reply "that the map [they] had was quite out of date." When the travelers rejoined that the official Italian version showed the same boundary line, "they said the Italian map was out of date." In an act of cordiality, Capt. Roberto Cimmaruta, the inspector of the frontier—conveniently stationed at Korahe within the Ethiopian border—took the War Office map and "most ingenuously" marked the nearly finished road and the new frontier, "according to Italian ideas." When the leader of the British group asked when the new line had been demarcated "and commented on how slack the map makers were in not having it properly marked," Cimmaruta admitted that a commission would quickly settle the matter, if only the Ethiopians would appoint their delegation. "It was all rather amusing—the commission is to sit apparently at any time but the boundary frontier, roads and forts have all been settled and established beforehand by the Italians."

Commenting on the information, Sir Sidney Barton, British minister since late 1929, warned London that the Italian post at Danot was sited in the intersection of the forty-seventh east meridian and the eighth north parallel, the point at which an impending joint demarcation of the British Somaliland–Ethiopian frontier would begin: "It will be observed that the Italians have lost no time in consolidating their position in this area since this junction point was recognized by us as such in connection with the Anglo-Italian frontier demarcation in 1930." [33] Thus, all the pieces were in place for the Welwel crisis of November 1934, including Addis Abeba's determination not to permit the Italians to retain illegally occupied parts of Ethiopia.

In August 1931, Ethiopian authorities advised Berbera and Mogadishu to withdraw their subjects from the Ogaden,[34] because an Ethiopian expedition would be operating there "with the firm intention of bringing order to the country." According to *Berhanena Selam*, the commander, Dej. Gebre Mariam, intended to establish administration and garrisons down to the district level; to construct government offices and markets where people normally congregated, in other words, at water holes and wells; and to build roads, especially between Jijiga, Degeh Bur, and Korahe.[35] The imperial army's excellent equipment, weapons, and well-maintained trucks so impressed the Italians that they reinforced their posts and put their army on alert.[36] The colonial authorities were clearly determined to retain their controversial posts, just as Gebre Mariam's expedition signaled Addis Abeba's resolve "to transform its rather theoretical domination over the Ogaden into a solid occupation." [37]

By the beginning of 1932, the Ethiopian consolidation was having a positive effect, at least in the Megalo region, where Dej. Gebre Mariam had succeeded in introducing "the most absolute tranquility." The bandits of earlier, less-policed times had disappeared, and the formerly terrorized population had turned away from the burden of constant defense to the tribulations of peaceful pursuits.[38] *Berhanena Selam* confirmed that the Ogaden expedition aimed to establish a government that would "guarantee security and . . . administer justice." [39] Throughout 1932, Dej. Gebre Mariam's officers called in regional and local leaders, sought their advice, and recruited them into the evolving administration as headmen.[40]

The new Ogaden government quickly prepared a network of mo-

torable tracks and established administrative centers, such as Kebri
Dehar, which were as much commercial hubs as district military
headquarters. The new towns were linked by telegraph to small outposts, largely manned by Ogadeni, who policed and regulated the
subdistricts and localities.[41] The activity unsettled Mogadishu, and
Governor Maurizio Rava cast about for a way to counter the show of
force and the increasingly effective administrative reorganization.
Although some of his own officers reported otherwise, the governor
informed Rome that the Ethiopian expedition had created anarchy
along the frontiers, and he asked permission to unleash his Somali
militia, the dubat, "to restore order and tranquility and to reaffirm
our prestige."[42] Rava really wanted war, because Gebre Mariam's
men had carefully avoided the most-forward Italian positions. General Emilio De Bono, the colonial minister, was not then looking for
a *casus belli*, and he advised prudence in the face of the "reawakened
and active Ethiopian Government," especially as he did not want to
provoke Addis Abeba into mounting other expeditions and accelerat-
ing its rearmament and military-training programs.[43]

In late 1932, however, De Bono accompanied King Victor Emmanuel III (r. 1900–1946) to Eritrea and Somalia and used the opportunity to survey colonial defenses. The general found the dependencies relatively weak in comparison to Ethiopia's growing strength, at
least as he surmised it.[44] He could easily imagine a future crisis in
which Ethiopian armies would push the Italians into the sea. Upon
returning to Rome, he reported to Mussolini that Eritrea, immediately adjacent to populous Tigray, was especially vulnerable and that
its future "depended on what Fascism wanted to do in East Africa and
what were its ultimate aims." Speaking to the Fascist Senate, De
Bono subtly posed the same questions but emphasized that Eritrea
and Somalia were "suffocating" in isolation from the rich Ethiopian
hinterland. He raised the possibility of armed intervention, no matter how costly in time and money, to open up the Solomonic Empire
to Italian aggrandizement. His colleagues nodded agreement, and
later Mussolini authorized the general to begin planning the conquest of Ethiopia.[45]

In 1932, "nothing concrete had been decided" about any aggression, for that choice was a political matter.[46] Nevertheless, the record
is clear that the ultimate *casus belli* was the success of Haile Sellas-

sie's programs of modernization and Rome's feeling that events in the Horn of Africa were moving beyond its control.[47] This conclusion is confirmed by archival materials, memoirs, and the logic of subsequent developments. By early 1934, however, purely local considerations became submerged in a welter of Italian national needs and international compulsions.[48] George W. Baer has summed up the Fascist predicament best:

Without a broad and viable program for the peaceful development of Italy, Mussolini came to lean more and more on the pursuit of militant nationalism to give the appearance of direction and energy to his regime. The Ethiopian adventure was almost certainly contrived, at least, in part, as an alternative to social reform; it was a way to glorify the Duce and, correspondingly, to divert social attention from domestic problems.[49]

Furthermore, through 1934, anxieties about Nazi Germany and the general European situation made the decision in favor of an Ethiopian war even more likely.[50] It should be stressed, therefore, that the Italian war in the Horn of Africa was conceived, if not timed, to counter an imagined local threat by Ethiopia against Somalia and especially Eritrea and to stop the Solomonic state, under Haile Sellassie, its agent of development, from attaining the status of a modern state in the eyes of the world.[51]

The emperor was busy during 1932–1934 implementing basic reforms that would have augured well for the future, had the war not intervened. Haile Sellassie was a whirlwind of activity: he was everywhere, so it seemed, doing everything. Projects and planning fell into place for roads, schools, hospitals, communications, administration, and public services. Given Ethiopia's limited resources and educated manpower, it is a wonder that so much was accomplished. The two-year period was a monument to Haile Sellassie's leadership and a testament to the wisdom of mixing idealism with personal benefit.

The road-building program is a good case in point.[52] The emperor understood the value of motorable roads, not only for government and the economy but also for his own exchequer. He often invested in toll roads or transport companies, as did other members of the royal family and the aristocracy. He had even sold government concessions in his name to road construction companies for fairly sizable annual payments.[53] Avarice was, however, only one part of the

emperor's devotion to road building. His basic motive was to facilitate commerce and to expand the range of government. By mid-1934,
thanks to Haile Sellassie's leadership, the Addis Abeba–Jima road
had passed the Omo River and was growing daily; Harer-Jijiga was
completed; and Mojo-Sidamo was finished and being extended to
Mega.[54] There were motorable connections from the capital to
Fiche, toward the Blue Nile, and to Dese. Dej. Gebre Mariam had
laid down a network of tracks in the Ogaden "to guard against Italian
encroachments and resist them if necessary." [55] Ras Desta Demtu
had completed rough tracks from Sidamo to Moyale via Mega and
thence toward Dolo via Arero: "It is now possible (though not easy)
to motor from Addis Abeba to Moyale." [56] Presiding at every ceremonial opening of a new bridge or road was a member of the royal
family, often the emperor himself, not to ensure profit, but to celebrate national development.

National needs accounted for the retirement of the Maria Theresa
dollar and its replacement by a new national currency. Because it
had proved impossible to obtain international loans during the Depression, the government was determined to obtain fiscal flexibility
and a mechanism to finance deficits. By 1932, however, revenues
were pouring into Addis Abeba from recently opened provincial
offices of the Ministry of Finance; from reorganized customs stations, which applied the new, higher tariffs; and from export taxes
applied to twenty-five thousand tons of coffee, triple the amount
shipped in 1928, but only one-third more in money terms.[57] As the
country's international commerce grew and as the needs of the development program and military procurements soared, the government wanted a control over foreign exchange impossible to impose
with the continued use of a specie that was a commodity itself. In
early 1933, therefore, the Bank of Ethiopia issued paper money in
denominations of E$5, 10, 50, 100, and 1,000, backed at the outset by a
reserve of silver for the full value of the notes outstanding. The bills
were legal tender for all transactions but were useful mainly in the
towns. For the countryside, the government distributed locally
minted nickel and bronze coins, a remarkable innovation in a country that hitherto had used salt bars and bullets as small change. In the
offing were a nickel dollar, one and two dollar bills, and an eventual
gold reserve for a gold standard currency.[58]

The government forced traders to use the paper money for all legal, public, and private transactions, and in September 1933, it banned the private import and export of Maria Theresa dollars, finally freeing the national economy from domination by the world silver market.[59] The government would henceforth be able to benefit from any rise in the value of silver by adjusting currency reserve requirements and then selling any surplus for international exchange, a procedure it followed from time to time after October 1934.[60] Given control over specie and currency, the Bank of Ethiopia could issue bonds and other bills, against its reserves, to raise funds to cover the government's short-term needs. Thus, the introduction of a national currency permitted the mobilization of relatively large sums to finance modernization programs and to pay for the rearming and retraining of the Ethiopian army.

On 1 December 1932, Addis Abeba informed the tripartite powers that it intended to spend ten million francs on arms and ammunition during the coming year.[61] It purchased some Oerlikon antiaircraft guns,[62] an obvious response to the Italian air force, then considered the best in Europe, and several hundred machine guns, ten thousand modern Mausers, one hundred fifty tons of ammunition, and a few thousand obsolete French rifles. The Italian military attaché, Lt. Col. Vittorio Ruggero, an arrogant racist and ardent Fascist, invariably exaggerated the importance of any military development, refusing to understand Ethiopia's need for internal security. His reports to Rome puffed up the strategic value of military imports by warning that Ethiopia's rearmament threatened Eritrea. He was particularly upset by the modern military training under way in Addis Abeba and in other towns.[63]

By February 1933, thanks to the four-man Belgian team that had arrived before the coronation, Haile Sellassie's Imperial Bodyguard consisted of a trained force of 2,100 infantry and 150 cavalry, whose high morale and discipline permitted deployment at the company level to such hostile places as Gojam, where they buttressed Ras Imru's authority.[64] A gratified monarch renewed the Belgians' contracts until 1935 and sent Major André Polet, the senior man, home to recruit four police, one cavalry, and three army officers, who arrived in Addis Abeba in April 1933.[65] The four gendarmes remained in the capital to begin the reorganization of the Ethiopian police, as did the horse soldier, but in early May, the three infantrymen left for Bale. They were accompanied by two St. Cyr–trained Ethiopian officers and fourteen noncoms from the bodyguard, all of whom were expected to establish a military headquarters and training center at Goba, the new capital and seat of Dej. Nasibu, the progressive governor who was to transform Bale into a model province.[66] The placement of a small modern force in Goba was to ensure internal security, as Bale was huge, its people troublesome, and its frontiers porous.

Ruggero, of course, believed that a military headquarters in Goba, at least 230 miles from the nearest Italian outpost, threatened adjacent Somalia. He imagined Ethiopian devils everywhere; in October 1933, he reported that the bodyguard in Addis Abeba was battle ready in terms of weapons, uniforms, discipline, and organization.[67] Although he exaggerated their preparedness, the guards did make an excellent impression on ceremonial parade and were competent at close-order drill. Their fighting skills were less honed because they had not received enough combat training, and there were too few instructors and competent Ethiopian officers and noncommissioned soldiers.[68] The emperor responded by sending more young men to military academies in Switzerland and France and by hiring seven more Belgian officers, five of whom went to Harer in September 1934 to open a regional training center for a three-thousand-man frontier force, while one each went to Yirga Alem (Sidamo) and Dese (Welo) to help train battalion-sized forces for local use.[69]

The developments — which Ruggero fully reported — gave the impression that Haile Sellassie was preoccupied with military power, even though there were few significant arms deliveries through the end of 1934. In September, for the Feast of the Holy Cross, only three thousand modern infantry paraded past the imperial reviewing stand. Each battalion deployed six Hotchkiss guns and twenty pack mules, and each soldier brandished a modern rifle, hardly the equipment that an aggressive army would muster.[70] Certainly the most important military event of 1934, the establishment of a military academy, was designed only to meet domestic needs. The idea came from Gen. Eric Virgin, a Swedish adviser, who told Haile Sellassie that only a national military academy would train officers sensitive to Ethiopia's conditions and security needs. He recommended a sixteen-month program, four months for basic training and a year for advanced instruction in one of the following specialties: infantry, artillery, communications, or engineering. Five Swedish officers, led by Capt. Viking Tamm, arrived in the Ethiopian capital shortly before Christmas 1934 to take up their duties of producing officers for the fledgling Ethiopian army.[71]

Meanwhile, an embryonic system of secular education and a concept of national indoctrination had developed. Between 1932 and 1935, the government opened Amharic-language schools in Ambo, Jima, Gonder, Debre Markos, Adwa, and Mekele, joining those established earlier in Addis Abeba, Gore, Jijiga, Nekemte, and Dire Dawa. There was a parallel system of mission schools, many of which, however, were placed in the countryside, especially in the more remote parts of the empire. By the time of the Italian invasion in October 1935, twenty government schools enrolled perhaps five thousand children, and another two thousand went to denominational schools.[72] Missionaries were expected not only to teach academic subjects but also to indoctrinate the empire's peoples with Addis Abeba's view of national unity; otherwise they were deported.

In December 1933, an article appeared in *Berhanena Selam* criticizing the foreign missions for teaching in local languages, "since it creates obstacles to unity." The newspaper asserted that government policy aimed "to have all the people in the country speak Amharic. With language unity there is also a unity of ideas." Sharing a common idiom would lead Ethiopia's peoples to greater mutual understanding and to intermarriage — "thus the border peoples and the central inhabitants [will] become related" and will treat each other as kin. "With such a foundation of mutual sympathy our country will remain united without orders from anyone. This is better than the best."[73] That the domination of Amharic might frustrate and alienate various ethnic groups was ignored by many nationalists, especially by the Young Ethiopians, who stared fixedly at a vision of a modern nation gleaned from Western textbooks.

The several hundred young men involved in this group — among them many Eritreans — also constituted Addis Abeba's intelligentsia. As the emperor's chosen instrument of change, its members were devoted to him and to his ideas about progress and politics.[74] Haile Sellassie used them as a counterweight to the traditional men he so often named as ministers of government. The latter charged that their educated underlings were un-Ethiopian, their nationalism and patriotism flawed by exposure to modernity. In fact, the young men were intensely proud of being Ethiopians and were outspokenly anti-foreign, if not truly xenophobic. They criticized what they considered the excessive profiteering by resident European shopkeepers and foreign concerns, and they were positively acid about the extraordinary salaries paid to expatriates generally.[75] They tended to view the emperor's major European advisers, no matter how skilled or devoted, as impediments to their careers.[76]

In early 1932, the government had about one hundred westerners on the payroll, mostly Russian émigré engineers and technicians, who worked in the municipality and in the Ministry of Public Works for less than US$100 monthly. The Ministry of War employed twenty Belgian and Swiss officers; the imperial Aviation Corps was served by eight Frenchmen; and the Ministry of Education had hired seventeen foreign teachers, mostly poorly compensated Egyptian Copts. Only five Europeans held the title of adviser: Eric Virgin, Swedish, Ministry of Foreign Affairs; Frank de Halpert, British, Ministry of the Interior; Jacques Auberson, Swiss, Ministry of Justice; E. A. Colson, American, Ministry of Finance; and F. E. Work, American, Ministry of Education.[77] The last man was an Afro-American and evidenced Haile Sellassie's conviction that his administration would benefit from the immigration of educated blacks, whose careers in Ethiopia would not be warped by "that superior feeling of arrogance ill concealed by white men or women."[78] Unfortunately, however, this attitude was not matched by an exchequer adequate to implement Professor Work's program of reform, and he remained a frustrated man throughout his stay in Ethiopia.

Equally frustrated was Frank de Halpert, who took up his job at Interior in August 1930. During his tenure through January 1934, he confronted a political economy so "highly profitable to the ruling and official classes" that the emperor easily accepted only those reforms that promised greater revenues but resisted "essential recommendations" that might lose him supporters.[79] The Englishman's ignorance of the sociopolitical situation merely deepened his sense of helplessness. He brightened up a bit when the government agreed in mid-1932, after a delay of only ten months, to establish a Slavery

Division in the Ministry of the Interior, to begin registering slaves, and to organize a special police unit to control the slave trade. He subsequently despaired when progress slowed, failing to appreciate how long change took in a traditional society guided by an under-staffed central administration.[80]

Yet Addis Abeba could move quickly when the emperor's orders were carried out by an energetic and progressive governor. In late 1932, de Halpert was asked to plan the reorganization of Bale's taxa-tion, police, judiciary, and finances, including the abolition of corvée labor. The adviser was delighted when Dej. Nasibu almost immedi-ately began implementing his recommendations. The governor, one of the most visible of the Young Ethiopians, had agreed to administer his province in a "European" fashion, sending all tax receipts to the central treasury, in return for which he and his staff would receive monthly fixed salaries ranging from E$300 for the governor to E$10 for a private soldier. Nasibu abolished the status of gabbar, to the immense dissatisfaction of the older officers; imposed an agriculture tax determined by income and paid in money; established a local administration drawn from indigenous leadership; and set up a mechanism for consulting the people. He built schools and clinics, constructed and maintained roads, and organized markets. Finally, with his few thousand trained soldiers, the governor was able to control the province's numerous brigands and to guarantee internal security. Even the Italian agent at Megalo commented approvingly on Nasibu's accomplishments and his plans for the future.[81] From Addis Abeba, de Halpert could not see the seedlings of achievement in the thicket of his frustrations, and he offered his resignation in late December 1933.[82]

Other advisers were more content with their impact on govern-ment: Virgin at Foreign Affairs, Colson at Finance, and Auberson at Justice worked well together, respected one another, and became, in 1934–1935, the emperor's "brain trust." Virgin recorded that Auber-son had "great forensic ability . . . great facility of style, and was invaluable in finding just the right turn of phrase in French." Colson, he believed, enjoyed "a truly American capacity for work, combined with great intelligence, conscientiousness, and a remarkable head for detail."[83] Outsiders saw Colson as the leading triumvir: "In strength of purpose and steadfastness of aim, he stood head and

shoulders above Virgin . . . and Auberson." The Yankee was always frank with Ethiopians and "was combatively anti-Imperial-
ist," as well as "brutally cool and steady." Colson did not deny his
leading role but declared that the trio discussed and decided all
matters collectively.[84]

When a consensus had been reached and a memo formulated, the
advisers would meet with the emperor, Blattangeta Herui and Tesfaye Tegegne of the Foreign Ministry, and Wolde Giorgis of the Ministry of Pen, who was also Haile Sellassie's private secretary. Because
the sessions were formal, the memo was read aloud in French and
then interpreted into Amharic by Wolde Giorgis. The emperor, of
course, understood the French as it was spoken, but the translation
allowed him time to organize his thoughts, probably explaining Virgin's accolade: "It was very impressive to note how rapidly the Emperor grasped a situation or a piece of reasoning, and how wise,
clear, and keen his observations were." The sessions were usually
long and hard and could be held at any time of day or night, very often
in Haile Sellassie's favorite palace room, "a turret-like pavilion
which commanded a fine view of the city below and surrounding
hills."[85]

In another capital, Asmera, Ras Gugsa Araya, governor of eastern
Tigray, lay dying from cirrhosis. He died on 26 April 1933,[86] and his
son, Dej. Haile Sellassie Gugsa, reasonably expected that he would
succeed his father, especially as he was the emperor's son-in-law. In
June 1932, he had married the fifteen-year-old princess Zanab Work
in a ceremony filled with pomp and happiness. Sadly, however, she
died from influenza on 25 March 1933, only a few months after she
and her husband had arrived in Mekele. The early and sudden death
of his favorite daughter devastated Haile Sellassie, even if he characteristically grasped the opportunity to reduce the period of deep
mourning, to moderate the various practices involved in public lam-
entation, and to simplify mourning attire.[87] The emperor was similarly opportunistic when he used Ras Gugsa's death to continue his
relentless program of centralization of authority.

Both Ras Seyoum, governor of western Tigray, and Dej. Haile
Sellassie came to the capital for consultations, and after considerable talk, the emperor agreed in May 1934 to make Seyoum, Yohannes IV's only surviving grandson, governor of Tigray, in return
for Addis Abeba's administrative control over the province's fi-

nances.[88] To become governor of eastern Tigray, Dej. Haile Sellassie had to acknowledge his uncle as overlord, a subordination that infuriated him.[89] He told the Italian minister in Addis Abeba, Count Luigi Vinci-Gigliucci, that he was on a collision course with the crown and condemned the Shewan-dominated central government for having "a limited view of how to treat affairs concerning the whole nation, while there were not lacking in all the peripheral provinces of the empire intelligent, educated people capable of providing the best results in the administration of the country." Vinci cabled Mussolini the substance of the conversation,[90] and one wonders whether he put the word *peripheral* in Haile Sellassie Gugsa's mouth. If not, then the Tigrayan must have been aware of Italian policy and must have understood that his treachery would help to convince Mussolini that the peripheral policy was finally working to weaken the central government, thereby encouraging Rome's decision to attack.[91]

En route to Tigray, Haile Sellassie Gugsa arrived in Asmera on 27 May 1934 and the next night held secret talks with the governor of Eritrea. The Ethiopian declared, "I intend from today to place myself in the service of Italy and faithfully to follow whatever orders are sent to me." He rationalized that his late father had been moving toward an accommodation with the Italians because Tigray could hope for nothing from the imperial regime, whose leader "only sought to procure riches for himself and his friends." The emperor's recent actions toward Tigray would finally divide the province, leading to the appointment of a Shewan as governor, a dire possibility Haile Sellassie Gugsa wanted to spare his fatherland. Patriotism demanded, therefore, that he unite with the Italians: "I am ready to obey whatever Italy orders; ready to join with Italian troops."

Astuto cautiously responded that Italy had only amicable intentions toward Ethiopia and had worked hard to foster commercial and economic links between the two countries. Yet he could not deny that Rome's efforts had been undermined by diffident, even hostile, Ethiopian officials. The Tigrayan interjected that "Italy's policy of friendship will never be appreciated by the Addis Abeba Government," and that relations would grow worse, "the work of the [Shewan] elements who surround the person of Haile Sellassie." In the dejazmach's opinion, "it was time for Italy to decide to liberate the Abyssinian people from the tyranny of Haile Sellassie," and, as "a

chief of the dynasty of King John . . . [and] a loyal friend of Italy,"
he would help.

The next night, Haile Sellassie Gugsa was even more assertive,
arguing that Italy should begin operations in Tigray immediately,
before Ras Seyoum returned from Addis Abeba. When the Italians
crossed the frontier, the dejazmach would move into western Tigray
and defend it against any counterattack by Seyoum, whom he swore
to kill. He imagined that an Italian attack would stimulate an immediate revolt in Ethiopia and lead to either the emperor's death or
exile in Europe to enjoy the riches he had banked there. "He is hated
and cursed by all: remaining faithful would be the very few people
with whom he shares the money extorted from the poor 'gebbar.' "
Haile Sellassie Gugsa was so "visibly aroused and agitated" that Astuto calmed him by offering his personal friendship and promising to
refer the matter to Rome. He repeated that Italy had only friendly
intentions toward Ethiopia but agreed that the emperor's policies
could lead to disaster. It was therefore the dejazmach's right, as
Yohannes's descendant, to think about saving Tigray from any catas-
trophe that might befall Ethiopia. When the governor insinuated that
salvation might be obtained through friendship with Italy, Haile Sellassie Gugsa "repeated that he considered himself in [Italian] hands
and that he awaited . . . our orders." Astuto believed that the dejazmach was sincere, full of good will toward Italy, and fully aware of
the implications of his offer. He recommended to Rome that Haile
Sellassie Gugsa be considered a potential ally should a "legitimate
war" with Ethiopia ensue.[92] Shortly thereafter, as the Welwel crisis
drew nigh, the Italian agent in Mekele was directed to tell the dejazmach that if fighting broke out, Italy would not forget his offer of
assistance, would regard him as an ally, and would help him in every
possible way.[93]

The year 1934 was Rome's fateful year of decision about Ethiopia,
and Astuto's use of the term *legitimate war* foreshadowed a crisis that
would lead inevitably to conflict and colonization. It is difficult to
provide detailed evidence about precisely when the choice for war
was made because continuing official Italian sensitivity about the
whole range of Fascist activities in Ethiopia has led to the withdrawal
of important papers from the archives. There are some glimmers of
light, however, from the work of other researchers and from memoirs. For example, General De Bono revealed that in the autumn of

1933, Mussolini promised him command of an operation against Ethiopia: "*Only he and I knew what was going to happen,* and no indiscretion occurred by which the news could reach the public."[94]

On 8 February 1934, Mussolini met with De Bono, General Pietro Badoglio of the War Ministry, and Fulvio Suvich, undersecretary of the Ministry of Foreign Affairs, to discuss possible war preparations; although various plans were discussed, no irreversible decisions were made.[95] Yet the various contingency plans led to a perceptible buildup in Eritrea, which the Ethiopian consul in Asmera, Lij Tedla Haile, reported to Addis Abeba in April 1934. His letters and telegrams were full of Italian war preparations and suggested countermeasures for Tigray.[96] The Fascist press also highlighted the extent of Eritrea's military expansion and belligerently asserted that Ethiopia was Rome's place in the sun. Both Tedla and the Italian media exaggerated the danger: in May 1934 the entire Eritrean military establishment consisted of 125 officers, 136 noncoms, 90 Italian soldiers, 4,300 askaris, a few irregulars, 800 pack animals, 70 motorized vehicles, and an out-sized 100-plane air force, perhaps a harbinger of the future but more likely the result of bad planning.[97] In Addis Abeba, the intelligentsia did not know the truth and imagined an Italian invasion from Eritrea,[98] more or less ignoring the imminent threat along the border with Somalia.

The Italians claimed a frontier in "direct contradiction to the Ethiopian program of consolidating the imperial domain in the Ogaden, which constitutes a dangerous and permanent source of incidents." Count Vinci believed that if Rome really wanted good relations with Ethiopia, the frontier had to be demarcated properly, or at the very least Mogadishu ought to be ordered not to take obvious and provocative actions.[99] Suvich, who was, of course, privy to Mussolini's plans, agreed with Vinci's observations, although he referred to "Ethiopia's . . . irredentist program."[100] His use of the word *irredentism* is interesting, because he thereby acknowledged that the Addis Abeba government made no claims on Italian holdings but sought to restore its own property.

A collision was therefore inevitable in the Ogaden, where the Ethiopian government continued to expand its administration. Jijiga, the region's administrative center, was also an important military and communications hub serving the twenty-two hundred soldiers stationed at seven widely separated garrisons. Their presence gave form and substance to Ethiopian sovereignty in the Ogaden[101] and helped Dej. Gebre Mariam to establish a Somali authority willing to mediate between the Imperial Government and the traditional clan leaders, to impose a new tax structure, and to help stop Italian infiltration into the region.[102] By 1933, the new Somali administration and the garrisons appeared "to have had an effect on the Italians, as road making by them over the border has ceased, and European resident officers have withdrawn from . . . Walwal [Welwel]."[103] Haile Sellassie wanted to push the Italians back across the frontier, or, as he put it, to provide "a stable remedy to the actual state of things" by proceeding to a delimitation.[104] Dej. Gebre Mariam was more outspoken, vowing to retake illegally occupied territory "one way or the other."[105]

In early 1934, Addis Abeba sent more men and modern war materiel to the Ogaden, some of which was given to a band of Somali led by Omar Samatar, a freedom fighter whom the Italians considered a "traitor and vulgar assassin."[106] As he and his men, accompanied by regular troops, moved slowly toward Italian positions, the governor of Somalia reminded Rome that the weakness of his illegal redoubts in the Ogaden would necessitate an air defense against the more numerous and better-equipped Ethiopians.[107] When Vinci orally protested Omar Samatar's activities and advised that Mogadishu would protect itself accordingly, Blattangeta Herui blandly asked the count to define the area under reference to establish its nationality. When the Italian "eluded the question, avoiding naming Warder and Walwal," Herui observed that the Ethiopians had never considered conducting operations in Somalia.[108]

By July 1934, Somalia's forces had been strengthened, particularly in armored cars and airplanes, to protect Warder and Welwel "against any sudden attack"[109] and "to safeguard our prestige and our indisputable rights."[110] Haile Sellassie appreciated that Rome was prepared to repel any Ethiopian reentry into its own national territory and was concerned about the Italian buildup in the Horn. He therefore sought to defuse the tensions by disclaiming any intention of using force to remove the alien posts.[111] In order to build a diplomatic case, he decided to use the imminent Anglo-Ethiopian border demarcation to reveal the extent of Italian infiltration into sovereign Solomonic territory.

Writing from Addis Abeba, Sir Sidney Barton pointed out that an Italo-Ethiopian Agreement of 1897 placed the border at 180 statute miles from the coast, but that article 4 of the treaty of 16 May 1908 stipulated that "all the territory belonging to the tribes towards the coast shall remain dependent on Italy." Only by stretching this principle could Warder and Welwel be considered Italian territory. Because Britain might want to exchange Zeila for Ogaden territory, Sir Sidney advised that the two wells be visited by the boundary commission to obtain "accurate information as to the nature of the Italian penetration at these points." [112] In London, lower-level Foreign Office officials were tilting toward Ethiopia: "It would seem logical that we should support the Emperor in the question as against the Italians. . . . Our own view appears to be that the Italians have no conceivable right to be in Walwal or Wardair." [113] They relished the possibility of tweaking the Italian nose, and they anticipated the report of the Anglo-Ethiopian commission as "an eye-opener to the Emperor," which might bring matters in the Ogaden "to a boil." [114]

Ranking officers were not so pleased with the possibility of Britain being caught in the middle of such a dispute. They believed that Barton should proceed very cautiously to avoid giving Haile Sellassie "the idea that we are so anxious for the all-around settlement that we will support him in all circumstances against the Italians and the French." London's interests in the Ogaden were limited to securing water and grazing rights for British-protected Somalis, and the acquisition of these rights "would not justify a major dispute with Italy." [115] These views were logical and strong, and Barton was instructed to make clear that Ethiopia could not rely on Britain in all circumstances. [116] From Rome, Sir Eric Drummond sought greater clarity because he thought that the Welwel and Warder questions were hardly significant enough to disrupt friendly relations between London and Rome, especially "at this particular moment, when Italy's political orientation is of the highest importance." [117] The foreign secretary, Sir John Simon, agreed: "I think you may be glad to learn that I am fully in agreement with your view that no Ethiopian or colonial question should be allowed to react adversely upon the general relations between . . . the United Kingdom and the Government of Italy." [118]

A month later, the British and Ethiopian sections of the border commission joined up twenty-one miles west northwest of Welwel at Ado, where there was a garrison of four hundred Somali Ishaak levies. The Ethiopian team was led by Fit. Tessema Banta; advised by the Eritrean-born Lorenzo Taezaz, a prominent Young Ethiopian who was also to act as interpreter in case of need; and protected by Fit. Shifferaw, the governor of Jijiga, and four hundred soldiers. The escort and most of the levies set off immediately for Welwel, reached there on 22 November, and encamped thirty to fifty yards from the Italian perimeter. On 23 November, the Anglo-Ethiopian commissioners arrived and established themselves on the northern edge of the wells, well back from the military bivouac. The next morning, at 11:00 A.M., Capt. Roberto Cimmaruta arrived to complain to Col. E. H. M. Clifford, the senior European officer, that the commission's arrival was a complete surprise and to advise that it could not proceed until he had orders from Mogadishu. When Fit. Shifferaw remarked that his men had insufficient water, Cimmaruta rudely refused to permit access to larger wells. Clifford and his officers tried to mediate but quickly realized that the Italian was a racist who refused "to . . . deal with black men."

At 4:00 P.M., two Italian planes appeared and buzzed the Ethiopian and British camps; "one of the observers was aiming a light automatic weapon at the members of the commission and at personnel in two camps, in each of which a national flag was flying." Clifford was outraged and expressed "to . . . Cimmaruta . . . disgust at such a provocative action, which, to say the least, was ill-mannered." When Fit. Shifferaw also complained, the captain considered that his honor as an Italian officer had been blackened "and retired in a towering rage." The Englishman thereupon decided to withdraw to Ado, and by the time the British team left the next morning, accompanied by their Ethiopian counterparts, the opposing forces had dug themselves into position, "the rifle pits in some cases being about waist-deep." The entire Ethiopian escort had remained behind, and Clifford concluded that "use has been made of the Commission in order to establish a footing at Walwal." [119]

On 27 November 1934, Governor Rava telegraphed a detailed chronological account of the Welwel events that differed little from Clifford's account. [120] By 3 December, however, he reported what had become a crisis: the Ethiopians were two meters from Italian lines, screaming insults at the dubat, warning that the defeat at Welwel would be as devastating as that at Adwa in 1896, only this time the Europeans would be pushed into the sea. The Ishaak levies continuously called on their dubat counterparts to desert, claiming that soon Somalia would be incorporated into Haile Sellassie's empire. When three men came over, the Ethiopian camp celebrated with an ostentatious war fantasia.[121] Rava advised Rome that he instructed his men not to respond to incitement but only to aggression.[122] At Welwel, however, the Italian officers must have feared for the morale of their troops, surrounded as they were by jeering, arrogant Ethiopian soldiers. The hotheaded Cimmaruta could not stand the insulting references to Adwa, and he engineered an incident.

At noon on 5 December, he sent a letter to Fit. Shifferaw, protesting a violation of the Italian lines allegedly being planned. At 3:00 P.M., according to British reports, a whistle was heard on the Italian line, the dubat began firing, and the Ethiopians responded. Ten minutes after the battle began, the dubat withdrew slightly toward the Italian zareba, and a flight of three planes bombed and strafed the Ethiopian lines. Immediately after the aircraft flew off to refuel and rearm, two armored cars, each mounting three machine guns, arrived and attacked the Ethiopian headquarters and line from the rear. Thereafter, the planes made several sorties, and the armored vehicles continued their devastating runs. By dusk, Ethiopian morale had cracked, and Shifferaw ordered a retreat under cover of darkness. His left flank, cut off by the dubat and the armor, continued resisting until the evening of 6 December and suffered heavy casualties. By noon on 7 December, all surviving Ethiopian troops had reached Ado, which they left the next day with the boundary commission.

Shifferaw's forces had suffered 107 dead and 45 wounded, whereas the Italian chargé in Addis Abeba reported the loss of 30 dubat. Lt. J. H. Collingwood, in command of the Somaliland Camel Corps unit escorting the British commissioners, wrote that "it would appear from information received that the Italians had every intention of a fight and were awaiting the arrival of their armoured cars and aeroplanes, whereas the Ethiopians appeared to be awaiting some form of arbitration between their respective Governments."[123] He could not have known it then, but he had written a commentary on the entire Italo-Ethiopian war of 1935–1936.

CHAPTER EIGHT

The War,
1935-1936

Raffaele Guariglia recalled that in late September 1934 he learned that Mussolini had decided "resolutely to deal with the Ethiopian question."[1] The Welwel hostilities provided a situation to exploit, although it remains unclear if at the outset the Italians intended to transform the incident into a war. Haile Sellassie thought the crisis could be settled peaceably, but when Blattangeta Herui invoked the arbitration provisions of the 1928 treaty,[2] the Italians refused to negotiate, claiming an aggression that rendered article 5 moot. Rome insisted that Ethiopia, as the culprit, should formally apologize at Welwel, rendering honors there to the Italian flag; pay an indemnity of MT\$200,000; and arrest and dismiss the officers responsible for the outrage.[3] Because Welwel was within Ethiopia, the emperor found the response so unreasonable that he decided to take the matter to the League of Nations,[4] which, Rome alleged, "marked a new stage in the controversy, if indeed it did not create a new situation." Italy continued to consider itself the aggrieved party, and any "argument that . . . [its] right to Walwal is in any case dubious is not admitted to be relevant." Italian stubbornness was fueled by Fascist notions of African social inferiority and by Mussolini's "profound hatred and contempt for the Abyssinians," whom he could not bring himself to treat "on an equal footing."[5]

Racism connived with rationalization to lead Mussolini to war. On 30 December 1934, he circulated to his closest advisers the "Directive and Plan of Action for the Resolution of the Italian-Abyssinian Question." The document claimed that only force would obtain Italy's goals in the Horn of Africa; that Ethiopia's armed forces had to be destroyed and the entire country conquered; that Haile Sellassie's program of modernization necessitated resolving "the problem as soon as possible"; that Italy would have to act before mid-1937, when Germany would be strong enough to take an initiative in Europe; and that consequently Ethiopia must be destroyed soon, to remove a threat to Italy's colonies during a general war. Mussolini recommended an immediate agreement with France over Ethiopia, to ensure European stability while Italy was preoccupied in Africa.[6]

In mid-1932, France had abandoned Ethiopia in principle and by 1934 was being driven to act by the implicit threat from Hitler's Germany, a fact that dominated European foreign policy. The Solomonic state was a coin the Quai d'Orsay was willing to exchange for Italy's adherence to an anti-German entente and, of course, for Rome's abdication of its rights in Tunisia.[7] In June 1933, Paris signaled the bargain by sending Henri de Jouvenal to Rome to open *pourparlers* about European security. Without the preliminary discussions, Laval and Mussolini would not have been able to undertake the negotiations of January 1935.[8] French disengagement from its hitherto consistent defense of Ethiopia's sovereign independence was, in fact, the "free hand" sought by the Italians.[9]

Pierre Laval was thus acting according to the script and was not, at least in this case, the malicious opportunist so reviled by his political enemies.[10] During a private conversation with Mussolini from midnight to 1:00 A.M. on 7 January 1935, Laval generally agreed to French economic disinterest in Ethiopia but not to an Italian military adventure.[11] In the sparse archival evidence found in the Quai d'Orsay, one repeatedly reads the phrase *economic disinterest*, seemingly confirming that Laval understood the arrangement as conceding economic primacy.[12] Alfred Mallet, Laval's biographer and longtime secretary, emphasized the premier's often repeated explanation that he abandoned Ethiopia to Rome's lire, not its legions.[13] Laval himself claimed that although he "urged Mussolini not to resort to force . . . he committed the blunder of going to war. He started war against my will and my solemn protest."[14]

The premier's disclaimers were ingenious and have proved mendacious. His efforts to check the Italians amounted to very little. Indeed, during the first half of 1935, he was so supportive of his Fascist allies that in July Mussolini thanked his counterpart for France's demonstrated "loyalty and friendship." The Frenchman was so moved that he instructed his ambassador in Rome to confirm his "determination to develop, in a general sense and in every way possible, the policy and collaboration that this declaration [of 7 January] has assigned as the goal of our common efforts."[15] Laval referred to what proved to be an ephemeral military alliance to counter any German invasion of Austria. "This treaty," he wrote, "was of paramount importance; as long as Italy was France's ally we had a bridge leading to all those countries of western and eastern Europe which were then our allies."[16]

As of January 1935, therefore, there was little any power, singly or in combination, could do to stop Italian war preparations. To be fair, leading members of the League believed that Rome could achieve its goals peaceably, and none foresaw Haile Sellassie's stubborn refusal to abandon his government's independence. With a consistency bordering on religious faith, the emperor clung to his belief that the League would muster collective security sufficient to defend Ethiopia against Italy. Haile Sellassie was as stubborn in upholding Ethiopia's honor as Mussolini was in asserting a question of honor where there was none. The British, who understood honor—even if they did not uphold it during the crisis—quietly agreed that since Welwel, Mussolini had been insolent and churlish, whereas Haile Sellassie had been "reasonable" and "statesmanlike."[17]

That respect could not overcome either European ignorance about Ethiopia or a racism that considered blacks incompetent and irresponsible. The general prejudice made Italian propaganda more convincing: when a cease-fire in the Ogaden broke down in January and February, the Italians loudly complained to London about Ethiopian perfidy and double-dealing. Without ever considering that the

Italians might have started the new fighting, virtually the entire Foreign Office sympathized with Rome. Indeed, in conversation with a member of the Italian Embassy, one officer volunteered that "it was quite impossible to deal with Abyssinia as though it was an advanced state with an established bureaucracy, proper systems of communications and so forth." The Englishman then launched into nonsensical speculation about "whether the Emperor's writ extended to chieftains now active in the Wal Wal area"; if not, then the monarch might diplomatically divest Addis Abeba of blame or responsibility "for skirmishes of the kind under discussion." [18]

From Addis Abeba, Sir Sidney Barton disclosed that the Italians had begun the fighting in order to force the evacuation of Ethiopia's posts in the Ogaden. He reminded London that the Ogaden was part of Haile Sellassie's patrimony, where only trusted officials governed: "Every move in this affair . . . has been made by direct orders from here [Addis Abeba] and the Emperor is now in direct wireless touch with the Webbe Shebelli." Barton advised that Ethiopian forces would remain in the Ogaden, particularly as Haile Sellassie feared that the Italians might exploit any withdrawal "to marshal the resources necessary to enable them to make that eventual forward movement which the press declares to be inevitable." [19]

Even had the emperor wished to evacuate forward positions, he was governed by public opinion and his compatriots' anti-Italian feeling.[20] Patriotic couplets and poems, popular art forms, already circulated widely in Addis Abeba, especially among the jingoistic Young Ethiopians.[21] One long and particularly unsubtle piece likened the European adversary to pasta and white bread.

Eat the macaroni . . .
It is not hard for the stomach but agreeable,
It is not strong for the teeth, but is a stuff which
dissolves in the mouth.
The moment it is available, eat it at once. . . .
How can we fail to devour a dish of macaroni
We must not miss the good luck of eating from the white bread.
The way we eat white bread is to break it in pieces.[22]

The Italians used such signs of hostility and European gullibility to explain calling up troops and otherwise preparing for war. Thus, Sir Eric Drummond could report from Rome in mid-February 1935: "It seems probable that while Italians have at present no aggressive intentions they are genuinely afraid of [an] overwhelming Abyssinian attack. Whatever happens, they will not be caught napping. [The] situation is therefore serious but hardly critical." [23] While Drummond was recording war preparations, Haile Sellassie was truthfully testifying to a French reporter that he had not mobilized a single soldier and that Ethiopia wanted peace, but that "his country and people would resist dishonor." [24] From Vatican City, the future Pope Pius XII told a French diplomat that "the Italians have informed us that they might march. They told us this before M. Laval's visit and repeated it afterward." [25] In Rome, the Ethiopian minister, Ato Afework, declared that recent military preparations provided convincing evidence that Mussolini would take the crisis to war. [26]

In Ethiopia, the emperor resisted the mounting evidence. He had neither sufficient weapons nor army to contain a modern force. His sole military interest had been to create an up-to-date army to ensure internal security, in other words, to retain himself in power. True, he could call up a traditional Ethiopian levy of half a million men, but such a mobilization was, the emperor knew, an act of defeat. [27] He therefore put on a brave face and prayed that France or the League would save him, although by the end of March 1935, he learned from Albert Bodard, Paris's new and unreliable minister, that France would continue to refuse to transship war materials from Djibouti, contrary to all relevant treaties. [28] The French apparently decided to believe Italian propaganda about the fabled Ethiopian war machine.

After reading through the copious documentation on the subject available in the Italian Foreign Ministry archives, one might conclude that during 1935–1936 Ethiopia purchased millions of the most modern rifles, tens of thousands of machine guns, squadrons of planes, thousands of bombs, and tanks and armored vehicles galore. [29] The truth was otherwise: because Ethiopia could not afford to buy the weapons needed for defense, only a trickle of armaments entered the country for distribution to an army that needed everything. [30] In May 1935, Barton reported that Ethiopia had only a small quantity of modern weapons, including 3 field batteries; 250 machine guns; 6 mortars; 600 automatic rifles; 50,000 rifles; 80 million rounds of ammunition, mostly of dubious quality; 5 tanks, 4 of which had not moved in four years; and 19 serviceable planes, all civilian models.[31] Meanwhile, reports were circulating that Mussolini had determined on an attack in September or October 1935, after the rainy season.[32] Even had Haile Sellassie been able to procure weapons at will, they would not have been delivered until late in 1936. His only hope was negotiation through the League of Nations.

On 17 March 1935, Bej. Tekle Hawariat officially informed the secretary general that "in consequence of the mobilization ordered by the Royal Italian Government, and of the continual despatch of troops and war matériel to the Italo-Ethiopian frontier, there now exists between Ethiopia and the Royal Italian Government a dispute likely to lead to rupture." The Ethiopian delegate complained that Rome had refused to arbitrate the Welwel dispute according to article 5 of the Italo-Ethiopian treaty of 1928: "It has not consented to enter into any real negotiations; it has proceeded by way of injunctions, demanding reparations before the matter is examined at all." The Ethiopian government was anxious that the Italians not use a "local incident . . . as a pretext for military action." Tekle Hawariat warned: *"The independence of Ethiopia, a Member of the League of Nations, is in peril* [italics mine]." The Addis Abeba government therefore asked implementation of article 10 of the Covenant of the League whereby member states "undertake to respect and preserve against external aggression the territorial integrity and existing political independence of all Members of the League." Ethiopia also asked the Council of the League to undertake a full investigation of its charges against Italy.[33]

Months before, Rome had concluded that "always taking bigger steps will lead to increasing suspicions about us" and that it would be best to "shilly shally, be indifferent; ignore the spite directed at us [and] that which offends our dignity"[34]—in other words, stonewall, prevaricate, dissimulate, and postpone. Therefore, the Italian reply of 22 March 1935 countered that the Ethiopian request was based on "unfounded or incorrect premises." Rome had not mobilized but was merely reinforcing its East African colonies to balance Ethiopian military measures. It was untrue that Italy had ignored the provisions of article 5 of the 1928 treaty, as Rome had requested mutual submission of documents to establish the facts and to expedite negotiations, and it was now willing to proceed to arbitration. In the circumstances, the Italians argued that implementation of article

10 was unnecessary, a ploy immediately agreeable to the council, whose members did not want to alienate Mussolini's government.[35]

In a speech to the council, Tekle Hawariat suspended his government's application but stressed Addis Abeba's fears about the scale of Fascist reinforcements, its anxieties about a country whose newspapers broadcast that the national government aimed "to establish . . . domination over the Ethiopian Empire," and its misgivings that the process of arbitration might occasion "fresh delays in the pacific settlement of a very simple dispute." The Ethiopian therefore imposed a thirty-day limit on the establishment of arbitration procedures, including the nomination of arbitrators, and asked that Rome cease sending men and war materials to the Horn, especially as both sides had agreed in mid-March to a neutral zone separating forces in the Ogaden.[36]

The emperor believed that the Italians would hide behind any convenient blind to prepare for war,[37] and he began the desperate job of building Ethiopia's defenses. In 1959, Haile Sellassie told an astonished French newspaperman that Germany had provided Ethiopia with the most assistance during the crisis.[38] In early 1935, persistent rumors to that effect were regularly denied by Germany,[39] although they were credible in terms of the longstanding Nazi-Fascist antagonism over Austria.[40] Berlin viewed the Welwel crisis as an excellent opportunity to keep Italy involved in East Africa while it worked for the *Anschluss*. The apparent Franco-Italian entente of January 1935 made the strategy more compelling, and Germany immediately offered Ethiopia assistance,[41] which Haile Sellassie accepted in March when it became clear that collective security would not protect his empire.[42]

In July 1935, the Ethiopian national David Hall, whose father was German, visited Berlin and asked for a loan of three million reichsmarks (RM) to purchase weapons. The request made its circuitous way to Hitler, who agreed to break "the neutrality up to then officially maintained" and to make funds available for the purchase of ten thousand Mausers, ten million cartridges, several hundred submachine guns and machine pistols, a few thousand hand grenades, a few planes, thirty antitank guns, and some field dressings.[43] The Nazi regime acted after the German minister in Addis Abeba had assured Count Vinci that it was "false and absurd" for Italy to believe that

Berlin would ever aid Ethiopia. Herr Kirchholte explained that he had been instructed "to observe the most rigid neutrality," and he confided to his colleague that "great powers ought to show the greatest spirit of solidarity in face of people of color." [44]

Hitler breached that unity of race by providing materiel that "permitted a prolongation of fighting, and later [allowed] the supply of guerrillas, to the great prejudice of the occupying power." [45] The German supplies found their way to Ethiopia through every possible access, coming through Djibouti in "piano" crates, more openly through British-controlled ports, and even by air. [46] The arrival of such excellent weaponry and munitions merely pointed to the general inadequacy of Ethiopia's arsenal in face of the modern and well-armed Italian force, before which Haile Sellassie could place "only valiant troops with limited resources." [47]

Meanwhile, in Geneva the jawing prefatory to warring went on. To say that the League was working against Ethiopia's interests would be generous. The controlling powers tried to force humiliating concessions on Ethiopia, so that an appeased Italy might then serve the needs of European politics. [48] Most scholars of the crisis have ignored considerations of territoriality and equity as seen from Addis Abeba, explaining that the Italo-Ethiopian imbroglio was important solely because of its European dimension. Certainly the main European players, with whom scholarship agrees, believed that the future of an unimportant African country — even more remote than Czechoslovakia — was an insignificant consideration in relation to the growing threat of another great war. This position was strongly held by Sir Robert Vansittart, the permanent undersecretary in the Foreign Office, who regarded Nazi Germany as the principal danger to world peace. Sir Robert, according to Anthony Eden, "was determined to keep the rest of Europe in line against Germany and would pay almost any price to do so. He did not discern that to appease Mussolini beyond a certain point in Abyssinia must break up the alignment which Italy was intended to strengthen." [49] The meeting at Stresa in April 1935 conclusively proved this theorem.

The conference was relentlessly concerned with Europe and had dual objectives: to keep the door open for Germany's return to the League and its proper role in the collective security of Europe; and to demonstrate the solidarity of Britain, Italy, and France in continental matters.[50] Stresa was indifferent about the world's many nooks and crannies, although Rome believed it "probable" that the Ethiopian question would be raised. Indeed, the Italians hoped for the démarche, for conversations à trois would undermine the peace moves at Geneva, where Rome and Addis Abeba were treated as equals, and would "underscore the connection which exists or should exist between the Ethiopian question and the whole of the more general European problems." The Fascist government was prepared to inform the British in particular of its firm intent to liquidate "the old Ethiopian problem" in order to secure its colonies from barbaric dangers and to bring civilization to the Solomonic state. Mussolini was ready and rehearsed to tell Sir John Simon about Italy's "irrevocable determination" to conclude the crisis with Ethiopia in its own way.[51]

To the dictator's surprise, nobody formally raised the Ethiopian issue, although it was discussed privately by staff officials. Maurice Peterson, who oversaw the Ethiopian crisis at the Foreign Office, was "bluntly" informed by two Italian colleagues that they "could not exclude the possibility of solving the Abyssinian question by force." Since hitherto the Italians had paid lip service to the principle of peaceful settlement, Peterson dutifully informed Ramsay MacDonald, the head of the British delegation, but the old man's "mental and physical powers were clearly on the wane," and he did not react. According to one participant, "it was a catastrophic error for the British delegation to have ignored the remorseless fact that the Abyssinian question existed," because its omission signaled that Mussolini could move to war with his European rear secured.[52] This message was apparently confirmed on 14 April, when the delegations composed a final statement: "The three Powers, the object of whose policy is the collective maintenance of peace within the framework of the League of Nations, find themselves in complete agreement by opposing, by all practicable means, any unilateral repudiation of treaties which might endanger the peace." At this point, Mussolini asked twice, "Of Europe?" After a long, silent pause, the fatal qualifier became part of Italy's license to attack Ethiopia. To use George Baer's words, "the French and the Italians drew an identical and instantaneous conclusion: the silence was a tacit consent given by the British Government to Italian ambitions in Ethiopia."[53] At the end of the conference, MacDonald asked Mussolini his opinion of the League; borrowing a candle from his experience at Stresa, the sly duce replied, "It might be quite useful if it confined itself to Europe." [54]

Stresa gave the Fascists confidence, and on 3 May 1935 Dino Grandi, the Italian ambassador in London, visited Sir John Simon at the Foreign Office to deliver a message from Mussolini asking the British to take "a friendly and helpful attitude in relation to Italy's activities in Ethiopia." Grandi classified the Solomonic state "as a cancer which had to be cut out," clearly implying that Rome "was contemplating a forward policy of the most serious dimensions." [55] A few days later, the ambassador told his French counterpart that Italy had never forgotten its humiliating defeat at Adwa and that it could no longer abide the Ethiopian threat to its colonies. Mussolini, he asserted, was not bluffing and would follow his rhetoric to war, since any retreat would admit weakness in the face of Nazi Germany. [56]

Meanwhile, Haile Sellassie had delivered an extraordinarily benign speech to parliament, laying out the government's position, explaining arms procurements, and appealing to the patriotism of his compatriots. [57] Citing a threat in the emperor's anodyne words, the Italians promptly increased the flow of men and munitions to the Horn. [58] The British found the additional "precautionary" measures to be "insulting to the intelligence of the world," especially as Ethiopia and Italy were scheduled for a period of conciliation and arbitration. [59] The Foreign Office's outrage became ridicule when, on 9 May, Sig. L. Vitetti, the Italian chargé, tried to activate article 9 of the treaty of 1930, which permitted neighboring states to deny transit of weapons and munitions in cases where the "attitude or disturbed condition of Ethiopia creates a threat to peace or public order." The Italian was told, rather undiplomatically, that too much "mental agility" was required to make Ethiopia responsible for the current threat to "peace and public order" in the Horn. [60]

This truth did not stop Britain, in May 1935, from joining France and other industrial countries in banning arms sales to both potential belligerents. This ban hit Ethiopia disproportionately hard because Italy was "quite capable of producing for herself sufficient arms and munitions for operations in Abyssinia." [61] Paris was, of course, acting in its own national interest: the Quai d'Orsay organized the embargo to win a secret Franco-Italian military convention, signed in June, pledging joint military action in case Germany invaded Austria. France was thereby enabled to move ten divisions from the Italian frontier to the German border, and Rome was able to send more troops to Ethiopia.[62] For France, the refusal to sell weapons to Ethiopia seemed a small price to pay for the new security, and the government sought to temper internal criticism by lifting its ban on transshipping arms to Addis Abeba via the railway.[63] Such cynicism sapped Haile Sellassie's morale, though he remained calm in the face of the growing "hopelessness" of Ethiopia's international position.[64]

As the awful prospect of war became evident, the emperor began planning Ethiopia's defenses. In May 1935, he traveled to Harer, met with the Ogaden's Somali leaders, and raised the specter of racial war to enlist their support. He told his listeners, "I am the emperor of all the blacks and all the blacks are my subjects," particularly those "currently enslaved by the whites in Somalia." All black men, the monarch contended, shared a responsibility to defend the black motherland from whites determined "to destroy your religion and mine, confiscate our goods, and place us under harsh discipline — incompatible with our love of liberty." Stressing the importance of integrating the Somalis into "Ethiopian political life," he mentioned that Ogadeni youth should be educated, "to learn and study not only your own language, but also Amharic because I intend to use them in the future . . . as functionaries in conditions of absolute equality with the Ethiopians." He promised to establish a coequal Somali court system and otherwise create institutions that would permit regional autonomy. When his audience repeatedly brought up past injustices, Haile Sellassie blamed Dej. Gebre Mariam for being old-fashioned and announced his replacement by Dej. Nasibu, a modern man who would build schools, hospitals, and other amenities.[65]

Nasibu was fully aware of the impossibility of defending the Ogaden and Ethiopia against the Fascists. He bitterly denounced the League as worthless, the British as perfidious, and the Italians as treacherous. He feared that Rome would use poison gas, "and how can we hold out against gas?" He knew, as did the emperor, "that war goes to the machine," but fight he would, though his plans were defensive: "They will beat us . . . but we will hold them as long as we can." Directly under his command was Geraz. Afework, the acting governor of Jijiga, an energetic young man "of character and intelligence," who believed in sanitation, roads, education, and order. "He wanted his country to fend for itself, and was ready to resist any foreign intrusion, whether the method was peace or war." With his well-trained troops and fleet of trucks, he tirelessly organized the defenses of the Ogaden.[66]

From May through September, Afework continuously demanded supplies and weapons from the emperor. As soon as Addis Abeba had satisfied one requirement or the other, he would send in new requests for food, cannon, armored cars, fuel, and machine guns. Nasibu's appointment merely provided Afework with another authority figure to badger for materiel. On 31 July, the gerazmach complained to the governor that he still had not received promised weapons and that if war came tomorrow, his men would be quickly defeated. The next day he telegraphed to Haile Sellassie, "Without arms and cartridges, it is not possible to defend ourselves." Throughout August and September, he nagged about food, money, rifles, and reinforcements, and ignored Nasibu's explanations about the priority of the northern front. Finally, on 4 October 1935, the day after the Italians invaded Tigray, the governor telegraphed Afework, "May the God of Ethiopia protect you."[67]

In the interim, Rome continued its buildup in the Horn and its delaying tactics in Geneva.[68] Each time an advance toward peace was made there, it was "closely followed by the mobilization of Italian forces for service in East Africa."[69] Mussolini justified his actions by pointing to the European-style training that he claimed was transforming the Ethiopian army into a modern force. Lamenting Addis Abeba's failure to carry out various provisions of the 1928 treaty, il duce claimed a right for Italy to clarify its relationship with Ethiopia, even "to resort to arms, in short to 'go to war.'" When reminded that an Italo-Ethiopian war might weaken or even destroy the League and Europe's political status quo, Mussolini retorted that "collective security should be confined to Europe; this had been specifically emphasized at Stresa." Besides, he told Drummond, "Abyssinia was . . . a blot on civilization . . . a collection of tribes, some warlike, who preyed on the others. He suggested the existence of cannibalism . . . he expatiated on Adowa (and the ensuing mutilations) and the need to avenge it."[70] The dictator's rancor and ignorance were matched by Italian media: "Little by little all consistency and juridical argument are disappearing from the press and the virtual inevitability of war is sedulously preached." [71]

Conditioned by his environment, Sir Eric could only believe that appeasement would retain Italy's devotion to the common front against Germany and even save the League from disaster. "I submit that the situation is so grave, and the threat to the League so serious, that every effort should be made to see whether, and, if so, to what extent, it is possible to assist Signor Mussolini in the difficulties he now finds himself." Drummond thought that the bedeviled duce might accept an Ethiopian-Italian relationship based on the Anglo-Egyptian model: the emperor would remain on his throne but would be guided by Italian advisers, Rome would garrison the empire at strategic points, and its nationals would dominate the economy. "To put it quite shortly, it seems essential to show the Italian Government that within certain limits we are prepared to help them both at Geneva and Addis Abeba." [72]

By June 1935, Mussolini's attitude was increasingly belligerent; he remarked to troops soon to leave for East Africa, "We have old and new accounts to settle; and we will settle them. We will take no account of whatever may be said beyond our frontiers, since we alone and exclusively . . . are the judges of our interests and guarantors of our future." [73] In response, Addis Abeba warned the League that the "inflammatory harangues and speeches" by ranking Fascists signaled the imminence of "an aggression upon the independence and integrity of Ethiopia." [74] London agreed that war was soon likely and, following Drummond's advice, sought to appease Mussolini with blandishments short of conceding Ethiopia's sovereignty to Italy. The cabinet even contemplated cession of a large portion of the Ogaden it would receive from Ethiopia for Zeila, that is, if negotiations proved successful. To sound out the Fascist government, Anthony Eden was sent to Rome. [75]

On 24 June 1935, Mussolini rejected the scheme because Ethiopia would have gotten Zeila, a coveted outlet to the sea through which to import arms at will. Addis Abeba could claim a victory over Rome, as it would have made no concession to Italy but instead would have transferred a property that London, in turn, had every right to cede to a third party. Mussolini believed that it was time for the British to stop trying to be Ethiopia's "protector and benefactor" and to understand that Italy wanted Menilek's conquered empire. The central Abyssinian plateau might remain under its own sovereignty, "but only on condition that it was under Italian control."[76] A few days later in Paris, Laval faithfully echoed that "the best solution would probably be for Italy to have some sort of protectorate over the whole of Abyssinia." Eden repeated his government's view that such an arrangement could not be reconciled with Ethiopia's membership in the League of Nations.[77] The conversations with il duce and the premier finally forced Whitehall officials to acknowledge that the crisis might destroy the League, "our collaboration with Italy for European purposes," and Ethiopia.[78]

On 18 July 1935, Haile Sellassie voiced his own pessimism about the crisis to parliament. He indicted Rome for having transformed a minor incident into a major crisis and for massing men and materiel on his country's borders prefatory to attack. He blamed the Fascists for having obstructed every effort to arrive at a peaceful settlement and for having mounted a defamatory propaganda attack on Ethiopia, a "name Italy seeks to extinguish." The Solomonic state, the emperor declared, would, of course, defend itself, as it had "even at the time of Adwa." Haile Sellassie exhorted his people to maintain their unity in the face of possible aggression and "to trust in God's divine plan."[79]

He also continued to hope that reason and negotiation would save the country. He wrote, "The Abyssinian has arbitration in his blood; the Abyssinian is the most subtle, the most persistent, the most passionate of litigants. . . . The idea of justice is deeply rooted among a people, the most wretched of whom have the right to go to law against the king." Haile Sellassie's belief that justice would be done was matched by "an unshakeable confidence in the League of Nations," and for a long time he "remained immobilized before those weapons that were being aimed at us."[80] By mid-July, the emperor was beginning to appreciate that collective security must give way to national security and that discussion had to yield to preparation. The Italians had constructed a line of fortifications along the Eritrean border, and it was time to respond to the challenge. He asked Th. Konovaloff, an ex-colonel in the imperial Russian air force, who had worked in the Ministry of Public Works for ten years, to go to Adwa and guide Ras Seyoum toward a workable military strategy.

Haile Sellassie was opposed to any frontal attack, "a veritable folly," but rather favored an offensive that would take Seyoum around the fixed Italian flank and into Eritrea. The emperor believed that the colony's population would thereupon join their Ethiopian brothers and so disrupt the enemy rear that the Italians would have to abandon the war: "If we penetrate their territory . . . it will be their end, I am certain of it." Meanwhile, Seyoum should withdraw before any challenge, permitting the Italians to enter Ethiopia, where they would be handled "precisely" as the Russians had treated the French in 1812.[81] Avoidance of positional warfare was a sound strategy, permitting Seyoum's soldiers to exploit their greater maneuverability by attacking in small units in the enemy rear, on the flanks, and especially along communications and supply lines, causing havoc and chaos, inflicting heavy casualties, and sapping the enemy's will to continue. The longer the war dragged on, the greater the chances that the League might be able to intervene effectively with a chastened and more flexible Italy.[82] Regrettably, however, such sound strategic thinking diverged from Seyoum's parochialism.

The ras had no patience for modern military tactics and proper fortifications. His front-line trenches permitted neither an adequate field of fire nor space enough for fallen wounded, and their design offered no obstacle at all for a determined and disciplined adversary. On a front of 150 to 180 kilometers, without organized communications, Seyoum had haphazardly placed about 20,000 to 25,000 men armed with obsolete rifles—he refused to hand out the new ones sent from Addis Abeba—several hundred machine guns of diverse makes, some small cannon, and tens of antiaircraft guns, the last distributed senselessly according to the political importance of area commanders. Equally ineffective, though not from want of trying, were about 150 trained soldiers sent from Addis Abeba to reform Seyoum's hodgepodge army into a disciplined force. The ras and his lieutenants considered the effort one of "the many caprices of the capital, which now and then decided to disturb the established order of the country."[83]

In Addis Abeba, soldiers and the home guard drilled everywhere, but there was "a very definite absence of panic." The emperor refrained from ordering general mobilization, continued to seek advice far and wide, but fully understood what the future inevitably held.[84] He was very tired, always, but never bitter or emotional in public: "His words were measured, his voice was gentle." He remained adamant about making concessions that would damage the integrity and sovereignty of Ethiopia. If it came to war, "I would be the first soldier in my army."[85] As such, he was privy to the dire thoughts of Ethiopia's military advisers.

When a quarter of a million men, armed with every device that science can contrive for killing, are facing, at a few kilometers distant, and in some cases, only a few yards distant, another army of equal size, but only half as well equipped, isn't it obvious there will be war? And coupled with that, one leader is shouting defiance at the other, promising fantastic rewards to his hypnotized followers, while the other leader is preaching restraint and a spirit of sweet reasonableness to warriors who are straining at the leash . . . isn't it absurd to think that the British Empire or the League of Nations or the entire world can stop this war?[86]

Certainly London's active support was needed to effectuate any decisive collective security. When the cabinet sought military advice, the royal navy reported that shortages of ships and shells in the eastern Mediterranean rendered problematic the defense of Alexandria and the Suez Canal against the locally powerful Italian fleet. Whitehall also had to consider that the success of the privately organized "peace ballot" revealed a public that preferred economic and diplomatic measures, rather than military means, to stop aggressors.[87] Finally, even the normally belligerent Winston Churchill advised the government to

go as far as the French will go, take them along with you, but remember their weakness and don't make impossible requests to Laval. It is doubtful whether the French will go as far as economic sanctions, but that is no reason for not pressing them. The real danger is Germany, and nothing must be done to weaken the anti-German front.[88]

The Churchillian rationale for appeasement was seriously pondered by Samuel Hoare, now the foreign secretary, and in August 1935 he accepted the findings of an interdepartmental committee chaired by Sir John Maffey (governor general of the Sudan from 1926 to 1933; thereafter, permanent undersecretary in the Colonial Office) that no "vital interest in and around Ethiopia . . . would make it essential for His Majesty's Government to resist an Italian conquest of Ethiopia [and] so far as local British interests are concerned, there is no balance of advantage in either direction, i.e., if Ethiopia remains independent or if it is absorbed by Italy." [89]

Meanwhile, the situation had grown yet more menacing; over 100,000 Italian troops were in the Horn of Africa, and another 140,000 were being processed for shipment. [90] In Geneva, the Ethiopian delegation reported the buildup and condemned the arms embargo as an

unequal combat . . . between two members . . . one of which, all powerful, is in a position to employ, and declared that it is employing, all its resources in preparing for aggression, while the other, weak and pacific, and mindful of its international undertakings, is deprived of the means of organising the defence of its territory and of its very existence, both of which are threatened. [91]

In response, Italian media attacked Ethiopia as a menace to Rome's colonies and insisted that Addis Abeba's power "must be destroyed." [92] In a letter to President Franklin D. Roosevelt, Mussolini emphasized "the necessity" of teaching the Ethiopian barbarians a lesson. [93] Finally, on 29 August, he advised an already convinced Whitehall that Italy did not threaten British imperial interests either directly or indirectly. He hoped, therefore, that Italy's activities in the Horn would not cause repercussions in Europe, "unless it is desired to run the risk of provoking a new world war with the object of preventing a great power such as Italy from bringing order into a vast country now given over to the most atrocious slavery and primitive conditions of life." [94]

On 3 September, the Italo-Ethiopian Commission of Conciliation and Arbitration released its report. The Italians were exonerated of blame for being in Welwel, on the grounds that their presence there had not been protested since their occupation in 1928. The Ethiopians were also found blameless, although they were criticized for having too many troops in and near Welwel, giving "the impression that they had aggressive intentions." The commission also concluded that incidents subsequent to Welwel were either accidental or "not serious and of very ordinary occurrence." [95] At Geneva on 4 September 1935, Baron Pompeo Aloisi, the Italian delegate, nonetheless indicted Ethiopia for the entire crisis. Italy, he declared, "had no further confidence in the Abyssinian Government and considered that Abyssinia was entirely incapable of understanding and realising

the principles of international morality." Then he brazenly proclaimed Rome's dictum that Ethiopia "had neither equality of rights
nor equality of duties with civilized states." Italy would therefore be
"deeply wounded in her dignity as a civilized nation if she continued
discussions in the League on a footing of equality with Abyssinia." As
usual, the Ethiopian delegation responded effectively, repeating the
findings of the Welwel commission and drawing attention to Italy's
threats, stressing Ethiopia's consistent efforts to keep the peace, and
warning of the imminence of a "war of extermination" against a
member state.[96]

The League worked to avoid hostilities, but its efforts resulted in
arrangements that tended to appease Italy at Ethiopia's expense.
After the commission report was issued, the Council of the League
established a special Committee of Five, including France and Great
Britain, to work out an arrangement acceptable to Rome and Addis
Abeba. From the beginning of its work, Laval sought to convince the
committee "to accept the assumption that under the cloak of the
League we were in truth preparing for what would in the long run
prove to be an Italian mandate." Anthony Eden was scandalized and
said so privately,[97] but the committee's final report of 19 September
was a jerry-built blind for a League protectorate with Italian economic interests predominating.[98] Notwithstanding immediate Ethiopian opposition "to a disguised form of Italian domination,"[99] Laval
advised Mussolini to accept, as rejection would justify the suspicion,
"already too widespread, of a systematic [Italian] opposition to all
peaceful resolution of the conflict." If il duce would make a concession here, Laval promised "to neglect nothing to sustain Italian pretensions in every way compatible with respect for the Covenant."[100]
He need not have bothered; on 21 September 1935, the Italian cabinet,
after a long harangue by Mussolini, totally rejected the proposals.[101]
The day before, the *Giornale d'Italia* had written: "Italy has not sent
200,000 men to East Africa to secure cession to the League of Nations
of certain powers exercised by the Negus."[102]

On 25 September, Haile Sellassie reported that Ethiopian troops
remained thirty kilometers from the frontiers so that the world
would know the aggressor "in the event of hostilities."[103] A few days
later, Tekle Hawariat told Eden that the emperor had signed the
order for general mobilization,[104] which he kept locked in his desk,

hoping against all reality for a diplomatic resolution to the crisis. The monarch was so embarrassed at the thought of any break with the ideal of collective security — to which he had entrusted his nation's future — that even at this late date he did not want "any public show of mobilisation," any ceremonials, any drums beating. On 2 October, only after the Italians had crossed the frontiers in Awsa, did Haile Sellassie act. That evening, foreign correspondents were invited to be present at the palace the next day at 11:00 A.M. to witness "an important event."

On the morrow, the journalists hurried to the gibbi, joining a stream of excited Ethiopians who also wanted to share the moment. In thinking about Addis Abeba and its inhabitants, George Steer of *The Times* (London), a gifted and sympathetic writer, revealed why Ethiopians would stubbornly fight for their country:

Amazing town — squalor and natural beauty sprawling side by side. For all its irregularity the African lived in Addis Abeba a happier, freer and cleaner life than in any other town of the continent. Accra, Freetown, the 'locations' of Capetown and East London, Djibouti passed through my mind: all these gifts of the white to the black were far more crowded, stank more, more gravely offending the eyes than the gift of Menelik and Haile Sellassie to unconquered Ethiopia.[105]

Throughout the capital sounded Menilek's great war drum, "beating a series of single thuds, slow as a tolling bell." It directed people to the palace gates, up through the emperor's garden, to the imperial residence itself, where on the balcony stood the royal family and high government officials. When the booming stopped, the court chamberlain loudly and clearly read the emperor's mobilization decree to a quiet crowd.[106]

Haile Sellassie compared his peoples' durable independence with the inhabitants of Eritrea and Somalia, where "our brothers . . . [bear] the yoke of serfdom," which Italy now sought to extend to Ethiopia. Without national independence, the emperor warned, there was only "bitter affliction" and "humiliation." He therefore called on his people to rally round their flag "for the sake of your religion and your freedom." [107] To the soldiers present, Haile Sellassie advised: "Be cunning, be savage, face the enemy one by one, two by two, five by five in the fields and mountains." He ordered them not to wear white, or to mass. "Hide, strike suddenly, fight the nomad war, steal, snipe, and murder singly."[108] As the crowd broke up, the news circulated that the Italians had invaded Tigray and the war was on.[109]

About six hours earlier, at 5:00 A.M., one hundred thousand Italian troops had crossed the Mareb River in three formations along a sixty-mile front: "As the sun burst forth, the three columns erupted into Ethiopia with banners waving and trumpets blaring triumphantly."[110] In Rome, Signor Suvich justified the invasion as a way of catching up with the numerically superior Ethiopians, who were now thirty kilometers from the frontiers. This bit of nonsense was followed by a bulletin explaining that the advance was "in the full sense of the word defensive"; that a "peaceful solution" was still possible, if it was "of a nature to satisfy legitimate Italian aspirations"; and that the attack "might render Abyssinia more ready to come to terms, thus facilitating a settlement."[111]

The Italian advance developed quickly because the border region was undefended, and Ethiopian commanders had orders to retire until mobilization would bring reinforcements and countermeasures. By 4 October, the enemy had reached Inticho and Adigrat, and on 6 October entered Adwa, after two bombing attacks that had demoralized Ras Seyoum.[112] Seated in an armchair in the center of a cave-shelter outside of town, the ras raised his eyes heavenward and asked, "Great God of Ethiopia, what is happening?" The answer was simple enough: Seyoum was witnessing the beginning of Ethiopia's defeat by the machine. He was so shocked by the experience that he ordered a hurried retreat, leaving behind large stocks of food, forcing his men to live off the countryside thereafter.[113] Adwa's fall prompted prideful statements in Rome.

Adowa had become a symbol of Italian failure which had thrown a shadow over the name of Italy at home and abroad. It was essential . . . that Italy should cancel this memory. It was essential that Abyssinia should cease to associate the name of Adowa with Italian defeat. Adowa was not a goal but a symbol.[114]

For the Ethiopians, the town's loss "without resistance and without a single drop of blood [spilled] on this historical earth [was] a great disgrace."[115] An even greater dishonor occurred in Mekele, when Dej. Haile Sellassie Gugsa defected with fifteen hundred well-armed men, perhaps a premature treachery, since he left no gap in an organized Ethiopian front.[116] Nonetheless, the Fascists were obviously moving from success to success. By 15 October, they had entered Axum, where they began to build an airfield, and later that month marched on Mekele. De Bono expected Ras Seyoum to put up a stiff fight there, but when Italian advance units entered the town's outskirts on 30 October, they found only a few hundred defenders. The general left behind two battalions to conquer the small garrison and, through mid-November, continued cautiously and slowly toward the Tekeze River, simultaneously consolidating his position and securing lines to the rear. From Addis Abeba came the comforting intelligence that Haile Sellassie had quashed all rumors of an immediate counteroffensive, "as his people intended to remain strictly on the defensive and to maintain guerrilla warfare." [117]

The emperor had ordered the same tactics for the southern front, where Korahe suffered its first air attack on 4 October, after which bombing became a daily occurrence. Nasibu ordered Afework to stop the Italian advance from Geregube, whose small garrison had been quickly overrun by troops from Welwel and Warder. The gerazmach pointed out that his 1,390 men were short of supplies of all kinds and could not be expected to withstand an enemy estimated at 30,000 soldiers. When he asked for massive reinforcements, Haile Sellassie ordered the immediate dispatch of supplies and of a battalion of trained troops, great recognition, indeed, of Afework's ability. The 450 new men and the ammunition and food did much for morale in bomb-battered Korahe, now increasingly isolated as the Italians took outlying forts.

Ethiopian soldiers had learned how to survive the air war by taking shelter in trenches while their officers fought off the planes with a relatively few antiaircraft guns. These guns were, of course, prime targets, and on 5 November, Afework, long concerned about Ethiopia's vulnerability from the air, was mortally wounded during a strafing attack.[118] His men continued a valiant defense, and Korahe's garrison did not yield until several days later, after having inflicted heavy losses on the army of Gen. Rodolfo Graziani. Korahe's defensive fortifications — constructed with the advice of Wehib Pasha, an Albanian general in the old Turkish army — caught the Italians in an enfilade while the trained battalion attacked from the flanks. Nevertheless, the Italian mass soon dominated, though Graziani, now respectful of his adversary's fighting abilities, had to rethink his strategy and consolidate his rear before marching on the sixty thousand men that Nasibu commanded in the Harer–Jijiga–Degeh Bur triangle.[119] With a lull in the fighting on both fronts came the last diplomatic effort to end the crisis.

On 7 October 1935, the Council of the League concluded "that the Italian Government had resorted to war in disregard of . . . Article 12 of the Covenant,"[120] thereby automatically raising the issue of sanctions. The British Government canvassed for significant action in combination with other states,[121] knowing full well that Paris would only agree to measures "of an anodyne nature." According to Pierre-Etienne Flandin, now foreign minister, "the French would fight for France, they would fight for the frontiers of Belgium and . . . they would probably fight for England, but otherwise they would never fight outside France and . . . would not if put to the test, even incur the risk of war for Austria or Czechoslovakia, much less for Russia."[122] Laval clarified that his government was willing, however, "to take part in collective economic pressure."[123] The Italians were properly scornful: Baron Aloisi told Eden that "it was impossible to arrest the course of history by the imposition of sanctions." Italy, he declared, as if he were addressing a crowd, was "now fulfilling [its] destiny," and he warned that the League ought to recognize his country's "imperious necessity to live."[124]

Mussolini wanted to obliterate Ethiopia's independence, by war if necessary, peacefully if possible. He again offered peace if Rome were ceded Menilek's conquests, Eritrea eastern Tigray, and Somalia the Ogaden—in return for which he would graciously permit Haile Sellassie to follow Italian advice in ruling his truncated state.[125] France, as usual, was willing to accept such an outrageous scheme, but Whitehall knew that Ethiopia would refuse.[126] Indeed, in Addis Abeba, on 17 October, the emperor had presided over a massive military review, an experience that buoyed him considerably. The march past took four hours and included all manner of soldiers, even "fierce fighting men from the provinces armed with nothing better than sticks and empty cartridge belts."[127] Many men rushed up to the reviewing tent and screamed their defiance of the Italians: "When he was a calf we drove him away with sticks; now he is a fat bull and we'll slaughter and eat him." "You have kept us [waiting] too long. All our enemies are already slain by the men of other provinces!" "Never fear; we shall soon be at the sea." [128]

From the fictitious glories of the parade ground, a quarter of a million men traveled north to join the reality of war against Italy. "There were no trim battalions marching four abreast, no wheeled transport of any kind, just a straggling procession of men and mules spread over a distance of five or six miles." [129] The mobilization raised the morale of most Addis Abebans, if not of the emperor and his government, who understood the power mustered against Ethiopia. As a matter of psychological necessity, Haile Sellassie continued to trust in the League: "If Signor Mussolini has staked his all on the conquest of Ethiopia, the Emperor had done the same on the efficacy of the Covenant." [130]

Yet Haile Sellassie refused negotiations "so long as Italian soldiers remained in occupation of Ethiopian territory as a result of aggression." Upon their withdrawal, he was prepared "to consider any terms which the League might put forward . . . offering a reasonable basis for discussion," if they did not compromise his nation's territory or its independence. The emperor also believed that any unilateral concession to Italy would "do a disservice to the League itself which had supported him by vindicating the justice of his cause." [131]

On 18 November 1935, Geneva imposed import and export sanctions on Italy. Though bothersome, the restrictions did not interfere with the Fascist war effort, and Mussolini used them to rally his people to the government. [132] More worrying to il duce was the possibility of an oil embargo, and he fumed about the threat, leading Britain and France to believe that he might undertake an act of madness — war against them — should his army's petroleum supplies be interrupted. [133] His own representatives successfully conjured up the image of a maniac to frighten their diplomatic colleagues: British officials, in particular, scurried around to assess potential support in case the Italians used bully boy tactics after the imposition of oil sanctions. [134] When the French complained that such an embargo was a "military sanction," Sir Samuel Hoare realized that a negotiated settlement was the only way to keep the peace. [135]

Laval agreed to help work out a new scheme, but his goal still was to retain his Italian ally by forcing Ethiopia to accept Roman hegemony. Hoare was amenable to any arrangement that did not "give the *appearance* of rewarding aggression" and was based on the report of the Committee of Five, already rejected by Rome. On 7 December 1935 — only six years before another day of "infamy" — the two men wrapped discredited ideas in new verbiage: an outlet to the sea for Ethiopia; no mandate as such for Italy; a judicious mixture of territorial exchange, including parts of recently conquered Tigray; and economic concessions for Italy.[136] Laval was well pleased with the reinvention of appeasement, as was Vansittart, who congratulated Hoare for "having reestablished the Anglo-French front."[137] Hoare and Laval had one night of satisfaction before a tide of indignation swept the world.

In Geneva, many commented bitterly that the effect of sanctions had been completely undermined by the Hoare-Laval pact.[138] In Paris, the entire liberal-left press united to denounce the service done the Fascists,[139] and the media in America were almost unanimous in seeing the newly hatched scheme as "a betrayal of Ethiopia" to the aggressor.[140] In Addis Abeba, Haile Sellassie announced that acceptance of the Anglo-French arrangement "even in principle . . . would be an act of cowardice and treason against Our people, the League of Nations, and all states which might have had confidence in the system of collective security."[141] In a formal response, the Addis Abeba government followed the imperial line, refused therefore to participate in its own dismemberment "under the pretext of a fallacious exchange of territories," and called on the League not to sponsor the "final ruin . . . [of the] system of guaranteed collective security provided for by the Covenant."[142]

In London, so general and so vehement was the obloquy directed at Hoare — even the establishment press participated — that he was forced to resign, although he continued to believe that nothing short of the arrangement he had negotiated with Laval would have saved Ethiopia and prevented "Mussolini from joining the Hitler front."[143] He neither concerned himself with il duce's earlier refusal of similar concessions[144] nor seriously considered that Haile Sellassie and his compatriots would prefer war to their country's dismemberment.[145] Hoare's lofty indifference to Ethiopia's fate combined with Laval's cynicism to destroy any chance of bringing the crisis to a just end. The failure led, according to Vansittart, to tragedy for Europe: "We lost Abyssinia, we lost Austria, we formed the axis, we made certain of Germany's next war." [146]

When it became clear that the peace process had disintegrated, Haile Sellassie decided to test the Italian line in Tigray. Ras Mulugeta, the minister of war and commander of Shewan forces, traveled to Temben to confer with Ras Kassa, the "Commander-in-Chief against the enemy coming by way of Tigre," Ras Seyoum, who led the Tigrayan army, and Ras Imru, who headed Gojami troops held in reserve.[147] On 20 December, Mulugeta told Colonel Konovaloff that soon Kassa and Seyoum would push forward frontally into Italian-occupied Tigray while he and his men would move eastward to outflank the enemy at Mekele and to cut their supply lines.[148] This simple maneuver was designed to punish the Italians, to forestall a renewed offensive, and to gain more time for the peace process to work.

The rases' major adversary was Gen. Pietro Badoglio, who on 17 November had replaced De Bono, signaling that the hitherto slow and careful Italian campaign would give way to ruthless struggle: "Badoglio . . . had only one end in view — to wipe out the enemy — and to achieve this purpose, he made use of every weapon he possessed, legal and illegal." [149] The new commander had concluded that his predecessor's advance to Mekele had opened the Italian flank to attack, and as the enemy deployed, he decided "to forestall his intentions, take the offensive in Temben, upset his plans, hamper his movements, and take advantage of this surprise action to launch an offensive south of Macallè." [150] Badoglio believed in massed artillery and air power, and he had no scruples about using poison gas bombs on 22–23 December to turn Ras Imru's army away from the supply depots at Adi Kwala.[151] Although his tactics foreshadowed subsequent Italian strategy, Badoglio was unable to clear the Ethiopians from Temben, even though their offensive failed to achieve any of its goals.[152]

The rases claimed victory, although they admitted that the Italians had been a tough adversary and that the artillery barrages had been difficult. Many Ethiopian officers generally became overconfident: "We know how to fight against the planes. . . . Beat the Italians on the ground." Usually cautious commanders concluded that in the end only personal valor counted on the battlefield, "which reinforced [the] conviction that . . . [Ethiopians] possessed a military talent without parallel." Even Ras Kassa, who sent frantic messages during the fighting to Addis Abeba for reinforcements and supplies, claimed, "Cannon, aircraft, they are only playthings; strength only shows itself in the final phase of combat, when the attackers come into contact with the enemy. Only at this moment can one judge who is the strongest." [153] Haile Sellassie was not fooled; he had sniffed the significance of mustard gas, which "no people on earth, even if they are a people descended from lions, could resist if they did not possess the technical means necessary." [154]

On the southern front, Desta Demtu's army became the first victim of massive gas attacks. Badoglio had instructed General Graziani to carry out "a very active defensive, in order to attract and to retain on the southern front the greatest possible number of the enemy's forces." [155] So literally did Graziani take his orders that his energetic defense became an offensive. From mid-December on, the Italians bombarded Ethiopian forward positions with gas "like a cloud." Without proper medications, the Ethiopian command could not relieve the suffering, and many troops deserted. Promised reinforcements and supplies never arrived, nor did the antitank guns needed to stop Graziani's armor. On 6 January, Desta reported imminent disaster for his army, now dug in sixty miles north of Dolo on both banks of the Juba: desertions were high, and his men were weak from hunger.[156]

On 10 January, Graziani attacked, and by the twelfth, thousands of Ethiopians had been killed. Italian tanks and armored cars terrorized survivors, who had fled into the bush after abandoning cannon and machine guns and most of their ammunition and food. By the time the ras ordered the retreat to Adola, he had only a few hundred men in his command. Unaware of the extent of his victory, Graziani halted his advance to consolidate his position and his lines of communication; otherwise he could have marched into Ethiopia's soft southern underbelly, by now largely empty of defenders.[157] The emperor quickly sent reinforcements southward and refused to criticize his son-in-law, although Addis Abebans openly expressed "scorn and anger at the [ras's] incapacity." [158] They, of course, did not know that Desta's defeat had been caused by modern weapons and tactics, not lack of courage or generalship. Haile Sellassie knew the truth but could not escape the same fate.

On 28 November, he left Addis Abeba for Dese, where he would remain with the bodyguard "as rearguard for the advance corps." [159] He traveled with the Duke of Harer, his favorite son, his secretaries and his *hommes de confiance*, his beloved little dogs, and a larder worthy of an emperor. At his headquarters, he put in his usual hard day: "It was a marvel . . . how this frail little man — the complete physical opposite of the brawny Italian dictator — could cram so much work . . . into twenty-four hours." Up at 5:00 A.M., he went to chapel for half an hour, dressed and looked over urgent messages; at 6:30 A.M., he ate a light breakfast and took a bit of coffee, except on fast days, when he ate a few handfuls of parched grain, washed down with water. Thereafter, he read reports, dictated responses, and met with officials and officers. After a lunch of fruit and cheese, he went for a walk and then returned to his desk, reading through and answering newly arrived telegrams, instead of taking the nap recommended by his physicians: "As the genuine Commander-in-Chief of his forces the whole strategy of war rested on his shoulders." [160]

He was mostly a cool leader, having "the gift of appearing at all times, even in the middle of war, completely detached and poised above the mêlée, pursuing his quiet, rather delicate and well dressed life without noting overmuch the noise which surrounded him." He matched sang-froid with courage, and on 6 December 1935, when airplanes bombed Dese, the emperor leapt from shelter to man his own personal Oerlikon, rattling away, perhaps, at Mussolini's flyer son. An approving crowd gathered around him, and Haile Sellassie grew angry: "Haven't I told you not to mass. . . . Do you want to make me a target? Take cover and let me fire!" After the attack was over, the emperor, surely totally ignorant of the dangers involved, had all the unexploded bombs collected and piled up in front of the small Dese palace. "Setting his foot on one of the biggest, he was photographed by a nervous press. They thought the bombs were on time-fuses and used the fastest exposures." After they fled, Haile Sellassie, obviously protected by the God of Ethiopia he often invoked, "settled down happily to weighing and measuring the bombs, investigating their contents, and precisely recording the results in his notebook." [161]

Through all of January into February, the Italians bombed the supply lines north of Dese. The largely Oromo population was traumatized by the violence and rebelled when the military requisitioned most of their food and animals. "Only at the great centres where there were armies, like Korem and Weldiya, was it safe to live."[162] From Dese, the emperor failed to secure his army's rear, as insurgent strength kept pace with peasant frustrations. From 10 February on, the increasingly unstable situation stimulated a persistent Italian offensive, which used air power and poison gas to separate, flank, and destroy the Ethiopian armies one by one. Within a four-week period, the Italians conquered Ras Mulugeta at Amba Aradam, demolished Ras Kassa's army at the second battle of Temben, and defeated Ras Imru at the battle of Shire.[163] The rapidity of the debacle confounded Haile Sellassie, whose orders to his commanders reveal a general remote from military reality,[164] incapable of countering Badoglio's war of maneuver and mass.

Mass of men, mass of fire, mass of artillery, mass of aviation. The mass of a civilised people, six times in population, greater and incalculably more advanced, smashing the wholly inferior mass of an African state.[165]

Modernity defeated Ethiopia — it was that simple. General Badoglio assumed that Haile Sellassie would be unable to counter: "Whether the Negus attacked or whether he awaited my attack, his fate was now sealed." The Italian expected Ethiopian withdrawal southward, "thus compelling me to organize a large-scale battle hundreds of miles from our bases"; or transformation of the war into a costly and protracted guerrilla struggle.[166] Instead, the emperor chose to fight an unwinnable battle at Maychew, directly in the path of the Italian advance. The terrain was all wrong for an attack, but a successful action was needed to give heart to the army, stem the rout, and delay the enemy advance.[167] A victory would vindicate the emperor, and a defeat might permit a soldier's death, converting him from monarch to martyr. By now he had little to lose; he was angry and frustrated, deeply wounded by the national calamity he witnessed and morally outraged by the devastating use of poison gas against Ethiopia's broad masses. He had found "corpses in each thicket, under each tree, in everything which could be a refuge. . . .

It was necessary to get used to living in a charnel-house."[168] The
emperor lost his sense of reality and, to satisfy honor, had to attack.

On 19 March, rases Seyoum and Kassa led the remnants of the
northern armies into Korem, where the emperor was waiting. The
next day, he closely interrogated Colonel Konovaloff about the rout
and retreat, even asking, "Are you convinced that Ras Kassa could
not hold on to the Temben any longer? Was he forced to retire?"
Konovaloff agreed that Kassa had no choice, sensibly holding back
details about poor leadership. When the Russian queried the current
situation, Haile Sellassie answered as Napoleon doubtless did after
Waterloo: "It is all going normally. Up to now we have resisted as best
we might and kept them back; I see nothing very dangerous in the
situation." The next day, however, the emperor opted for peril by
deciding to attack the newly established enemy camp at Maychew.
Haile Sellassie could marshal an estimated forty to fifty thousand
men, including five thousand modern troops; several hundred machine guns of all types; and nine cannon, six heavy mortars, and eight
antiaircraft guns.

During the night of 20 March, Haile Sellassie's army began its
move to the front at Hayo: "As the night was dark, We directed the
army to prepare torches . . . and since the road was very narrow,
the march took many hours." The Ethiopians managed to avoid no-
tice until 22 March, when "enemy aircraft dropped many bombs and
were spraying yperite poison [mustard gas] that was flowing like
water." Konovaloff overheard some ranking officers say "that they
were determined to give up their salaries . . . and even, if need be, a
gasha [about forty hectares] . . . to get aeroplanes and crews." The
Russian reflected:

The moral effect of aviation in this war is enormous. . . . From their heights
[Italian aircraft] penetrated our life, turning it upside down . . . they
blocked our movements . . . after a heavy march they prevented us from
eating and warming ourselves around our camp fires, which we were afraid
to light. They turned us into moles who dashed into their caves at the slight-
est alarm . . . each Ethiopian thought he was the special target of the bom-
bardment.

Between air attacks on 22 March, Colonel Konovaloff and three
Ethiopian St. Cyr graduates reconnoitered Italian positions at Maychew. After hearing their report, the emperor laid plans to attack that

night, an intent frustrated by his overcautious generals, who wanted to prepare for the offensive. By conceding the point, Haile Sellassie lost the element of surprise, and he also agreed to several other delays, permitting the Italians time to build up their strength to forty thousand troops, to fortify their positions, and to bomb and gas an increasingly demoralized Ethiopian army. In any case, Badoglio learned about the impending counterattack through intercepted messages; on 27 March, at 4:30 P.M., Haile Sellassie telegraphed Empress Menen: "Since our trust is in our Creator and in the hope of his help, and as we have decided to advance and enter the [Italian] fortifications, and since God is our only help, confide this decision of ours in secret to the Abun, to the ministers and dignitaries, and offer up to God your fervent prayers." The next day, the emperor drew up a complex and completely unrealistic set of general orders for his army, probably written more with posterity and autobiography in mind than with a clear appreciation of imminent hostilities. After further delays, Ethiopia's last organized force, comprising thirty-one thousand men, finally began advancing at 4:00 A.M. on 31 March 1936.

From its onset, the attack was a disaster. Even local surprise was lost when some Ethiopian soldiers fired prematurely, forcing the emperor to open the battle immediately.[169] It is perhaps best to turn to the emperor for a recapitulation of the worst defeat of his life.

As Our army moved forward with enthusiasm and reached the enemy's fortifications, the enemy troops abandoned the forward positions and were seen to defend a second more heavily fortified line towards the rear.

Within four or five hours enemy aircraft arrived, dropped bombs, and cut off Our army at the rear preventing it from coming to the aid of the advance troops at the front. At this time the enemy army was recovering once again and began fighting hard to re-enter the strongholds it had abandoned.

Our forces spent the whole day fighting with an ardent spirit and with daring. The battle did not cease until five o'clock at night (= 11 p.m.). In this day's fighting many nobles and army officers died sacrificing their life for their country.[170]

The battle was so hard fought that the Italians did not immediately pursue the retreating enemy. By the evening of 3 April, however, the Fascists were moving on the right and left flanks of Haile Sellassie's rear guard, seeking to cut the Ethiopians off. At 9:30 P.M., well after the possibility of air attack, the emperor and his army abandoned their equipment and took the road for Korem. On the march to Lake Ashange, the rebellious Azebo Oromo shot stragglers and otherwise harassed the survivors. At 7:00 A.M., on 4 April, finding the retreating columns near the lake in the open, Italian planes began an all-day attack with bombs and gas that completely broke what remained of an organized Ethiopian army. For Haile Sellassie, it was a nightmarish day of massacre and cruelty: "If I could speak of what I saw, no one would believe me. I can only reflect on it to myself. Isn't it all a dream?" [171] Ethiopians at the rear of the retreating mass, among them both the emperor and the high command, managed to survive.

Though the emperor despaired, "my brain no longer works," he had enough sense to march southward toward safety, quitting the temporary sanctuary of the caves at Enda Agafari, near Korem, at 6:00 P.M. on 5 April. Two days later, Haile Sellassie confided to Konovaloff, "It is beyond our strength to hold them back." Yet he sought personal renewal on 12 April, near Lasta, when he and "the highest lords of the land" celebrated Easter mass in a small parish church and ate a meager meal. The next day, the emperor and entourage entered Lasta proper, where the Solomonic writ still ran, and received an enthusiastic welcome and lavish hospitality. His spirits obviously buoyed, Haile Sellassie continued on to nearby Lalibela, a town made holy by its many rock-hewn churches. For the emperor, the visit was "something . . . mystical and in the nature of a pilgrimage. Lalibela is a monument of Ethiopian glory; perhaps the emperor was seeking new moral strength in this contact with a holy place." More likely he was seeking to understand Ethiopia's defeat. That he received no divine revelation is obvious from the preface to his autobiography:

It is a subtle secret which a creature, after even much exploring, cannot know but which You alone do know; why . . . You have made the Ethiopian people, from the ordinary man to the Emperor, sink in a sea of distress for a time, and why You have made the Italian people up to its King swim in a sea of joy for a time. [172]

While Haile Sellassie was seeking divine revelations, the Council of State in Addis Abeba was deciding on worldly salvation for the government in the remote interior and for the imperial family abroad.[173] When the emperor finally reached the capital on the afternoon of 30 April, he went into an immediate meeting with the Council of Ministers. It was a quiet session, during which the participants "conferred in hushed tones for hours," and convened again the next day before convincing Haile Sellassie to leave with his family.[174] Although unprecedented and certainly dramatic, it was the correct move to make: as long as the sovereign was free and unbowed, Italian rule could have no legitimacy. For the emperor to have remained in Ethiopia — and it took all the strength and conviction of the government and empress to convince him to leave — would have been vainglorious, for he would have risked a humiliating capture, death, or, even worse, submission to the conqueror. Haile Sellassie could not withstand the logic of the case for exile, and as subsequent events would amply prove, withdrawal to Europe ensured that Ethiopia would be free in five short years.

The emperor was by now operating on nerves alone: "He was very tired and worn and his usual calm dignity seemed at times to be tinged with despair."[175] He appeared to be at the edge of reality: "Vigour had left his face, and as he walked forward he did not seem to know where he was putting his feet. His body was crumpled up, his shoulders drooped; the orders on his tunic concealed a hollow, not a chest." He tried to change his mind about exile during the night of 1 May but did not have the strength to withstand the empress's four-hour rebuke. Instead, he sat in the palace, listening to the trucks that took boxes of Maria Theresa dollars, his family's possessions, and even his royal lions to the railroad station to load on a special train. At about 4:00 A.M., on 2 May 1936, the emperor, the empress, their children, and a retinue of high-ranking officials left Addis Abeba for Djibouti.[176]

That evening, the special train stopped in Dire Dawa for a few hours to allow the emperor to take on some passengers and to discharge others and then went on to Djibouti, arriving at 10:30 A.M. on 3 May. The next day, Haile Sellassie met the captain of the two-ship British task force that was to transport him to Palestine. "My very first impression on being presented to His Majesty was how very tired he looked. I felt somehow that he was almost at his last gasp and from his first remarks I knew he was a very frightened man. He had a hunted look in his eyes." Haile Sellassie's first questions concerned his own personal safety, and the Englishman assured him that once he stepped over the ship's gangway, "he would be as safe as the Bank of England." The Ethiopian smiled for the first time, a memorable moment: "There is something about his smile that you cannot resist, and you are always hoping that you will say something of which he approves or do some little thing that will please him, so that you can see him smile."

The captain nevertheless gently advised the emperor that one hundred people and the two lions must remain in Djibouti. "When this information was communicated . . . they all held up their hands in horror and said it could not be done. . . . The Emperor looked so weary and fragile that I felt a perfect brute." While the remaining fifteen tons of baggage and about MT$250,000 to MT$300,000 (£25,000) was being loaded, Haile Sellassie, his family, and about forty others went aboard. The emperor "went fast asleep," and during the next few days en route to Port Suez he pulled himself together and once again became sovereign of Ethiopia. "I have seldom been so impressed with any man, black or white, and his consideration, courtesy, and above all his dignity, has left a deep impression on every officer and man in my ship." Before disembarking, Haile Sellassie presented the captain with a gold coronation medal, not the gift of a man who had abandoned his throne.[177] Nevertheless, he would have five troubled years of exile and self-doubt in England before returning to power in 1941, thanks to the Ethiopian patriots, who had never stopped fighting the Fascists, and to the British, who in 1940 finally began fighting them.

NOTES

Works frequently cited have been identified by the following abbreviations:

Archives Capucins	Archives of the Capucins, Province of Toulouse, Toulouse, France.
Autobiography	Haile Sellassie I. *My Life and Ethiopia's Progress.* Vol. 1. Edited and translated by Edward Ullendorff as the *Autobiography of Emperor Haile Sellassie I, 'My Life and Ethiopia's Progress,' 1892–1937.* Oxford, 1976.
FFM	Archives of the French Foreign Ministry, Paris.
FO	Archives of the British Foreign Office, Public Record Office, London.
IFM	Historical Archives of the Italian Foreign Ministry, Rome.
IFM/MAI	Historical Archives of the Italian Foreign Ministry, Ex-Ministry of Italian Africa, Rome.
SD	Archives of the State Department, National Archives, Washington.

PREFACE

1. Edwin R. A. Seligman, *The Economic Interpretation of History,* 2d ed. (New York, 1907), pp. 3, 67, 100, 149.

2. Peter Worsley, *The Three Worlds* (London, 1984), pp. 41–60.

3. Karl Marx, "The Eighteenth Brumaire of Louis Bonaparte," in *Karl Marx and Frederick Engels, Selected Works* (New York, 1969), p. 97. Joanna Mantel-Niećko provides a more specific view in *The Role of Land Tenure in the System of Ethiopian Imperial Government in Modern Times* (Warsaw, 1980). For a plea to regard Haile Sellassie as "a particularly articulate and successful representative of his class rather than a unique phenomenon," see Bahru Zewde, "Economic Origins of the Absolutist State in Ethiopia," *Journal of Ethiopian Studies* 17 (Nov. 1984): 18.

4. Perry Anderson, *Lineages of the Absolutist State* (London, 1974), pp. 17, 40, 47; Dessalegn Rahmato, "Political Power and Social Formation Under the Old Regime," in *Collected Papers of the Eighth International Conference of Ethiopian Studies*, vol. 2, B-E (Institute of Ethiopian Studies, Addis Abeba University, 1984), pp. 420–426; Shiferaw Bekele, "Prince-Merchants and Tujars: A Preliminary Study of Class Evolution (c. 1900–1935)," in *Papers, Eighth International Conference*, vol. 6, P-S, pp. 421–423.

5. S. N. Eisenstadt, *The Political System of Empires* (Glencoe, Ill., 1963), pp. 21–22, 24, 117, 118, 138, 141–144, 150.

CHAPTER ONE

1. *Bath Weekly Chronicle and Herald*, 10, 19 Oct. 1936.

2. Even Ryszard Kapuściński got this right in his otherwise misguided and absurd *The Emperor: Downfall of an Autocrat* (New York, 1983), p. 16.

3. *My Life and Ethiopia's Progress*, vol. 1 (Addis Abeba, 1973); later edited and translated by Edward Ullendorff as the *Autobiography of Emperor Haile Selassie I, 'My Life and Ethiopia's Progress,' 1892–1937* (Oxford, 1976) (hereafter cited as *Autobiography*). See my review in *International Journal of African Historical Studies* 10 (1977): 495.

4. *Autobiography*, p. 14; Pierre Pétridès, *Le Héros d'Adoua: Ras Makkonen, Prince d'Ethiopie* (Paris, 1963), pp. 31–32.

5. *Autobiography*, p. 15.

6. Augustus B. Wylde, *Modern Abyssinia* (London, 1901), p. 430; Capt. M. S. Wellby, *'Twixt Sirdar and Menelik* (London, 1901), p. 31; Rodd to Salisbury, Harer, 4 June 1897, Public Record Office, London, Foreign Office (hereafter cited as FO) 403/255; Robert P. Skinner, *Abyssinia of Today* (London, 1906), p. 21n; Asfa Yilma, *Haile Selassie, Emperor of Ethiopia* (London, 1936), p. 113.

7. *Autobiography*, p. 17; "Mgr. Jarosseau, vicaire apostolique des Gallas," *La Croix* 1–2 (Jan. 1925); "L'Oeuvre de Mgr. Jarosseau," *Le Petit Parisien*, 6 July 1938.

8. *Autobiography*, p. 15; Alaka Imbakom Kalewold, *Traditional Ethiopian Church Education* (New York, 1970); Bairu Tafla, "Education of the Ethiopian Makwannent in the Nineteenth Century" (Seminar paper, Addis Abeba University, 1972).

9. *Autobiography*, p. 19; Henri de Monfried, "Vers les Terres hostiles d'Ethiopie," *Le Petit Parisien*, 6 July 1938; Aleme Eshete, "The Influence of the Capucin Bishop of Harer (1900–1940), Mgr. Andre Jarosseau on Taffari Makonnen, Later Emperor Haile Sellassie," *Ethiopian Journal of Education* 7, no. 2 (1975): 22–30.

10. Harold G. Marcus, *The Life and Times of Menelik II: Ethiopia, 1844–1913* (Oxford, 1975), pp. 193–194; Donald N. Levine, *Wax and Gold: Tradition and Innovation in Ethiopian Culture* (Chicago, 1965), pp. 2–3.

11. Marcus, *Menelik*, p. 193.

12. Blattangeta Herui Wolde Sellassie, *Biographie. Sa Majesté Hailé Sélassié Premier, Empereur d'Ethiopie* (Addis Abeba, 1930), p. 4; *Autobiography*, p. 20.

13. *Autobiography*, pp. 21–22; Donald N. Levine, "Legitimacy in Ethiopia" (Conference paper, American Political Science Association, 1964).

14. Pétridès, *Makkonen*, pp. 277–278; *Autobiography*, p. 23; André Jarosseau, "Vicariat apostolique des Gallas, 1846–1925," Unpubl. ms., Archives de la Mission, Archives des Frères Mineurs Capucins, Province of Toulouse (hereafter cited as Archives Capucins). Compare the last with Marcus, *Menelik*, p. 226, who incorrectly claimed death by cancer. Also see Marse Hazan Wolde Qirqos, "BaDagmawi Minilik Zaman KeYahutna KeSamehut" (Unpubl. ms., Institute of Ethiopian Studies, Addis Abeba University, probably 1938), p. 14. This volume and others cited subsequently are memoirs of palace events and personalities. I am indebted to James McCann for bringing the manuscript to my attention and for permitting me to use his valuable notes, which contain translations from the Amharic typescript.

15. Entry for 23 March 1906, Journal de Mgr. Jarosseau, 1905–1906, vol. 3, Archives Capucins; Pétridès, *Makkonen*, pp. 279–280.

16. *Autobiography*, p. 23; Jarosseau to Abbé Frement, Harer, 29 March 1906, Correspondance Jarosseau, Archives Capucins.

17. Marcus, *Menelik*, p. 227.

18. Herui, *Biographie*, p. 4; *Autobiography*, p. 25.

19. Basile to Jarosseau, Addis Abeba, 31 July 1906, Correspondance Jarosseau, Archives Capucins.

20. Peter Garretson, "A History of Addis Ababa from Its Foundation in 1886 to 1910" (Ph.D. diss., University of London, 1974); Eduard Berlan, *Addis Ababa, la plus haute ville d'Afrique* (Grenoble, 1965); Marcus, *Menelik*, p. 200.

21. Harold G. Marcus, "The Infrastructure of the Italo-Ethiopian Crisis: Haile Sellassie, the Solomonic Empire, and the World Economy, 1916–1936," in *Proceedings of the Fifth International Conference of Ethiopian Studies*, edited by Robert L. Hess (Chicago, 1979), p. 570. Perry Anderson describes a similar process in Europe during the Renaissance; see Perry Anderson, *Lineages of the Absolutist State* (London, 1974).

22. Marcus, *Menelik*, pp. 214–215.

23. Asfa Yilma, *Haile Selassie*, pp. 116–118; Georges Rémond, "L'Agonie de l'empereur Ménélik," *Le Correspondant* 244 (25 July 1911): 342.

24. Naggiar to Pichon, Dire Dawa, 14 Oct. 1907, Archives of the French Foreign Ministry (hereafter cited as FFM), Ethiopie, Politique Intérieure, I, April 1898–August 1908.

25. Brice to minister, Addis Abeba, 8 April 1908, ibid.; *Autobiography*, p. 28.

26. Ababa Kiflayasus, "The Career of Liul Rās Imru Hāyla Sillāse" (B.A. essay, Addis Abeba University, 1973), p. 14; *Autobiography*, p. 29.

27. *Autobiography*, p. 29.

28. Marcus, *Menelik*, pp. 225–237.

29. *Autobiography*, pp. 30–31.

30. Marcus, *Menelik*, pp. 242–243.

31. Marse Hazan, "Minilik," p. 53; *Autobiography*, pp. 34–35; Marcus, *Menelik*, pp. 246–248.

32. "Le Prince Taffari, Fils du Ras Makonnen," *Le Semeur d'Ethiopie* 6 (July 1910): 707–708; entries for 11 and 13 March 1910, Journal de Mgr. Jarosseau, 1909–1911, vol. 6, Archives Capucins.

33. "Faits divers," *Le Semeur d'Ethiopie* 7–8 (Aug.-Oct. 1910): 726, 760.

34. *Autobiography*, pp. 37–41.

35. Allan Hoben, "Perspectives on Land Reform in Ethiopia: The Political Role of the Peasantry," *Rural Africana* 28 (Fall 1975): 58–63; Negussay Ayele, "Is There Feudalism in Ethiopia?" (Conference paper, Addis Abeba University, 1976); Gene Ellis, "The Feudal Paradigm as a Hindrance to Understanding Ethiopia," *Journal of Modern African Studies* 14 (June 1976): 281–284; Aleme Eshete, "A General Survey of Ethiopian Feudalism" (Conference paper, Addis Abeba University, 1976); Donald N. Levine, "Individualism in Feudal Ethiopia" (Conference paper, Addis Abeba University, 1976); Donald Crummey, "State and Security: Nineteenth-Century Ethiopia," in *Modes of Production in Africa: The Precolonial Era*, edited by D. Crummey and C. Stewart (Beverly Hills, 1981).

36. "Faits divers," *Le Semeur d'Ethiopie* 7 (Aug. 1911): 114; Gontran de Juniac, *Le Dernier Roi des Rois: L'Ethiopie de Hailé Sélassié* (Paris, 1979), pp. 49–50; *Autobiography*, pp. 41–42.

37. Marcus, *Menelik*, pp. 252–264.

38. Journal de Mgr. Jarosseau, 1912–1914, vol. 7, Archives Capucins.

39. *Autobiography*, p. 44.

40. Marcus, *Menelik*, pp. 265–269.

41. *Autobiography*, pp. 44–45; Peter Garretson, "The Naggadras, Trade, and Selected Towns in Nineteenth and Early Twentieth Century Ethiopia," *International Journal of African Historical Studies* 12, no. 3 (1979): 430.

42. Brice to minister, Addis Abeba, 4 May 1916, FFM, Guerre, Affaires politiques générales, Ethiopie III, 1916, vol. 1619.

43. Colli Memo. of Conversation with Lij Iyasu, Addis Abeba, 24 May 1916, Historical Archives of the Italian Foreign Ministry (hereafter cited as IFM), Affari Politici, Etiopia, n. 65, file 1145/2.

44. Gebre Egzabieher Elyas, "YeTarik Mestawasha, 1901–1922 E.C."

(Unpubl. ms., no. 23, National Library, Addis Abeba, n.d.); see also Aby Demissie, "Lij Iyasu: A Perspective Study of His Short Reign" (B.A. essay, Addis Abeba University, 1964), p. 140.

45. Jarosseau to Pascal, Harer, 12 Sept. 1916, Correspondance Jarosseau, Archives Capucins; Aby Demissie, "Lij Iyasu."

46. Brice to minister, Addis Abeba, 28 Nov., 12 and 26 Dec. 1914, FFM, Guerre, Affaires politiques générales, Ethiopie I, 1914, vol. 1617.

47. Charles L. Geshekter, "Anti-Colonialism and Class Formation: The Eastern Horn of Africa Before 1950," *International Journal of African Historical Studies* 18, no. 1 (1985): 16.

48. *Autobiography*, pp. 42–43; Jarosseau to DeLoue, Harer, 8 June 1915, Correspondance Jarosseau, Archives Capucins; Colli to minister, Addis Abeba, 6 Feb. 1916, IFM, Archivio Politico, Etiopia, 1915–1918, n. 65, file 1114/2; Marcus, *Menelik*, pp. 270–271.

49. Brice to minister, Addis Abeba, 4 May 1916, FFM, Guerre, Affaires politiques générales, Ethiopie III, 1916, vol. 1619; Thesiger to Grey, Addis Abeba, 7 and 18 May 1916, FO 371/2593.

50. Brice to minister, Addis Abeba, 24 Aug. 1916, FFM, Guerre, Affaires politiques générales, Ethiopie III, 1916, vol. 1619; see also Colli to minister, Addis Abeba, 17 Aug. 1916, IFM, Affari Politici, Etiopia, n. 65, file 1145/2.

51. Thesiger to Grey, Addis Abeba, 18 May 1916, FO 371/2593.

52. *Autobiography*, pp. 46–47; Harold G. Marcus, "Genesis of an Ethiopian Monarch: Haile Sellassie, 1916–1918," *Horn of Africa* 3, no. 4 (1980–1981): 46; Colli to minister, Addis Abeba, 5 Sept. 1916, Historical Archives of the Italian Foreign Ministry, Records of the ex-Ministry of Italian Africa (hereafter cited as IFM/MAI), file 37/11; Brice to minister, Addis Abeba, 1 Sept. 1916, FFM, Guerre, Affaires politiques générales, Ethiopie III, 1916, vol. 1619.

53. Entries for 27 July, 14 and 16 Sept. 1916, Journal de Mgr. Jarosseau, 1916–1918, vol. 9, Archives Capucins.

54. See, for example, Colli to minister, Addis Abeba, 11 Sept. 1916, IFM/MAI, 37/11.

55. Copy of Note in Thesiger to Grey, Addis Abeba, 14 Sept. 1916, FO 371/2595.

56. Marcus, *Menelik*, pp. 276–277.

57. Entries for 21 and 26 Sept. 1916, Journal de Mgr. Jarosseau, 1916–1918, vol. 9, Archives Capucins.

58. *Autobiography*, pp. 48–49.

59. Testimony of Ato Wolde Mariam, present at the meeting, and second interpreter of the French Legation, in "Summary of Events," in Brice to minister, Addis Abeba, 6 Oct. 1916, FFM, Guerre, Affaires politiques générales, Ethiopie IV, 1916, vol. 1620. Cf. Marcus, *Menelik*, p. 277, who did not have the benefit of data only recently available at the Quai d'Orsay. Cf. Marse Hazan, "YeZaman Tarik Tezzetaye BaNegesta Negastat Zawditu Zamana Mangist" (Unpubl. ms., Institute of Ethiopian Studies, Addis Abeba Univer-

sity, n.d.), pp. 2, 24, who claims that Tafari was then named only heir apparent, not crown prince.

60. Southard to Secretary of State, Addis Abeba, 24 Nov. 1916, United States National Archives, microfilmed Records of the Department of State relating to the Internal Affairs of Ethiopia, 1910–1929 (hereafter cited as SD, Records); cf. *Autobiography*, p. 50.

61. Dodds to Thesiger, Harer, 7 Oct. 1916, enclosed in Thesiger to Grey, Addis Abeba, 21 Oct. 1916, FO 371/2594; entries for 28 and 30 Sept., 1 Oct., Journal de Mgr. Jarosseau, 1916–1918, vol. 9, Archives Capucins.

62. Entries for 3–9 Oct., Journal de Mgr. Jarosseau, 1916–1918, vol. 9, Archives Capucins; entry for 21 Oct. 1916, Brice Diary, in Brice to minister, Addis Abeba, 2 Nov. 1916, FFM, Guerre, Affaires politiques générales, Ethiopie V, 1916, vol. 1621.

63. Enclosure in Thesiger to Grey, Addis Abeba, 3 Oct. 1916, FO 371/2594; Brice to minister, Addis Abeba, 1 Oct. 1916, FFM, Guerre, Affaires politiques générales, Ethiopie IV, 1916, vol. 1620.

64. Thesiger to Grey, Addis Abeba, 3 and 11 Oct. 1916, FO 371/2594; Colli, "Rapporto," in Colli to minister, Addis Abeba, 27 Oct. 1916, IFM/MAI, 37/11; entry for 16 Oct. 1916, Brice Diary, FFM, Guerre, Affaires politiques générales, Ethiopie V, 1916, vol. 1621.

CHAPTER TWO

1. Entry for 16 Oct. 1916, Brice Diary, FFM, Guerre 1914–1918, Affaires politiques générales, Ethiopie IV, 1916, vol. 1620; Harold G. Marcus, "Genesis of an Ethiopian Monarch: Haile Sellassie, 1916–1918," *Horn of Africa* 3, no. 4 (1980–1981): 47.

2. The previous few pages were drawn largely from reports, dispatches, and other documents found in FFM, Guerre, Affaires politiques générales, Ethiopie IV, 1916, vol. 1620; IFM, Archivio Politico, 1915–1918, n. 66/file 1145–3, which contains a unique record of tapped telephone conversations between the palace and the front; Marse Hazan Wolde Qirqos, "Ye-Zaman Tarik Tezzetaye BaNegesta Negastat Zawditu Zamana Mangist" (Unpubl. ms., Institute of Ethiopian Studies, Addis Abeba University, n.d.), pp. 47–84; *Autobiography*, pp. 53–56, which, as usual, offers little besides the conventional lore; and Harold G. Marcus, *The Life and Times of Menelik II: Ethiopia, 1844–1913* (Oxford, 1975), pp. 278–281, whose recapitulation, written in 1970, was based largely on British archives and some Italian documentation.

3. Colli to minister, Addis Abeba, 3 Nov. 1916, IFM, Archivio Politico, 66/1135; Brice Diary in FFM, Guerre, Affaires politiques générales, Ethiopie IV, 1916, vol. 1620; Ministry of War, Intelligence Report on Ethiopia, 7 Dec. 1916, Affaires politiques générales, Ethiopie V, 1916, vol. 1621; Thesiger to Grey, Addis Abeba, 3 Nov. 1916, FO 371/2594.

4. *Autobiography*, p. 56.

5. De Rossi to de Martino, Dese, 11 Nov. 1916, and de Rossi to Colli, Dese, 17 Nov. 1916, IFM, Archivio Politico, 66/1145–3.

6. Brice to minister, Addis Abeba, 18 Dec. 1916, FFM, Guerre, Affaires politiques générales, Ethiopie V, 1916, vol. 1621.

7. De Rossi to ?, Dese, 20 Nov. 1916, IFM, Archivio Politico, 66/1145–3.

8. De Martino to Minister of Colonies, Asmera, 11, 21, 22, 28 Dec. 1916, and Colli to minister, Addis Abeba, 21 Dec. 1916, ibid., 65/1135; Marse Hazan, "Zawditu," pp. 95–98.

9. De Coppet to minister, Addis Abeba, 20 Feb. 1917, and enclosure, FFM, Guerre, Affaires politiques générales, Ethiopie VI, 1917, vol. 1622; Archer to Colonial Office, Berbera, 27 March 1917, FO 371/2854; Marse Hazan, "Zawditu," pp. 100–105.

10. De Coppet to minister, Addis Abeba, 21 Feb. 1917, FFM, Guerre, Affaires politiques générales, Ethiopie VI, 1917, vol. 1622; Marse Hazan, "Zawditu," pp. 122–124.

11. Ambroise to Jarosseau, Addis Abeba, 23 and 30 March and 6 April 1917, Correspondance Jarosseau, Archives Capucins; de Coppet to minister, Addis Abeba, 19 March 1917, FFM, Guerre, Affaires politiques générales, Ethiopie VI, 1917, vol. 1622; Archer to Colonial Office, Berbera, 27 March 1917, FO 371/2854. See the many letters from this period in "The Collected Letters of Tafari Makonnen," Book One, National Library of Ethiopia, Addis Abeba.

12. Marse Hazan, "Zawditu," p. 129; Brice to minister, Addis Abeba, 30 Nov. 1916, FFM, Guerre, Affaires politiques générales, Ethiopie V, 1916, vol. 1621; Thesiger to Wingate, Addis Abeba, 29 Dec. 1916, FO 371/2594; Ababa Kiflayasus, "The Career of Liul Rās Imru Hayla Sillase" (B.A. essay, Addis Abeba University, 1973), p. 24; Tesfaye Ababa, "The Life and Career of Dejjazmatch Takala Walda Hawariat" (B.A. essay, Addis Abeba University, 1971), p. 8.

13. De Martino to minister, Asmera, 9 March 1917, and Colli to de Martino, ? March 1917, IFM, Archivio Politico, 66/1145–3; de Coppet to minister, Addis Abeba, 1 March 1917, FFM, Guerre, Affaires politiques générales, Ethiopie VI, 1917, vol. 1622; Thesiger to Balfour, Addis Abeba, 27 Feb. 1917, FO 371/2854.

14. Harold G. Marcus, "The Embargo on Arms Sales to Ethiopia, 1916–1930," *International Journal of African Historical Studies* 16, no. 2 (1983): 265; Colosimo to Minister of Foreign Affairs, Rome, 13 Sept. 1916 and 26 Jan., 24 Feb., 14 Mar. 1917, IFM, Archivio Politico, 66/1135. Concerning Tafari's efforts to obtain the use of military aircraft, see the lengthy correspondence in FO 371/2853.

15. De Coppet to minister, Addis Abeba, 13 Aug. 1917, FFM, Guerre, Affaires politiques générales, Ethiopie VIII, 1917, vol. 1624.

16. Reports from the Italian agent in Dese, enclosed in Cora to minister, Addis Abeba, 6 Aug. 1917, Archivio Politico, 66/1145–3.

17. Thesiger to Balfour, Addis Abeba, 27 Aug. 1917, FO 371/2854; cf. *Auto-*

biography, p. 62, for an admission that Iyasu's freedom had given heart to "some idlers [who] had not ceased causing trouble."

18. De Coppet to minister, Addis Abeba, 30 Aug. and 15 Sept. 1917, FFM, Guerre, Affaires politiques générales, Ethiopie VIII, 1917, vol. 1624; Thesiger to Balfour, Addis Abeba, 29 Aug. 1917, FO 371/2854; *Autobiography*, pp. 58–59; Marse Hazan, "Zawditu," pp. 130–133.

19. Colli to minister, Addis Abeba, 23 March 1917, IFM, Archivio Politico, 66/1135.

20. Archer to Colonial Office, Berbera, 27 March 1917, FO 371/2854.

21. De Coppet to minister, Addis Abeba, 25 April 1917, Guerre, Affaires politiques générales, Ethiopie VII, 1917, vol. 1623.

22. Thesiger to Balfour, Addis Abeba, 27 Sept. 1917, FO 371/2854; Marse Hazan, "Zawditu," p. 138.

23. Thesiger to Balfour, Addis Abeba, 21 May 1918, FO 371/3125.

24. Victor Dervaniades to Messrs. Dervaniades and Co. of Alexandria, Addis Abeba, 27 May 1918, ibid.

25. Campbell to Balfour, Addis Abeba, 26 April 1918, FO 371/3126.

26. I alluded to the beginnings of Addis Abeba's proletariat and underclass in *Menelik*, p. 221.

27. Campbell to Balfour, Addis Abeba, 16 March 1918, FO 371/3126.

28. Thesiger to FO, Addis Abeba, 8 July 1918, ibid.

29. De Coppet to minister, Addis Abeba, 28 March and 13 April 1918, and "Diary of Events Leading up to the Dismissal of the Ethiopian Ministers," Addis Abeba, 20 March 1918, FFM, Guerre, Affaires politiques générales, Ethiopie IX, 1918, vol. 1625; Thesiger to FO, Addis Abeba, 26 March 1918, FO 371/3126; Colli to minister, Addis Abeba, 9 July 1918, IFM, Archivio Politico, 66/ 1145–3; *Autobiography*, p. 59; Marse Hazan, "Zawditu," pp. 148–155.

30. De Coppet to minister, Addis Abeba, 3 June 1918, Archives of the French Foreign Ministry, K-Série, Afrique, 1918–1930, (hereafter cited as K-Afrique), Ethiopie, Questions générales, 1918–1919, vol. 6.

31. De Coppet to minister, Addis Abeba, 31 July 1918, ibid.

32. Campbell to Sperling, Addis Abeba, 2 Dec. 1918; Campbell to Balfour, Addis Abeba, 11 Dec. 1918; Thesiger to Balfour, Addis Abeba, 31 Dec. 1918; Curzon to Cecil, London, 20 Feb. 1919, FO 371/3494; de Coppet to minister, Addis Abeba, 30 Sept. 1918, K-Afrique, Ethiopie, Questions générales, 1918–1919, vol. 6; Richard Pankhurst, "The Hedar Baseta of 1918," *Journal of Ethiopian Studies* 13, no. 2 (1976): 59.

33. De Coppet to minister, Addis Abeba, 21 June 1918, FFM, Guerre, Affaires politiques générales, Ethiopie IX, 1918, vol. 1625.

CHAPTER THREE

1. Colisimo to Minister of Foreign Affairs, Rome, 24 Feb. and 14 March 1917, IFM, Archivio Politico, 66/1135; Thesiger to Balfour, Addis Abeba, 22 Feb. 1917, FO 371/2855; Giovanni Buccianti, *L'Egemonia sull'Etiopia* (Milan, 1977), pp. 18–33.

2. Colli to minister, Addis Abeba, 11 Nov. 1918, IFM, Archivio Politico, 66/1145–3.

3. Memo. of Mayer and Baldassare, no date, in de Coppet to minister, Addis Abeba, 30 April 1917, FFM, Guerre, Affaires politiques générales, Ethiopie VIII, 1917, vol. 1623.

4. Cora Memo., "Etiopia 1918, Finanze Etiopiche," IFM/MAI, 54/3–71. Boucoiran to minister, Addis Abeba, 19 Dec. 1919, and enclosures; Boucoiran Memo., "L'Ethiopie économique, 1916–1925," in Gaussen to minister, Addis Abeba, 1 Dec. 1926, FFM, K-Afrique, Ethiopie, Affaires commerciales, 1918–1929, vol. 34. For information about early concession-seekers, refer to FO 371/3125 and 3495. Also see Harold G. Marcus, "The Infrastructure of the Italo-Ethiopian Crisis: Haile Sellassie, the Solomonic Empire, and the World Economy, 1916–1936," in *Proceedings of the Fifth International Conference of Ethiopian Studies,* edited by Robert L. Hess (Chicago, 1979), pp. 559–561.

5. De Coppet to minister, Addis Abeba, 19 Dec. 1918, 17 and 27 Jan. 1919, 28 March 1919, FFM, K-Afrique, Ethiopie, Questions générales, 1918–1919, vol. 69; *Autobiography,* pp. 559–561.

6. Southard to Secretary of State, Addis Abeba, 20 April 1919, SD, Records.

7. Campbell to Curzon, Addis Abeba, 12 May 1919, FO 371/3491.

8. Boucoiran to minister, Addis Abeba, 23, 24, 28 June and 2 July 1919; minister to Boucoiran, Paris, 3 July 1919, FFM, K-Afrique, Ethiopie, Affaires générales, vol. 7.

9. French Foreign Ministry to British Embassy, Paris, 22 July 1919, FO 371/3497.

10. Buccianti, *Egemonia,* pp. 16, 329.

11. Note of the Italian Embassy, London, 8 April 1919, and FO to Italian Embassy, London, 16 April 1919, FO 371/3494.

12. Campbell to Curzon, Addis Abeba, 22 June 1919, FO 371/3496.

13. *Autobiography,* p. 6.

14. Note of Tripartite Powers addressed to Empress Zawditu, Addis Abeba, 17 Aug. 1919, FO 371/3497.

15. Campbell to Curzon, Addis Abeba, 3 July 1919, ibid.

16. Campbell to Curzon, Addis Abeba, 13 Sept. 1919, ibid.; Marse Hazan Wolde Qirqos, "YeZaman Tarik Tezzetaye BaNegesta Negastat Zawditu Zamana Mangist" (Unpubl. ms., Institute of Ethiopian Studies, Addis Abeba University, n.d.), pp. 179–181.

17. Boucoiran to minister, Addis Abeba, 15 Aug. and 29 Sept. 1919, FFM, K-Afrique, Ethiopie, Affaires générales, vol. 7; Colli Memo., "Situazione politica, amministrativa e militare dell'Abissinia," Addis Abeba, 30 March 1920, Historical Archives of the Italian Foreign Ministry, Archivio degli Affari Politici, 1919–1930 (hereafter cited as Affari Politici), pacco 1020. Tafari's supporters were Dej. Wolde Gabriel, the minister of the palace, and Dej. Katama, the minister of the interior; Zawditu's Dej. Habte Mariam, minister

of finance, and Tsehafi Tazaz Wolde Maskal, minister of pen; and Habte Giorgis's, Afanegus Stefanos, the minister of justice.

18. Dodds to Sperling, Addis Abeba, 21 Oct. 1919, FO 371/3497.

19. Boucoiran to minister, Addis Abeba, 14 Nov. 1919, FFM, K-Afrique, Ethiopie, Affaires générales, vol. 7.

20. De Coppet to minister, Addis Abeba, 21 Jan. 1920, ibid.; Dodds to Curzon, Addis Abeba, 3 Dec. 1919, FO 371/3497.

21. Dodds to Curzon, Addis Abeba, 5 and 18 Feb. 1920, FO 371/4392; de Coppet to minister, Addis Abeba, 18 March 1920, FFM, K-Afrique, Ethiopie, Affaires générales, vol. 7.

22. Dodds to Curzon, Addis Abeba, 20 April 1920, FO 371/4394.

23. Boucoiran to minister, Addis Abeba, 31 Oct. 1919, FFM, K-Afrique, Ethiopie, Affaires générales, vol. 7. Ato Sahle was among the first of a long line of officials who owed their positions and status to Tafari. The regent habitually chose more or less educated men of humble family background as trusted advisers or confidential messengers rather than choosing men from the traditional nobility. The perfect Young Ethiopian, Sahle owed his education at Menilek's school to his parents, both of whom were palace workers. During his six-year education, Sahle learned French, English, and arithmetic; he also met Tafari, to whom he owed his career.

24. De Coppet to minister, Addis Abeba, 17 May 1920, FFM, K-Afrique, Ethiopie, Affaires générales, vol. 7.

25. Dodds to minister, Addis Abeba, 20 Aug. 1920, FO 371/4394.

26. Same to same, Addis Abeba, 6 Sept. 1920, ibid.

27. Same to same, Addis Abeba, 21 Jan. 1921, FO 371/5505.

28. Same to same, Addis Abeba, 20 Dec. 1920, ibid.; *Autobiography*, pp. 61–62; Marse Hazan, "Zawditu," p. 195.

29. De Coppet to minister, Addis Abeba, 7 and 10 Feb. 1921, FFM, K-Afrique, Ethiopie, Affaires générales, vol. 8.

30. Telegram of 28 Jan. from Commercial Agent Brielli in Adwa, as quoted in Pollera to Colonies, Asmera, 1 Feb. 1921, IFM/MAI, "Ligg Yasu, Cattura, 1917–1921," 54/37–150a.

31. Pollera to Colonies, Asmera, 10 Feb. 1921, ibid.

32. Telegram of 11 Feb. from Commercial Agent Brielli in Adwa, as quoted in Pollera to Colonies, Asmera, 11 Feb. 1921; Legation to ministry, Addis Abeba, 9 March 1921, ibid.

33. Same to same, Addis Abeba, 4 Aug. 1921, ibid.; de Coppet to minister, Addis Abeba, 2 and 31 May, 21 June, 30 July 1921, and Report by Dr. Mouzel, "Expédition à Dessie, 6 May–20 July 1921," Addis Abeba, 20 Aug. 1921, in de Coppet to minister, Addis Abeba, 31 Aug. 1921, FFM, K-Afrique, Ethiopie, Affaires générales, vol. 8; *Autobiography*, p. 62; Marse Hazan, "Zawditu," p. 195.

34. See articles in *Westminster Gazette*, 18 Jan., 1 and 2 May, 6 June 1922; Marcus, "Infrastructure," pp. 560, 565–566, nn. 10 and 13. In certain parts of northern Ethiopia, the demands of the changing economy and emergent

central government might have revitalized slavery. See James McCann, "Children of the House: Slavery and Its Suppression in Lasta, Northern Ethiopia, 1916–1975," in *The Suppression of Slavery in Africa*, edited by Suzanne Miers and Richard Roberts (Madison, forthcoming). Jon Edwards, however, generally discounts the importance of the world economy in undermining slavery, suggesting instead that a decline in the supply of slaves killed the institution; see Jon R. Edwards, "Slavery, the Slave Trade, and the Economic Reorganization of Ethiopia, 1916–1935," *African Economic History* 11 (1982). For a middle view, see Tekalign Wolde Mariam, "The Slave Trade in the Economy of Jimma," in *Collected Papers of the Eighth International Conference of Ethiopian Studies*, vol. 7, T-2 (Institute of Ethiopian Studies, Addis Abeba University, 1984), pp. 84, 89–90.

35. De Coppet to minister, Addis Abeba, 7 and 25 July 1922, FFM, K-Afrique, Ethiopie, Affaires générales, vol. 9; Dodds to Balfour, Addis Abeba, 7 July 1922, FO 371/7148. As late as 1919, Tafari himself was profiting from slavery in Ethiopia; see the many letters on the subject from Tafari to provincial governors in "The Collected Letters of Tafari Makonnen," Book One, National Library of Ethiopia, Addis Abeba. As is obvious from remarks in his autobiography, Tafari really understood the problem only in terms of international relations, not as a major internal drama; *Autobiography*, pp. 78–81.

36. Marse Hazan, "Zawditu," pp. 247–250.

37. Dodds to Curzon, Addis Abeba, 23 Aug. 1922, FO 371/7148.

38. G. Barrett, First Asst. Resident, Aden, "An Account of the Visit to Aden of His Highness Ras Taffari, Regent of Ethiopia, 2–3 Nov. 1922, Aden, 8 Nov. 1922," FO 371/7152; "S.A.I. Le Ras Taffari à Aden," *Le Courrier d'Ethiopie*, 18 Nov. 1922.

39. De Coppet to minister, Addis Abeba, 17 Nov. 1922, FFM, K-Afrique, Ethiopie, Affaires générales, vol. 9.

40. Internal Memo., Paris, 22 Nov. 1922, ibid.; French Note for the British Embassy, Paris, 27 Dec. 1922, FO 371/7147; French Note for the Italian Embassy, Paris, 9 Jan. 1923, IFM, Affari Politici, pacco 1025.

41. Minister of Colonies to Minister of Foreign Affairs, Rome, 16 Feb. 1923, IFM, Affari Politici, pacco 1025.

42. Précis of Conversation between Col. D. Sandford and Ras Tafari, Addis Abeba, 24 Feb. 1922, FO 371/7147.

43. Minute A4773, by Dodds, London, 6 July 1921, FO 371/5503; Buccianti, *Egemonia*, pp. 269ff.

44. Russell to Curzon, Addis Abeba, 12 May 1922, FO 371/7146.

45. Marginalis by M. Paretti, Director for African Affairs, in de Coppet to minister, Addis Abeba, 25 March 1920, FFM, K-Afrique, Ethiopie, Affaires générales, vol. 7.

46. "Renseignements communiqués par le Gouvernment Français sur L'Esclavage," in Poincaré to Secretary General of the League of Nations, Paris, 12 June 1923, FFM, K-Afrique, Ethiopie, Affaires générales, vol. 10.

47. H. M. Consul, Geneva, to FO, Geneva, 4 July 1923, FO 371/8405.

48. Goub to minister, Geneva, 5 July 1923, FFM, K-Afrique, Ethiopie, Affaires générales, vol. 10.

49. Resolution adopted by the Council of the League of Nations, C.459 (1)1923.VI, as found in FFM, K-Afrique, Ethiopie, Affaires générales, vol. 11.

50. Minister to Boucoiran, Paris, 14 July 1923, and Boucoiran to minister, Addis Abeba, 23 July 1923, FFM, K-Afrique, Ethiopie, Affaires générales, vol. 10.

51. Boucoiran to minister, Addis Abeba, 30 July 1923, ibid.

52. "Abyssinia and the League," *Near East,* 20 Sept. 1923. This piece is dated Addis Abeba, 20 Aug. 1923, and bears the unmistakable style of Col. D. Sandford, a close acquaintance of the regent.

53. Tafari to Drummond, Addis Abeba, 1 and 12 Aug. 1923, FO 371/8410.

54. *Autobiography,* p. 77.

55. Arlotta to legation, Rome, ? Aug. 1923, IFM, Affari Politici, pacco 1024.

56. FO to delegation, Geneva, 15 Sept. 1923, FO 371/8410.

57. League of Nations, Admission of Ethiopia, "Proposal by the Special Sub-Committee," A.VI, 5, 1923, as found in FO 371/8410.

58. Mussolini to della Torreta, Rome, 1 Sept. 1924, IFM, Affari Politici, pacco 1026, fasc. 3047; "Note sur L'Ethiopie et la Société des Nations," FFM, K-Afrique, Ethiopie, Affaires générales, vol. 13.

59. Tafari to Baldwin, Addis Abeba, 18 Sept. 1923, FO 371/8410; Tafari to Mussolini, Addis Abeba, 18 Sept. 1923, IFM, Affari Politici, pacco 1024.

60. Buccianti, *Egemonia,* pp. 339, 343.

61. Mussolini to della Torreta, Rome, 1 Sept. 1924, IFM, Affari Politici, pacco 1026, fasc. 3047; "Note sur L'Ethiopie et la Société des Nations," FFM, K-Afrique, Ethiopie, Affaires générales, vol. 13.

62. Nado to Tafari, Geneva, 22 Sept. 1923; Boucoiran to minister, Addis Abeba, 26 Sept. 1923; Clauzel to minister, Geneva, 28 Sept. 1923, FFM, K-Afrique, Ethiopie, Affaires générales, vol. 11.

63. Extract from League of Nations, 4th Assembly 1923, Verbatim Report of the 17th Plenary Meeting, 28 Sept. 1923, as found in FO 371/8410.

64. *Autobiography,* p. 77.

65. Maj. H. C. Maydon, *Simen: Its Heights and Abysses* (London, 1925), pp. 153–155.

66. C. F. Rey, *Unconquered Ethiopia as It Is Today* (London, 1923), p. 145. There was so much forest that some "suggested that Addis Ababa's name might appropriately be changed to Eucalyptopolis." See Ronald J. Horvath, "Addis Ababa's Eucalyptus Forest," *Journal of Ethiopian Studies* 6, no. 1 (1968): 15–16.

67. Demetre Nicopoulos, *Addis Ababa ou Fleur Nouvelle* (Marseilles, 1923), pp. 107, 130–132.

68. Maydon, *Simen,* p. 165.

69. Rosita Forbes, *From Red Sea to Blue Nile* (New York, 1925), p. 131.

70. Harry Harlan, "A Caravan Journey Through Abyssinia," *National Geographic* 47 (1925): 629, 636.

71. C. F. Rey, "Abyssinia of Today," part 3, *Journal of the Royal African Society* 22 (1922–1923): 119.

72. Ibid., part 2, 21 (1922–1923).

73. Rey, *Unconquered Ethiopia*, p. 111.

74. Nicopoulos, *Addis Ababa*, p. 130.

75. Forbes, *From Red Sea*, p. 141.

76. The city was relatively better served than the countryside, where an infinitesimal number of children went to school in Tigray, Harerge, Arsi, and in one or two other provinces; Daniel Ayana, "Some Notes on the Role of Village Schools in Planting Protestantism in Wollega, 1898–1935," in *Collected Papers of the Eighth International Conference of Ethiopian Studies*, vol. 2, B-E (Institute of Ethiopian Studies, Addis Abeba University, 1984), pp. 334–343.

77. Thomas Jesse Jones, *Education in East Africa* (New York, 1925), pp. 326–332.

78. Rey, *Unconquered Ethiopia*, p. 111.

79. Ibid., p. 175; Forbes, *From Red Sea*, p. 141; Harlan, "A Caravan Journey," p. 615.

80. *Autobiography*, p. 84.

CHAPTER FOUR

1. Legation Memo., "Viaggio di Ras Tafari in Italia. Questioni ad esso connesse," Addis Abeba, 25 March 1924, IFM, Affari Politici, pacco 1026, fasc. 3056; Gaussen to minister, Addis Abeba, 4 Jan. 1924, FFM, K-Afrique, Ethiopie, Affaires générales, vol. 12.

2. *Autobiography*, p. 83.

3. Pierre Alype to Léonce Lagarde, Addis Abeba, 19 Jan. 1923, FFM, Léonce Lagarde Papers, vol. 11.

4. Imperial Ethiopian Government Edicts "Regarding the Possession of, and Traffic in, Arms and Munitions," Addis Abeba, 9 April 1924, as enclosed in Tafari to the Secretary General of the League of Nations, Addis Abeba, 12 April 1924, FO 371/9887.

5. "Report from the Government of Abyssinia on the Question of Slavery," Addis Abeba, 12 April 1924; "Regulations for the Emancipation of Slaves and Their Condition of Life," Addis Abeba, 31 March 1924, in Tafari to Secretary General of the League of Nations, Addis Abeba, 12 April 1924, FO 371/9985.

6. Russell to minister, Addis Abeba, 18 April 1924, FO 371/9985.

7. "Freeing the Slaves," *Westminster Gazette*, 9 June 1924.

8. Gaussen to minister, Addis Abeba, 8 April 1924, FFM, K-Afrique, Ethiopie, Affaires générales, vol. 13.

9. *Autobiography*, p. 84.

10. Ibid., pp. 84–88; Allenby to MacDonald, Cairo, 18 May 1924 (here-

after cited as the Allenby Report); Samuel to Russell, Jerusalem, 30 April 1924, FO 371/9889.

11. *Autobiography*, pp. 88–89; Allenby Report.

12. Crewe to MacDonald, Paris, 24 May 1924 (hereafter cited as the Crewe Report), FO 371/9889.

13. "Black Ruler Thanks Parisians," *Daily Express*, 17 May 1924; "Ras Tafari in Paris," *The [London] Times*, 17 May 1924.

14. *Autobiography*, p. 91.

15. Crewe Report.

16. Toasts of President Millerand and Ras Tafari at Official Dinner, Elysée Palace, 16 May 1924, *Journal Officiel*, 17 May 1924.

17. Memo. of Conversation between Bellefon and Tafari en route to Fontainebleau, 20 May 1924, FFM, K-Afrique, Ethiopie, Affaires générales, vol. 13; Grahame to MacDonald, Brussels, 26 and 30 May 1924, FO 371/9889; "Le Prince D'Ethiopie à Bruxelles," *Le Soir* (Brussels), 24 May 1924.

18. "Un Brut Incroyable," *Dépêche Coloniale*, 2 May 1924; "L'Invraisemble peut être Vrai," ibid., 3 May 1924; Notes of the Meetings of the Inter-Ministerial Committee, 24 and 27 May 1924, and Memo. of Conversation between Tafari and de Peretti, 31 May 1924, FFM, K-Afrique, Ethiopie, Affaires générales, vol. 13.

19. Notes of the Meeting of the Inter-Ministerial Committee, 3 June 1924, and Note pour Monsieur le Directeur des Affaires Politiques et Commerciales, 5 June 1924, FFM, K-Afrique, Ethiopie, Affaires générales, vol. 13.

20. R. Graham to MacDonald, Rome, 20 June 1924, FO 371/9990.

21. He later wondered, "When they think of this today, how extraordinary must this appear to them?!" *Autobiography*, p. 98.

22. Ibid., pp. 99–100.

23. Serge Groussard, "Entretien avec Hailé Sélassié Ier," *Le Figaro*, part 1, 25 March 1959, p. 5.

24. Revised Draft of 22 June 1924, IFM, Affari Politici, pacco 1026, fasc. 3045; cf. *Autobiography*, pp. 101–102, for a much softer version; and Alan Cassels, *Mussolini's Early Diplomacy* (Princeton, N.J., 1970), p. 295, who claims that the Italian government was merely humoring Tafari by offering the draft agreement.

25. Visite du Ras Tafari à M. de Beaumarchais, Paris, 1 July 1924, FFM, K-Afrique, Ethiopie, Affaires générales, vol. 14.

26. Governor of Djibouti to Minister of Colonies, Djibouti, 29 June 1924, ibid.

27. William Bolitho, "Ras Tafari in Paris," *Manchester Guardian*, 17 June 1924.

28. Minute by Malet, n. 2731, 29 March 1924, FO 371/9988.

29. Stamfordham to Selby, Buckingham Palace, 31 March 1924, ibid.

30. Minute by Tyrell, n. 3256, n.d., ibid.

31. Russell to Murray, Sussex, 13 June 1924, FO 371/9990.

32. Murray to Stamfordham, Foreign Office, 17 June 1924, ibid.

33. Stamfordham to Murray, Windsor, 18 June 1924, ibid.

34. "Ras Tafari at the Tower," *Daily Express*, 9 July 1924.

35. "Ras Tafari Arrives," *Manchester Guardian*, 8 July 1924.

36. "Prince Tafari of Abyssinia," *The [London] Times*, 7 July 1924.

37. "Our New Royal Visitor," *The Observer*, 6 July 1924.

38. MacDonald to Bullock, Foreign Office, 31 July 1924, FO 371/9992; *Autobiography*, pp. 106–107.

39. "Record of Conversation between the Prime Minister and His Highness Taffari Makonnan at 9:30 A.M. on 16 July 1924, at No. 10, Downing St.," FO 371/9992; *Autobiography*, p. 108.

40. Asfa Yilma, *Haile Selassie, Emperor of Ethiopia* (London, 1936), pp. 8, 15.

41. Ibid., pp. 10, 13.

42. *Autobiography*, p. 112.

43. Deladier to Herriot, Paris, 28 July 1924, FFM, K-Afrique, Ethiopie, Affaires générales, vol. 14.

44. Enclosure in Deladier to Herriot, ibid.

45. Note for Tafari, Paris, 13 Aug. 1924, ibid.

46. *Autobiography*, p. 115.

47. "Un entretien avec le Ras Tafari," *Echo de Paris*, 30 Aug. 1924.

48. "Ras Tafari of Abyssinia," *Near East*, 10 July 1924.

49. *Autobiography*, pp. 115–121.

50. Ibid., pp. 121–123; Laurent d'Arce, *L'Abyssinie. Etude d'Actualité (1922–1924)* (Avignon, 1925).

51. Bentinck to Murray, Addis Abeba, 22 Oct. 1925, FO 371/10878.

52. Legation to minister, Addis Abeba, 21 Jan. 1925, IFM/MAI, 54/31–128.

53. "Present Council of Advisers of Abyssinian Central Government at Addis Abeba," in Bentinck to Chamberlain, Addis Abeba, 8 July 1925, FO 371/10877; Annual Report for 1925, in Bentinck to Chamberlain, Addis Abeba, 15 May 1926, FO 371/11574.

54. Memo for Gaussen, Paris, 16 Jan. 1925, FFM, K-Afrique, Ethiopie, Affaires générales, vol. 15.

55. Tafari to President of the Council, Addis Abeba, 12 March 1925, FO 371/10871.

56. Cantalupo to minister, Rome, 1 May 1925, IFM, Affari Politici, pacco. 1027, fasc. 3067. Also see above, chapter 3, page 54.

57. Ministry to Berthelot, Paris, 27 Oct. 1925, FFM, K-Afrique, Ethiopie, Affaires générales, vol. 15.

58. Onslow to FO, Geneva, 28 May 1925, FO 371/10871.

59. Wingfield to Chamberlain, Brussels, 24 June 1925, ibid. Cf. Cassels, *Early Diplomacy*, p. 296, who comments that Ethiopia won only a "token victory" at Geneva.

60. Minute J171, 25 June 1925, FO 371/10871.

61. Chamberlain to Bentinck, London, 14 Oct. 1925, ibid.

62. See Alexander Mikhailovich, *Always a Grand Duke* (New York, 1933), p. 167.

63. Gaussen to minister, Addis Abeba, 10 Nov. 1925, FFM, K-Afrique,

Ethiopie, Affaires générales, vol. 15; "Prince Tafari's Plans," *The [London] Times*, 9 Oct. 1924.

64. Bentinck to Chamberlain, Addis Abeba, 17 Oct. 1925, FO 371/10875.

65. Park to Secretary of State, Aden, 20 Oct. 1925, SD, Records.

66. Hodgson to Chamberlain, Moscow, 29 July 1925, FO 371/10874.

67. Marse Hazan Wolde Qirqos, "YeZaman Tarik Tezzetaye BaNegesta Negastat Zawditu Zamana Mangist" (Unpubl. ms., Institute of Ethiopian Studies, Addis Abeba University, n.d.), p. 267.

68. Summary of Intelligence for 1925, Addis Abeba, 10 Oct. 1925, FO 371/10878.

69. Bentinck to Chamberlain, Addis Abeba, 5 Aug., 17 Oct., and 3 Dec. 1925, FO 371/10878.

70. "Reform in Ethiopia," *The [London] Times*, 20 June 1925.

71. Gaussen to minister, Addis Abeba, 10 Oct. 1925, FFM, K-Afrique, Ethiopie, Affaires générales, vol. 15; Bentinck to Chamberlain, Addis Abeba, 24 Aug. and 28 Sept. 1925, and Philip Zaphiro, "Memorandum on Abyssinian Affairs" (hereafter cited as the Zaphiro Memo.), in Bentinck to Chamberlain, Addis Abeba, 28 Sept. 1925, FO 371/10877.

72. Colli to minister, Addis Abeba, 1 Oct. 1925, IFM/MAI, 54/26–99; Bentinck to Chamberlain, Addis Abeba, 13 July and 24 Aug. 1925, and Zaphiro Memo., FO 371/10877.

73. Graham to Mussolini, Rome, 14 Dec. 1925, FO 371/11560.

74. Mussolini to Graham, 20 Dec. 1925, ibid.

75. Lt. Col. G. Schuster, "Note on Italian Negotiations for Concessions in Abyssinia," 2 June 1925, FO 371/10872.

76. Bentinck to FO, Addis Abeba, 27 Jan. 1926, FO 371/11560.

77. Minister to heads of mission in London, Rome, Washington, Brussels, Madrid, Berlin, Moscow, Constantinople, Cairo, Addis Abeba, Tunis, and Rabat, n.d., FFM, K-Afrique, Ethiopie, Affaires générales, vol. 16.

78. Memo. by Phipps, Paris, 27 Jan. 1926; Record of Conversation between M. Ponsot and Mr. R. F. Wigram, Paris, 30 Jan. 1926, in Crewe to Chamberlain, Paris, 1 Feb. 1926, FO 371/11560. Cf. Cassels, *Early Diplomacy*, p. 299, who asserts that the accords did not transcend the provisions of the 1906 agreement and "were more symbolic than substantive." The Ethiopians and the French clearly saw matters differently and, later, so did Italian officials. See Edwardo Susmel and Duilio Susmel, eds., *Opera Omnia di Benito Mussolini*, vol. 27 (Florence, 1959), p. 79; Fulvio Suvich et al., *Il Processo Roatta* (Rome, 1945), p. 19; and Antoinette Iadorala, "The Anglo-Italian Agreement of 1925: Mussolini's 'Carte Blanche' for War Against Ethiopia," *Northeast African Studies* 1, no. 1 (1979).

79. FO to Bentinck, London, 22 Feb. 1926, FO 371/11560.

80. Graham to FO, Rome, 23 Feb. 1926, FO 371/11561.

81. Crewe to FO, Paris, 24 Feb. 1926, ibid.

82. Bentinck to Chamberlain, Addis Abeba, 20 March 1926, ibid.

83. Bentinck to FO, Addis Abeba, 7 June 1926, FO 371/11563.

84. Extract of a Note Verbale delivered to Count Colli, Addis Abeba, 9 June 1926, as quoted in FFM, K-Afrique, Ethiopie, Affaires générales, vol. 17. At the Italian Foreign Ministry, I was never able to track down any of the files relating to the accord. My experience was not unusual, given the disorganized and partial nature of the files, the archive's permissiveness in allowing certain Italian scholars to withdraw materials for scrutiny elsewhere, and the outdated secretiveness and sensitivity of officials when dealing with Ethiopia. The most recent Italian scholar to have spoken out publicly about these problems is Alessandro Triulzi, "Italian Colonialism and Ethiopia," *Journal of African History* 23, no. 2 (1982): 237 – 238.

85. Bentinck to FO, Addis Abeba, 15 June 1926, FO 371/11563.

86. *Autobiography*, pp. 134 – 137; cf. Tafari to Avenol, Addis Abeba, 19 June 1926, FO 371/11564.

87. Colli to minister, Addis Abeba, 2 July 1926, IFM/MAI, 50/20 – 64.

88. See especially *Berhanena Selam*, 16 Sept. 1926.

89. Graham to Murray, Rome, 18 June 1926, FO 371/11563.

90. Graham to Chamberlain, Rome, 29 Oct. 1926, FO 371/11566.

91. Instructions for General Malladra, Rome, 10 July 1926, IFM/MAI, 50/24 – 64. It is important to point out that the instruction about gas was in the form of a handwritten postscript — *not* in Badoglio's hand, although, strictly speaking, the request was his responsibility as chief of staff.

92. See, for example, the editorial in the *Washington Post*, 8 Aug. 1926.

93. Murray to Avenol, FO, 3 Aug. 1926, FO 371/11565.

94. Grandi to Avenol, Rome, 7 Aug. 1926, ibid.

95. Maclean to Chamberlain, Addis Abeba, 23 Sept. 1926, FO 371/11566.

96. Tafari to Avenol, Addis Abeba, 4 Sept. 1926, ibid.; cf. *Autobiography*, pp. 142 – 143.

97. George W. Baer, *The Coming of the Italo-Ethiopian War* (Cambridge, Mass., 1967), p. 18.

98. Esmonde M. Robertson, *Mussolini as Empire-Builder* (London, 1977), p. 8.

CHAPTER FIVE

1. Charles W. McClellan, "Land, Labor, and Coffee: The South's Role in Ethiopian Self-Reliance," *African Economic History* 9 (1980): 76 – 77; Tessema Ta'a, "The Basis for Political Contradictions in Wollega: The Land Apportionment Act of 1910 and Its Consequences," *Northeast African Studies* 6, no. 1 – 2 (1984): 184 – 192; Bahru Zewde, "Economic Origins of the Absolutist State in Ethiopia," *Journal of Ethiopian Studies* 17 (Nov. 1984): 12 – 13.

2. Enrico Cerulli, "Le popolazioni ed i capi dell'Etiopia Sud-occidentale," enclosure in Zoli to Minister of Foreign Affairs et al., Rome, 8 Jan. 1927, IFM/MAI, 54/34 – 137.

3. British records are full of reported border violations and raiding; see especially FO 371/10875 and /10878. The incidents may have comprised Ethiopian efforts to push the political frontier southward; see Edward Keefer,

"Great Britain and Ethiopia, 1897–1910: Competition for Empire," *International Journal of African Historical Studies* 6 (1973): 468ff.

4. Bentinck to Chamberlain, Addis Abeba, 18 Dec. 1926, FO 371/12339.

5. Same to same, Addis Abeba, 1 Feb. 1927, ibid.

6. As quoted in Park to Secretary of State, Addis Abeba, 17 March 1927, SD, Records.

7. Ibid; Bentinck to Chamberlain, Addis Abeba, 28 Feb. 1927, FO 371/12339; Gàussen to minister, Addis Abeba, 25 Feb. 1927, FFM, K-Afrique, Ethiopie, Affaires générales, vol. 18.

8. Mega in extreme southwestern Sidamo is a fine case in point: it began as a fortified government post situated atop a small mountain. Its several hundred soldiers and functionaries attracted a local population of Somali traders and Oromo herders, altogether comprising a sufficiently high density of population to stimulate the marketing of produce, salt, finished products, animals, and hides. The town's hinterland remained, however, firmly embedded in the traditional pastoral mode of production, but it was a place for the Oromos to come to sell animals and hides when they needed the money to satisfy taxes of MT$16 per one hundred cattle, or, less frequently, to buy cotton goods and other imported products. See Miles to Colonial Secretary (Nairobi), Mega, 27 April 1925, FO 371/10876.

9. Alexander Powell, *Beyond the Utmost Purple Rim* (London, 1925), p. 69.

10. Charles W. McClellan, "Reaction to Ethiopian Expansionism: The Case of Darassa, 1895–1935" (Ph.D. diss., Michigan State University, 1978), chapter 5. The process described by McClellan bears an uncanny resemblance to the changes stimulated in Adaba, Arsi Administrative Region, in the late 1960s, when a new road opened the area to the national economy and settlers from Shewa. See Hector Blackhurst, "A Community of Shoa Galla Settlers in Southern Ethiopia" (Ph.D. diss., University of Manchester, 1974), pp. 64–66.

11. Arnold Wienholt Hodson, *Seven Years in Southern Abyssinia* (London, 1927), p. 103.

12. Plowman to Bentinck, Harer, 29 June 1925, FO 371/10877.

13. Cora Memo., "L'Attivita economica del Belgio e le Azienda agricole nell'Etiopia sud-Orientale," Addis Abeba, 4 Feb. 1927, IFM/MAI, 54/43–137.

14. See the hodgepodge of statistics and reports included in FFM, K-Afrique, Ethiopie, Affaires commerciales, 1918–1929, vol. 34; "Der Maria-Therasien Thaler" and "La Situation en Ethiopie," *Correspondance d'Ethiopie*, 21 July 1927, 1–2; Jon Edwards, "An Introduction to Foreign Office File 915: The British Consular Court in Ethiopia, 1912–1938" (London, 1981); Dunbar to Chamberlain, Addis Abeba, 2 April 1929, and Plowman to Dunbar, Harer, 10 April 1929, FO 371/13833.

15. C. F. Rey, "A Recent Visit to Gudru and Gojjam," *Geographical Journal* 67 (1926): 482, 493.

16. Wilfred H. Osgood, "Nature and Man in Ethiopia," *National Geographic* 54 (1928): 129, 164.

17. Others went after coffee profits with the finesse of Attila the Hun. For example, Lij Fikre Sellassie devastated Maji, whose population he impoverished, to get his hands on all available coffee, thereby shattering agricultural productivity and the local economy for years to come. Addis Abeba Intelligence Report for April 1924, FO 371/9994; Report by Consul Hodson, Maji, 17 March 1925, excerpted in Kenya Monthly Intelligence Report for May 1925, FO 371/10878; Kenyazmach Kurri to Ras Tafari, Maji, 24 March 1927, IFM/MAI, 54/26–97; Osgood, "Nature and Man," pp. 129, 164.

18. Adi Cooper et al., "Class, State, and the World Economy: A Case Study of Ethiopia," (Conference paper, University of Sussex, 1975), p. 1; Catherine Coquery-Vidrovitch, "La Mise en Dépendance de l'Afrique Noire: essai de periodisation, 1800–1970," *Cahiers d'études Africaines* 16 (1976): 36.

19. FO to Colonial Office, London, 15 April 1926, FO 371/11567.

20. Addis Abeba Intelligence Summary, 10 Oct. 1925, FO 371/10878.

21. Tafari to Bentinck, Addis Abeba, 13 Nov. 1925, and Bentinck to Tafari, Addis Abeba, 19 Nov. 1925, FO 371/10875.

22. Vivalba to the Governor of Somalia, Addis Abeba, 5 June 1923, IFM/MAI, 54/26–99.

23. Roberto Cimmaruta, *Ual Ual* (Milan, 1936), p. 64. Indeed, Italian officers were ordered to collect the oral traditions of trans-frontier Somali to see "if history might support claims to pasture and wells in Ethiopian territory"; see Lee V. Cassanelli, *The Shaping of Somali Society* (Philadelphia, 1982), p. 33.

24. Colli to minister, Addis Abeba, 30 Oct. 1926, IFM, Affari Politici, pacco 1028, fasc. 3083.

25. De Vecchi di Val Cismon to Minister of Colonies, Torino, 5 Sept. 1927, IFM/MAI, 54/26–99.

26. Luigi Villari, "The Italian Case," *Journal of the Royal African Society* 34 (1935): 369.

27. Raffaele Guariglia, *Riccordi, 1922–1946* (Naples, 1950), p. 54.

28. *Autobiography*, p. 146.

29. Cora to minister, Addis Abeba, 19 May 1927; Report of Capt. L. Ornati, Jibuti, 29 May 1927; Report of the Duke of Abruzzi, n.p., 20 Aug. 1927, IFM, Affari Politici, pacco 1029, fasc. 3104.

30. Bentinck to Chamberlain, Addis Abeba, 27 May 1927, FO 371/12350.

31. Cora to minister, Addis Abeba, 3 May 1927, IFM/MAI, Affari Politici, pacco 1029, fasc. 3105.

32. *Autobiography*, p. 147.

33. Guariglia, *Riccordi*, pp. 56–58.

34. Cora to Mussolini, Addis Abeba, 18 March 1928, IFM, Affari Politici, pacco 1031, fasc. "Trattato di Amicizia Italo-etiopico."

35. Mussolini to Cora, Rome, 26 March 1928, ibid.

36. Cora to Mussolini, 30 March 1928, ibid.

37. Federzoni to Mussolini, 10 April 1928, ibid.

38. Mussolini to Cora, Rome, 20 April 1928, ibid. As Sven Rubenson has maintained, "The Italian infiltration into the Ogaden . . . speaks . . . of

deliberate disregard for [treaty] obligations." See Sven Rubenson, "The Genesis of the Ethio-Somali Conflict," in *Proceedings of the Fifth International Conference of Ethiopian Studies*, edited by Robert L. Hess (Chicago, 1979), p. 653.

39. Cora to Mussolini, Addis Abeba, 10, 15, 16 June 1928, and Mussolini to Cora, Rome, 1 July 1928, ibid.

40. Cora to Mussolini, Addis Abeba, 20 and 22 July 1928, ibid.

41. Treaty of 2 Aug. 1928, Road Agreement and Lease for a Free Zone in Aseb, in Cora to Mussolini, Addis Abeba, 2 Aug. 1928, ibid.; for the conventional Italian view, which, however, eschews analysis, see Giuseppe Vedovato, "Gli Accordi Italo-etiopici dell'Agosto 1928," *Rivista di Studi Internazionali* 22 (1955): 560ff.

42. Guariglia, *Riccordi*, pp. 56–58.

43. Zoli to Minister of Colonies, Asmera, 27 Oct. 1928; Cora to Mussolini, Addis Abeba, 12 Nov. 1928; Mussolini to Cora, Rome, 12 Nov. 1928, IFM, Affari Politici, pacco 1031, fasc. "Trattato di Amicizia Italo-etiopico."

44. *Autobiography*, p. 150.

45. FFM, K-Afrique, Ethiopie, Affaires commerciales, vol. 34.

46. For details, see FO 371/12351. Tokyo and Addis Abeba were sentimental about each other: the two were historical empires, they were anomalies in the Western-dominated world, they had defeated major European powers to make good their independence, and both were attempting modernization, with Japan already successful. Blattangeta Herui, Ethiopia's longtime foreign minister, visited there in 1931 and subsequently wrote a glowing account of his experiences: *Mahdere Berhan Ha-Ager Japon* (The example of light, the country of Japan) (Addis Abeba, 1931).

47. Memo. "Au sujet des relations Franco-Italiennes en Abyssinie," 12 Jan. 1928, FFM, K-Afrique, Ethiopie, Affaires générales, vol. 19.

48. Bentinck to Chamberlain, Addis Abeba, 26 Sept. 1927, FO 371/12341.

49. Same to same, Addis Abeba, 15 Jan. 1927, FO 371/12339.

50. Same to same, Addis Abeba, 25 July 1927, FO 371/12341.

51. Record of Colonial Office and Foreign Office Discussions about Lake Tana, London, 10 Oct. 1927, ibid. For a complete study of the Anglo-Ethiopian negotiations about the dam, see James McCann, "Ethiopia, Britain, and Negotiations for the Lake Tana Dam Project," *International Journal of African Historical Studies* 14 (1981).

52. Howard to Foreign Office, Washington, 4 and 5 Nov. 1927, FO 371/12342.

53. "Abyssinia Sees Independence at Stake in Tsana Dispute," *New York Times*, 13 Nov. 1927.

54. "Abyssinian Dam Flurry Called Publicity Bid," *New York Herald Tribune*, 13 Nov. 1927.

55. "The U.S. Insists on Open Door in Abyssinia," *San Francisco Chronicle*, 13 Nov. 1927.

56. "Two African Visitors Entertained by Harlem," *New York World*, 20 Nov. 1927.

57. FO to Lord Lloyd, London, 19 Dec. 1927, FO 371/12343.
58. Especially productive provinces were vulnerable. Addis Abeba wanted to control Jima, autonomous by treaty since 1884, which had a thriving coffee business. In 1928, the city-state paid an annual tribute of MT$102,000, of which MT$15,000 was delivered directly to regional army units for maintenance. Understanding how precarious his authority really was, Abba Jifar sought to buy Tafari's support; he helped pay for the ras's trip to Europe, the marriage of Princess Tenenya Work to Fit. Desta Demtu in November 1924, holiday costs, weapons acquisitions, and the like. In 1927, such additional demands amounted to MT$120,000, not counting gifts for visiting central government or provincial officials and those sent to important nonroyal Addis Abebans. The supplementary donations kept pace with Jima's growing economy, which it guarded zealously from northerners and the central government. Enrico Cerulli, Report, "Jimma Abbajifar," enclosure in Cora to minister, Addis Abeba, 27 March 1928, IFM/MAI, 54/34–137. See also above, chapter 6, pp. 120–121.
59. Bahru, "Absolutist State," p. 22; Charles W. McClellan, "Politics and Change in Ethiopia's Southern Periphery—Darasa in the 1920s and 1930s" (Conference paper, Stanford University, 1982), pp. 17–18.
60. *Autobiography*, p. 151.
61. Cora to minister, Addis Abeba, 18 April 1928, IFM/MAI, 54/34–137.
62. *Autobiography*, p. 151.
63. Ibid., p. 152.
64. Cora to minister, Addis Abeba, 18 April 1928, IFM/MAI, 54/34–137.
65. Marse Hazan Wolde Qirqos, "YeZaman Tarik Tezzetaye BaNegesta Negastat Zawditu Zamana Mangist" (Unpubl. ms., Institute of Ethiopian Studies, Addis Abeba University, n.d.), pp. 395–396.
66. Bentinck to Chamberlain, Addis Abeba, 21 Feb. 1928, FO 371/13101; Cora to minister, Addis Abeba, 18 April 1928, IFM/MAI, 54/34–137.
67. Cora to minister, Addis Abeba, 18 April 1928, IFM/MAI, 54/34–137; Notizario politico, Nov.-Dec. 1928, IFM/MAI, 54/26–99.
68. Report on Leading Personalities in Abyssinia, in Bentinck to Chamberlain, Addis Abeba, 18 Feb. 1928, FO 371/13112.
69. Southard to Secretary of State, Addis Abeba, 19 June 1928, SD, Records.
70. Bentinck to Chamberlain, Addis Abeba, 4 April 1928, FO 371/13101.
71. Abyssinian Intelligence Report n. 7 for July and August 1928, FO 371/13103; Reffye to minister, Addis Abeba, 7 Aug. 1928, FFM, K-Afrique, Ethiopie, Affaires générales, vol. 19.
72. Guillon to Minister of War, Addis Abeba, 8 Sept. 1928, FFM, K-Afrique, Ethiopie, Affaires générales, vol. 19.
73. *Autobiography*, p. 153.
74. Southard to Secretary of State, Addis Abeba, 7 Sept. 1928, SD.
75. Reffye to minister, Addis Abeba, 8 Oct. 1928, FFM, K-Afrique, Ethiopie, Affaires générales, vol. 19.

76. *Autobiography*, pp. 153–155; Marse Hazan, "Zawditu," p. 146; Dunbar to Cushendon, Addis Abeba, 22 Oct. 1928, FO 371/13103.

77. Reffye to minister, Addis Abeba, 29 Sept. 1928, FFM, Ethiopie, Affaires générales, vol. 19.

78. Dunbar to Cushendon, Addis Abeba, 22 Oct. 1928, FO 371/13103.

79. "La cérémonie de Courronnement du Négous Tafari Makonnen," *Correspondance d'Ethiopie*, Dec. 1928, 66.

80. See the Amharic text beneath the autographed picture that Hailu gave to an Italian visitor, IFM, Affari Politici, pacco 1031, fasc. 3119.

81. Scey to minister, Addis Abeba, 7 Feb. 1928, FFM, K-Afrique, Ethiopie, Affaires générales, vol. 19.

82. Gizachew Adamu, "A Historical Survey of Taxation in Gojjam, 1901–1969" (B.A. essay, Addis Abeba University, 1971), pp. 2–11.

83. Southard to Secretary of State, Addis Abeba, 11 Dec. 1928, SD, Records.

84. And Alem Mulaw, "Begemdir and Simiem (1910–1930)" (B.A. essay, Addis Abeba University, 1971), pp. 41–42, 53; Brielli to Cora, Dese, 23 June 1928, IFM/MAI, 54/26–98.

85. Southard to Secretary of State, Addis Abeba, 14 Jan. 1929, SD, Records.

86. Reffye to minister, Addis Abeba, 22 May 1929, FFM, K-Afrique, Ethiopie, Affaires générales, vol. 20; same to same, Addis Abeba, 10 April 1930, Archives of the French Foreign Ministry, Afrique, 1930–1940, Ethiopie, Correspondance générale politique, vol. 59 (hereafter cited as FFM, Afrique-Eth., 1930–1940, politique, vol. 59, et seq.).

87. Reffye to minister, Addis Abeba, 11 June 1929, FFM, K-Afrique, Ethiopie, Affaires générales, vol. 20.

88. Reffye to minister, Addis Abeba, 27 July 1929, ibid.

89. Same to same, Addis Abeba, 29 Aug. 1929, ibid. For the best description of the rebellion, see James McCann, "The Political Economy of Rural Rebellion in Ethiopia: Northern Resistance to Imperial Expansion, 1928–1935," *International Journal of African Historical Studies* 18 (1985): 601ff.

90. Zoli to Colonies, Asmera, 12 Dec. 1929, IFM/MAI, 54/26–99; same to same, Asmera, 17 Dec. 1929; same to same, Asmera, 8 Feb. 1930; Lij Abbai to Kidana Mariam, Gonder, 3 Feb. 1930; Cora Report, "Situazione Politica in Etiopia," Addis Abeba, 30 April 1930, IFM/MAI, 54/26–100.

91. Southard to Secretary of State, Addis Abeba, 20 Jan. 1930, 12 Feb. 1930, United States National Archives, Decimal Files of the Department of State, 1930–1949 (hereafter cited as SD, followed by a decimal classification), 884.00/177, /184; Barton to FO, Addis Abeba, 8 Oct. 1930, FO 371/13834; *Autobiography*, pp. 158–161.

92. "The Victory of Dejazmatch Mulugeta, Minister of War, over Ras Gugsa Wolie," *Berhanena Selam*, 10 April 1930; Zoli to ministry, Asmera, 14 and 21 Feb., 13 and 17 March 1930, IFM/MAI, 54/26–100.

93. Legation to minister, Addis Abeba, 17 March 1930, IFM/MAI, 54/26–

100; Southard to Secretary of State, SD 884.00/186; Barton to Henderson, Addis Abeba, 4 March 1930, FO 371/14595.

94. Reffye to minister, Addis Abeba, 10 April 1930, FFM, Afrique-Eth., 1930–1940, politique, vol. 59; Park to Secretary of State, Addis Abeba, 1 April 1930, SD 884.00/190; Marse Hazan, "Zawditu," p. 520.

95. Cf. Harold G. Marcus, *The Life and Times of Menelik II: Ethiopia, 1844–1913* (Oxford, 1975), p. 234.

96. Barton to Henderson, Addis Abeba, 17 April 1930, FO 371/14595; Reffye to minister, Addis Abeba, 10 April 1930, FFM, Afrique-Eth., 1930–1940, politique, vol. 59; Park to Secretary of State, Addis Abeba, 5 April 1930, SD 884.0011/13.

97. Barton to Henderson, Addis Abeba, 17 April 1930, FO 371/14595.

98. "Proclamation," *Berhanena Selam*, 17 April 1930.

CHAPTER SIX

1. *Autobiography*, p. 172.

2. John H. Spencer, "Haile Sellassie: Leadership and Statesmanship," *Ethiopianist Notes* 2, no. 1 (1978): 29–31.

3. Barton to Henderson, Addis Abeba, 25 April 1930, FO 371/14595.

4. Fan C. Dunckley, *Eight Years in Abyssinia* (London, 1935), p. 29.

5. Plans were made to link Addis Abeba to Gojam and Begemdir, to Bale, and to Jima; Gambela to Gore and Sayo; Jijiga to Hargeisa in British Somaliland; and Dese to Aseb. Barton to Henderson, Addis Abeba, 7 Jan. 1930, FO 371/14595.

6. "Motor Cars in Abyssinia," *Morning Post*, 1 Feb. 1929.

7. Henri Rebeaud, *Chez le Roi des Rois d'Ethiopie* (Paris, 1935), p. 119.

8. Olle Erickson, "Education in Abyssinia," *Africa* 5 (1932): 341.

9. Rebeaud, *Roi des Rois*, pp. 136, 142, 156.

10. "Une étude retrospective des achèvements de la régence," *Le Courrier d'Ethiopie*, 16 May 1930.

11. Ibid.

12. Intelligence Report for January 1929, from H.B.M. Consul Western Abyssinia, Gore, FO 371/13838.

13. James McCann, "Households, Peasants, and Rural History in Lasta, Northern Ethiopia, 1930–35" (Ph.D. diss., Michigan State University, 1984), p. 213.

14. Salvatore Tedeschi, "La carrière et les idées de Heruy Wäldä-Sellasié (1878–1938)," in *Trois Essais sur la Littérature Ethiopienne*, issued by Bibliotèque Peiresc (Antibes, 1984), pp. 40–43, 66–67, 83; "Blattengeta Herui," in Martino Moreno, compiler, *Biografie Etiopiche*, transmitted to the Minister of Foreign Affairs, 30 June 1935, Historical Archives of the Italian Foreign Ministry, Etiopia, Fondo de Guerra, 1935–1941, busta 5 (hereafter cited as Moreno, *Biografie*, IFM, Guerra); Bentinck to Chamberlain, Addis Abeba, 26 Aug. 1927, FO 371/12339.

15. Southard to Secretary of State, Addis Abeba, 8 Nov. 1928, SD,

Records; Barton to Henderson, Addis Abeba, 19 Oct. 1929, FO 371/13840; Reffye to minister, Addis Abeba, 4 Oct. 1930, FFM, Afrique-Eth., 1930–1940, politique, vol. 59.

16. FO to War Office, London, 28 Oct. 1929, FO 371/13831.

17. Astuto Memo. of Conversation with Murray, Paris, 16 Nov. 1929, IFM, Affari Politici, pacco 1035, fasc. 3151.

18. Astuto Memo. of Conversation with Murray, Paris, 19 Nov. 1929, ibid.

19. Minutes of Meeting of the Seventh Session, Paris, 29 Nov. 1929, FFM, K-Afrique, Ethiopie, Réunion de Paris, 1929–1930, vol. 29.

20. Minute by Noble, Paris, 4 Dec. 1929, FO 371/13832.

21. Southard to Secretary of State, Addis Abeba, 16 Jan. 1930, and State Department Internal Memo., Washington, 7 March 1930, SD 884.113. For complete details, see Harold G. Marcus, "The Embargo on Arms Sales to Ethiopia, 1916–1930," *International Journal of African Historical Studies* 16, no. 2 (1983).

22. "Renseignements présentées par la Délégation éthiopienne sur le program d'achats de matériel militaire au cours des prochaines années," encl. 2 in Tyrell to Henderson, Paris, 27 May 1930, FO 371/14587.

23. Murray to Campbell, London, 31 May and 2 June 1930, ibid.

24. French Government Note, 6 June 1930, FFM, Afrique-Eth., 1930–1940, Armes. Exportations. Importations. Conference des Armes, Convention du Août 1930, vol. 129.

25. Murray to Osborne, London, 14 July 1930, and Aide Mémoire delivered to the Italian Foreign Ministry, 18 July 1930, FO 371/14587.

26. Osborne to FO, Rome, 18 July 1930, ibid.

27. Minutes of the Ninth Session, Paris, 31 July 1930, FFM, K-Afrique, Ethiopie, Réunion de Paris, 1929–1930, vol. 29.

28. Ibid.

29. Campbell to Henderson, Paris, 14 Aug. 1930, FO 371/14588.

30. Treaty between the United Kingdom, Abyssinia, France, and Italy, regarding the Importation into Abyssinia of Arms, Ammunition, and Implements of War, Paris, 21 Aug. 1930, HMG, *British and Foreign State Papers, 1931* (London, 1936), pp. 332–351.

31. Adugna Amanu, "The Ethiopian Orthodox Church Becomes Autocephalous" (B.A. essay, Addis Abeba University, 1969), pp. 3–6, 10–13.

32. Lloyd to Chamberlain, Cairo, 19 June 1927, FO 371/12349.

33. Bentinck to minister, Addis Abeba, 28 Feb. 1927, ibid.; Adugna, "Ethiopian Orthodox Church," p. 15.

34. Bentinck to minister, Addis Abeba, 29 April 1927, FO 371/12349.

35. Lloyd to Chamberlain, Cairo, 30 March 1929, FO 371/13830; Adugna, "Ethiopian Orthodox Church," p. 19; *Autobiography*, p. 169.

36. Dunbar to Lloyd, Addis Abeba, 14 May 1929, FO 371/13830; *Autobiography*, p. 170–171. The quintet included Etchege Gebre Manfas Keddus of Debra Lebanos (then ailing), later Abuna Sawiros of Southern Ethiopia; Mahmer (teacher-priest) Haile Mariam, Tafari's confessor, who would be-

come Abuna Petros of Wello and Yeju; Mahmer Kidane Wold, Ras Kassa's confessor, later Abuna Yeshaq of Tigray, Lasta, Wag, and environs; Mahmer Desta, head of the palace's St. Gabriel's Church, subsequently called Abuna Abraham of Gojam and Begemdir; and Mahmer Haile Mikail, pastor of Addis Abeba's St. Ureal's Church, who would be known as Abuna Mikail of western Ethiopia.

37. Lloyd to minister, Cairo, 5 June 1929, FO 371/13830.

38. Dunbar to Henderson, Addis Abeba, 20 June 1929, ibid.

39. *Autobiography*, p. 171.

40. Memo. by Southard, "Money and Exchange Difficulties in Ethiopia," Addis Abeba, 20 Nov. 1929, SD 884.5151; Barton to FO, Addis Abeba, 17 March 1930, FO 371/14595.

41. Hoare to Henderson, Cairo, 11 April 1930, and Barton to FO, Addis Abeba, 20 June 1930, FO 371/14595.

42. In 1930, a commissioned report by the Morgan Guaranty Bank and Trust Co. of New York convinced the emperor to buy the bank and then to introduce a national monetary policy. See enclosure in Southard to Blattangeta Herui, Addis Abeba, 18 Aug. 1930, SD 884.51/8.

43. Haile Sellassie to Park, Addis Abeba, 7 July 1930, in Park to Secretary of State, Addis Abeba, 8 July 1930, SD 884.516-State/7.

44. Chancery to FO, Cairo, 6 Dec. 1930, FO 371/14596.

45. Barton to FO, Addis Abeba, 14 July 1931, FO 371/15385.

46. Southard to Secretary of State, Addis Abeba, 2 Jan. 1928, and 4 Feb. 1929, SD, Records.

47. Southard to Secretary of State, Addis Abeba, 21 Sept. 1929, ibid.; Jon R. Edwards, " 'And the King Shall Judge': The Capitulary Regime in Ethiopia, 1908–1936," in *Proceedings of the Seventh International Conference of Ethiopian Studies*, edited by Sven Rubenson (Addis Abeba, Uppsala, East Lansing, 1984), passim, pp. 373–380.

48. Ethiopia, for example, was determined to keep control over its communications. The government decided that telephone and telegraphic installations would be an official monopoly and advised all legations that transmitters would be forbidden once the Ethiopian stations were operating, although diplomats were allowed to retain their receivers. See Dunbar to FO, Addis Abeba, 15 Feb. 1929, FO 371/13833.

49. See IFM/MAI, 54/22, which reveals the failure of Italy's policy of economic penetration.

50. Lloyd to FO, Cairo, 9 Feb. 1929, FO 371/13835.

51. Cora Report, "Finanze etiopiche," in Cora to minister, Addis Abeba, 14 Sept. 1929, IFM/MAI, 54/36–147.

52. Ibid.; "Appunti sulla Riunione Tenutsi a Palazzo Chigi il 27/6/1930," IFM, Affari Politici, pacco 1036.

53. Cora to minister, Addis Abeba, 27 May 1930, IFM/MAI, 54/4–3.

54. Barton to Henderson, Addis Abeba, 6 Feb. and 5 Aug. 1930, FO 371/14592.

55. Curle to Barton, in the Ogaden, 21 June 1930, FO 371/14598.

56. Minute J2666 by A. Noble, 8 Aug. 1930, commenting on above, ibid.

57. Park to Secretary of State, Addis Abeba, 7 May 1930, SD 884.00/203.

58. Same to same, Addis Abeba, 21 May 1930, SD 884.00/205.

59. *Autobiography*, p. 172.

60. Troutbeck to FO, Addis Abeba, 7 May 1930, FO 371/14596.

61. *Autobiography*, pp. 174–175; Reffye to minister, Addis Abeba, 24 May 1930, FFM, Afrique-Eth., 1930–1940, Couronnement de l'Empereur Hayle Sellassie Ier, vol. 61. Dunckley (*Eight Years*, p. 213) claimed MT\$4 million, but Barton put the figure closer to MT\$20 million; Barton to Murray, Addis Abeba, FO 371/15388.

62. Dunckley, *Eight Years*, pp. 181–183; Rebeaud, *Roi des Rois*, pp. 172–173.

63. Reffye to minister, Addis Abeba, 14 Nov. 1930, FFM, Afrique-Eth., 1930–1940, Couronnement, vol. 61.

64. Evelyn Waugh, *When the Going Was Good* (London, 1948), p. 90.

65. Dunckley, *Eight Years*, pp. 189, 204.

66. W. Robert Moore, "Coronation Days in Addis Ababa," *National Geographic* 59 (1931): 738–739.

67. Brig. Gen. William W. Harts, Aide to the Special Ambassador, "Report of Mission on Visit to Ethiopia," Paris, 12 Jan. 1931, SD 884.001-Sell. 1/226 (hereafter cited as the Harts Report).

68. Waugh, *When the Going Was Good*, p. 102.

69. Harts Report; Asfa Yilma, *Haile Selassie, Emperor of Ethiopia* (London, 1936), p. 213.

70. Harts Report.

71. Ibid.

72. Evelyn Waugh, *Waugh in Abyssinia* (London, 1936), p. 8.

73. Moore, "Coronation Days," p. 743.

74. Ibid., p. 745.

75. Harts Report.

76. Barton to Henderson, Addis Abeba, 17 Nov. 1930, FO 371/14598.

77. Moore, "Coronation Days," p. 745.

78. Park to Secretary of State, Addis Abeba, 5 July 1930, SD 884.002/9; Southard to Secretary of State, Addis Abeba, 22 Sept. 1931, SD 884.002/16; Tesfaye Ababe, "The Life and Career of Dejjazmatch Takala Walda Hawariat" (B.A. essay, Addis Abeba University, 1971), pp. 10, 12–13.

79. "Confidential Biographic Data" Sheets on Biru Menilek, SD 884.00, and Nasibu Zamanuel, SD 884.002; Park to Secretary of State, Addis Abeba, 24 June 1930, SD 884.00/209; Southard to Secretary of State, Addis Abeba, 26 June 1931, 884.002/13; Paterno to minister, Addis Abeba, 23 Jan. 1931, IFM/MAI, 54/37–149.

80. Gaussen to minister, Stockholm, 3 March 1931, and Legation to minister, Addis Abeba, 25 July 1931, FFM, Afrique-Eth., 1930–1940, Correspondance politique, vol. 59.

81. Troutbeck to FO, Addis Abeba, 21 April 1931, FO 371/15382.
82. Legation to minister, Addis Abeba, 17 Feb. 1931, IFM/MAI, 54/37–149.
83. Paterno to minister, Addis Abeba, 24 April 1931, IFM/MAI, 54/4–3.
84. Barton to Henderson, Addis Abeba, 9 Feb. 1931, FO 371/15389.
85. *Autobiography*, pp. 178–179; Southard to Secretary of State, Addis Abeba, 6 Dec. 1930, SD 884.01/26.
86. John Markakis and Asmelash Beyene, "Representative Institutions in Ethiopia," *Journal of Modern African Studies* 5 (1967): 201.
87. Southard to Secretary of State, Addis Abeba, 16 July 1931, SD 884.011/1.
88. Translation of Decree, Haile Sellassie Speech of 16 July 1931, and List of Signatories of the Ethiopian Constitution, enclosures, SD 884.011/1; Barton to Henderson, Addis Abeba, 22 July 1931, and enclosures, FO 371/15389; cf. *Autobiography*, pp. 180–185.
89. Constitution of Ethiopia in Barton to Henderson, Addis Abeba, 27 July 1931, FO 371/15389.
90. Asrat Tassie, "The Status and Role of the Ethiopian Parliament: A New Appraisal" (B.A. essay, Addis Abeba University, 1971), p. 3.
91. Markakis and Asmelash, "Representative Institutions," p. 203.
92. Southard to Secretary of State, Addis Abeba, 4 and 7 Nov. 1931, both with many enclosures, SD 884.03/3 and /4; Moreno to minister, Addis Abeba, 17 Nov. 1931, IFM/MAI, 54/31–124; Reffye to minister, Addis Abeba, 21 April 1932, FFM, Afrique-Eth., 1930–1940, Correspondance politique, vol. 59.
93. There is at least one report that Hailu paid ridiculously little— MT$6,000 for 1928–1929—to the central treasury as tribute. See Zoli to minister, ? March 1929, IFM/MAI, 54/4–3.
94. See, for example, Southard to Secretary of State, Addis Abeba, 7 Aug. 1930, SD 884.00/212.
95. Guariglia Relazione a Sua Eccellenze il Capo del Governo, Rome, 21 Aug. 1929, IFM/MAI, 54/4–3.
96. Barton to Simon, Addis Abeba, 18 April 1932, FO 371/16102.
97. Legation to minister, Addis Abeba, 14 March 1932, IFM/MAI, 54/36–147. In the provinces, the following rhyme was then popular:

> Oh! Ras [Hailu]!
> You have taken my cattle; you robbed my wealth,
> You have left me my empty belly!
> Oh! do take the belly . . . which means hunger and want
> For me,
> All the hunger with the belly take,
> So that I may rest and sleep in peace!

(As quoted in Mehari Yohannes, "Debra Markos Awraja-Gojjam. Local Administration: The Role of Traditional Elements" [B.A. essay, Addis Abeba University, 1970], p. 12.)

98. Southard to Secretary of State, Addis Abeba, 9 April 1932, SD 884.00/235.

99. Reffye to minister, Addis Abeba, 21 April 1932, FFM, Afrique-Eth., 1930–1940, Correspondance politique, vol. 59.

100. Legation to minister, Addis Abeba, IFM/MAI, 54/36–147.

101. Southard to Secretary of State, Addis Abeba, 23 May 1932, SD 884.00/243.

102. Editorial, *Berhanena Selam,* 5 May 1932.

103. "Kindness to the Country and to the People," ibid., 12 May 1932.

104. Haile Sellassie sought to characterize Hailu as an Italian agent, but there is nothing in the Italian archives to indicate any treachery. *Autobiography,* pp. 201–206; cf. "Ligg Jasu-Fuga e Cattura," IFM/MAI, 54/37–150b.

105. Kenefe-Regb Zelleke, "The Episode of Eyasu Menelik (1896–1935)" (Conference paper, Lund, 1982); Philip Zaphiro, "The Story of Lij Yasu's Escape and Recapture," in Barton to Simon, Addis Abeba, 28 June 1932, FO 371/16102; Ruggero to Minister of War, Addis Abeba, 20 June 1932, IFM/MAI, 54/37–150b; Southard to Secretary of State, Addis Abeba, 13 June 1932, SD 884.00/248.

106. "The Judgment of Ras Hailu," *Berhanena Selam,* 30 June 1932.

CHAPTER SEVEN

1. Southard to Secretary of State, Addis Abeba, 28 June 1932, SD 884.00/256.

2. Medici to legation, Debre Markos, 30 July 1932, IFM/MAI, 54/37–149.

3. Southard to Secretary of State, Addis Abeba, 18 Oct. 1932, SD 884.00/267.

4. "Small Incident in Debre Markos, Gojam," *Berhanena Selam,* 20 Oct. 1932.

5. Medici to legation, Debre Markos, 22 December 1932, IFM/MAI, 54/37–149.

6. Falconi to legation, Debre Markos, 15 September 1934, IFM/MAI, 54/37–150b.

7. Ababa Kiflayasus, "The Career of Liul Ras Imru Hayla Sillase" (B.A. essay, Addis Abeba University, 1973), pp. 32–33.

8. Southard to Secretary of State, Addis Abeba, 24 Oct. 1932, SD 884.00/268.

9. Ibid. See also M. S. Lush, "Abyssinia 1932," National Records Office, Khartoum, Sudan, Palace, Class 4/Box 4/File 13.

10. John H. Spencer, "Haile Selassie: Triumph and Tragedy," *Orbis* 18 (Winter 1975): 1142; Ryszard Kapuściński, *The Emperor: Downfall of an Autocrat* (New York, 1983), p. 11.

11. Lessona to minister, Rome, 27 July 1931, IFM/MAI, 54/31–124.

12. Astuto to De Bono, Asmera, 18 Feb. 1931, IFM/MAI, 54/36–147. See Harold G. Marcus, "Disease, Hospitals, and Italian Colonial Aspirations in Ethiopia, 1930–1935," *Northeast African Studies* 1, no. 1 (1979).

13. Relazione per Sua Eccelenza il Capo del Governo, Rome, 12 Jan.

1932, Historical Archives of the Italian Foreign Ministry, Etiopia, Serie Affari Politici, 1931–1935, (hereafter cited as IFM, Serie Affari Politici), busta 21.

14. See the entire file, IFM/MAI, 54/22, which details the Italian failure; Record of Conversation with Paterno, n.d., in Southard to Secretary of State, Addis Abeba, 20 Oct. 1931, SD 884.00/224.

15. Paterno, "Schematico Riassunto della Situazione Etiopica," Rome, 19 Aug. 1932, IFM, Serie Affari Politici, busta 6.

16. Guariglia Memo. of 18 Feb. 1932, for Grandi, ibid., busta 13.

17. Guariglia's appreciation of Haile Sellassie's nation building differed sharply from the hostile and competing media view, later wartime propaganda, that the emperor only exercised power in Addis Abeba, outside of which lived a population hostile to "the Abyssinians . . . ethnically different, speaking diverse languages, where the laws emanating from the government are ignored and where they are tyrannized by local chiefs." The so-called Abyssinians were inherently corrupt, decadent, reactionary, and rapacious, unwilling to abandon slavery and feudalism. See, for example, Paterno to minister, Addis Abeba, 20 June 1931, ibid., busta 2.

18. Relazione Guariglia sull'Etiopia, 27 Aug. 1932, ibid.

19. See above, chapter 5, pp. 86–87.

20. "Abyssinia," *Near East*, 4 May 1931.

21. Reffye to minister, Addis Abeba, 2 April 1931, FFM, Afrique-Eth., 1930–1940, Relations et Conventions commerciales, Tarifs douaniers, vol. 135.

22. Legation to ministry, Addis Abeba, 18 Nov. 1931, ibid.

23. Reffye to minister, Addis Abeba, 2 April 1931, ibid.

24. Note pour le Ministre, Paris, 10 March 1931, FFM, Afrique-Eth., 1930–1940, Projet d'Alliance entre la France et l'Ethiopie, vol. 62.

25. Beaumarchais to Briand, Rome, 25 April 1931, ibid.

26. Renzo de Felice, *Mussolini, il Duce, gli Anni del Consenso* (Turin, 1974), pp. 397–398; Grandi to Mussolini, 25 July 1931, Rome, Archivo Centrale del Stato, Grandi Papers, F3/SF2. The British also noted the same tendency; see Tyrell to Henderson, Paris, 1 Aug. 1931, FO 371/15255. I want to thank Dr. Peter C. Kent of the University of New Brunswick for having made the last two documents available to me.

27. Guariglia Memo. of 18 Feb. 1932 for Grandi, IFM, Serie Affari Politici, busta 13.

28. Relazione Guariglia sull'Etiopia, 27 Aug. 1932, ibid.

29. Reffye to minister, Addis Abeba, 9 Nov. 1932, FFM, Afrique-Eth., 1930–1940, Correspondance politique, vol. 59.

30. Reffye to minister, Addis Abeba, 9 and 16 March, 14 April 1932; and military attaché, "Etudes sommaire du refus ou de l'acceptation des offres d'alliance faites par l'Ethiopie à la France," Addis Abeba, 5 April 1932, FFM, Afrique-Eth., 1930–1940, Projet d'Alliance, vol. 62.

31. Tardieu to Reffye, Paris, 2 May 1932, ibid.

32. Reffye to minister, Addis Abeba, 13 and 24 May 1932, and Tardieu to Reffye, Paris, 26 May 1932, ibid. Also see Reffye to minister, Paris, 21 July and 8 Sept. 1932, FFM, Afrique-Eth., 1930–1940, Projet d'Alliance, vol. 63.

33. Barton to Reading, Addis Abeba, 23 Oct. 1931, and enclosed extract of Wetherbe to Barton, n.p., 7 Oct. 1931, FO 371/15384.

34. Kittermaster to Thomas, Sheikh, 4 Sept. 1931, ibid.

35. Editorial, *Berhanena Selam*, 24 Sept. 1931.

36. Wetherbe to Barton, n.p., 7 Oct. 1931, in Barton to Reading, Addis Abeba, 23 Oct. 1931, FO 371/15384.

37. Moreno Memo., Addis Abeba, 16 Dec. 1931, IFM/MAI, 54/12–34.

38. Fuccio to legation, Magalo, 1 Jan. 1932, ibid.

39. Editorial, *Berhanena Selam*, 5 Nov. 1931; "Ogaden Expedition," *Berhanena Selam*, 31 Dec. 1931.

40. See the many relevant despatches in IFM/MAI, 54/12–34.

41. Ibid.

42. Rava to Minister of Colonies, Mogadishu, 22 June 1932; cf. "Bollettino Informazioni sull'Ogaden dal 18 Febbraio al 14 Marzo 1932," ibid.

43. De Bono Memo. to Minister of Foreign Affairs, n.d., ibid.

44. I remain perplexed by the view from a very remote scholarly vantage that "De Bono overestimated the Emperor's internal achievement." The comparative situation showed that Haile Sellassie's accomplishment was great in terms of the economic stagnation in Eritrea and Somalia. See Esmonde M. Robertson, *Mussolini as Empire-Builder* (London, 1977), pp. 10, 28.

45. Emilio De Bono, *La Preparazione e le Prime Operazioni* (Rome, 1937), p. 2; Giorgio Rochat, *Militari e Politici nella Preparazioni della Campagna d'Etiopia* (Milan, 1971), pp. 26–27.

46. De Bono, *Preparazione*, p. 5.

47. Renato Mori, *Mussolini e la Conquista dell'Etiopia* (Florence, 1978), p. 4.

48. Felice, *Mussolini*, p. 418.

49. George W. Baer, *The Coming of the Italo-Ethiopian War* (Cambridge, Mass., 1967), p. 31.

50. Manfred Funke, *Sanktionen und Kanonen* (Düsseldorf, 1970), p. 35.

51. Cf. Dennis Mack Smith, *Mussolini's Roman Empire* (New York, 1976), pp. 60, 65.

52. "The Inauguration of a Bridge at Akaki, near Addis Ababa," *Berhanena Selam*, 24 Sept. 1931.

53. Southard to Secretary of State, Addis Abeba, 5 Jan. 1932, SD 884.154/56; Bahru Zewde, "The Fumbling Debut of British Capital in Ethiopia: A Contrastive Study of the Abyssinian Corporation and the Ethiopian Motor Transport Company Ltd.," in *Proceedings of the Seventh International Conference of Ethiopian Studies*, edited by Sven Rubenson (Addis Abeba, Uppsala, East Lansing, 1984), p. 335.

54. Addis Abeba Intelligence Report for the Quarter ending 31 Dec. 1932, FO 371/16997.

55. Addis Abeba Intelligence Report for the Quarter ending 31 Dec. 1933, FO 371/18031.

56. Addis Abeba Intelligence Report for the Quarter ending 30 June 1934, ibid.

57. Reece to FO, Nairobi, 20 Oct. 1932, FO 371/16989; Reffye to minister, Addis Abeba, 13 July 1932, FFM, Afrique-Eth., 1930–1940, Affaires commerciales, vol. 134.

58. Southard to Secretary of State, Addis Abeba, 24 Jan. 1933, SD 884.515/12; Broadmead to Simon, Addis Abeba, 6 Oct. 1933, FO 371/16995.

59. Southard to Secretary of State, Addis Abeba, 11 Sept. 1933, SD 884.515/15.

60. Same to same, Addis Abeba, 11 Oct. 1934, SD 884.515/20.

61. Same to same, Addis Abeba, 3 Jan. 1933, SD 884.242/3.

62. Same to same, Addis Abeba, 21 March 1933, SD 884.24/41.

63. Lt. Col. Ruggero, Notizario del Mese di Marzo 1933, Maggio 1933, Luglio 1933, Agosto 1933, Ottobre 1933, Novembre 1933, IFM/MAI, 54/25–93.

64. Campion to Wallinger, War Office, 6 Feb. 1933, and Barton to Simon, Addis Abeba, 20 Feb. 1933, FO 371/16996.

65. Southard to Secretary of State, Addis Abeba, 6 April 1933, SD 884.20/18.

66. Barton to Simon, 8 April and 16 May 1933, FO 371/16996.

67. Ruggero, Notizario del Mese di Ottobre 1933, IFM/MAI, 54/25–93.

68. Col. H. R. G. Stevens to H. M. Chargé, Addis Abeba, 20 Dec. 1933, FO 371/18029; Lt. Jacques Dargis reported that he had trouble getting his soldiers to appear for drill, that Ethiopian officers resented their European counterparts and obstructed training, and that guardsmen did not receive promised equipment because of embezzlement in the high command. See Henri Rebeaud, "Au Service du Négous [Récit inédit]," I, *Tous les Vendredis*, 8 March 1935.

69. Barton to Simon, Addis Abeba, 29 May 1934, FO 371/18029; Memos. by military attaché, Addis Abeba, 29 Sept. 1934, FFM, Afrique-Eth., 1930–1940, Affaires politiques, dossier général, vol. 60.

70. Southard to Secretary of State, Addis Abeba, 20 Sept. 1934, 884.20/22; about arms acquisitions, see FO 371/18028, most of which is devoted to the subject.

71. Gen. Eric Virgin, *The Abyssinia I Knew* (London, 1936), pp. 118–121.

72. Maaza Bekele, "A Study of Modern Education in Ethiopia: Its Foundations, Its Development, Its Future, with Emphasis on Primary Education" (Ph.D. diss., Columbia University Teachers College, 1966), pp. 61–65.

73. Zelleke Tachbele, "Unity," *Berhanena Selam*, 28 Dec. 1933.

74. G. L. Steer, *Caesar in Abyssinia* (London, 1936), pp. 73–74.

75. Southard to Secretary of State, Addis Abeba, 12 Feb. 1934, 884.4016/6; Ladislas Farago, *Abyssinia on the Eve* (London, 1935), p. 66.

76. See the two-part article on Eritrea in *Berhanena Selam*, 20 Sept. and 18 Oct. 1934.

77. Southard to Secretary of State, Addis Abeba, 23 Jan. 1932, SD 884.01A/22.

78. Same to same, Addis Abeba, 30 July 1930, SD 884.01A/8.

79. Same to same, Addis Abeba, 14 April 1931, SD 884.42A-Work/8.

80. Report by Mr. de Halpert on His Period of Service with the Ethiopian Government, Addis Abeba, 22 May 1934, in Barton to Simon, Addis Abeba, 18 June 1934, FO 371/18030 (hereafter cited as de Halpert Report).

81. Vinci to minister, Addis Abeba, 18 April 1933, IFM/MAI, 54/4–3; Fuccio to legation, Magalo, 27 Oct. 1933, 54/14–44.

82. De Halpert Report.

83. Virgin, *Abyssinia*, pp. 79–80.

84. Steer, *Caesar*, pp. 28–29.

85. Virgin, *Abyssinia*, pp. 82, 84.

86. Dr. Lecco Report on the Death of Ras Gugsa, in Astuto to De Bono, 16 May 1933, IFM/MAI, 54/38–159.

87. Southard to Secretary of State, Addis Abeba, 16 June 1932 and 27 March 1933, SD 884.0011/50 and 55; see also "The Dead Shall Rise and Their Works Shall Follow Them," *Berhanena Selam*, 30 March 1933.

88. Southard to Secretary of State, Addis Abeba, 19 May 1934, SD 884.00/293.

89. Vinci to minister, Addis Abeba, 11 May 1934, IFM/MAI, 54/38–158.

90. Pollici, Appunto per Sua Eccellenza, Addis Abeba, 17 May 1934; Vinci to Mussolini, Addis Abeba, 21 May 1934, ibid.

91. For a similar conclusion, see Haggai Erlich, "Tigre in Modern History," in *Proceedings of the Seventh International Conference of Ethiopian Studies*, edited by Sven Rubenson (Addis Abeba, Uppsala, East Lansing, 1984), p. 328.

92. Astuto to De Bono, Asmera, 9 June 1934, IFM/MAI, 54/38–158.

93. Appunto per S.E. l'Alto Commissario, Asmera, 5 Feb. 1935, ibid.

94. De Bono, *Preparazione*, p. 9. The comments above in chapter 4, note 84, are equally apt here.

95. Rochat, *Militari e Politici*, p. 39.

96. Intercepted Messages of Lij Tedla Haile, April 1934 to Feb. 1935, IFM/MAI, 54/6–17.

97. Rochat, *Militari e Politici*, pp. 24, 29.

98. Reffye to minister, Addis Abeba, 7 Jan. 1934, FFM, Afrique-Eth., 1930–1940, Affaires politiques, Italie-Ethiopie, 1931–1934, vol. 65; William Shorrock, "The Jouvenal Mission to Rome and the Origins of the Laval-Mussolini Accords, 1933–1935," *Historian* 46, no. 1 (1982): 20–35.

99. Vinci to minister, Addis Abeba, 22 May 1934, IFM, Serie Affari Politici, busta 20.

100. Suvich to Vinci, Rome, 22 June 1934, ibid.

101. Concerning the treaties, see David Napier Hamilton, "Ethiopia's Frontiers: The Boundary Agreements and Their Demarcations, 1896–1956" (Ph.D. diss., Trinity College, Oxford University, 1974).

102. Campini to Vinci, Harer, 30 Oct. 1933, IFM/MAI, 54/13-37.

103. Lt. Collingwood, "A Report on Ethiopia," supplementary to "Protectorate Quarterly Report for Quarter ended March 31, 1933," FO 371/16997.

104. Vinci to minister, Addis Abeba, 22 April 1933, IFM/MAI, 54/4-3.

105. Same to same, Harer, 15 Nov. 1933, IFM/MAI, 54/13-37.

106. Roberto Cimmaruta, *Ual Ual* (Milan, 1936), p. 72.

107. Rava to minister, Mogadishu, 27 Feb. and 14 March 1934, IFM/MAI, 54/13-39.

108. Vinci to minister, Addis Abeba, 28 April 1934, ibid.

109. Caroselli to minister, Mogadishu, 16 July 1934, ibid.

110. De Bono to Rava, Rome, 15 (?) July 1934, ibid.

111. Haile Sellassie to Geraz. Afework, Addis Abeba, 21 Sept. 1934, IFM, Serie Affari Politici, busta 20.

112. Barton to Simon, Addis Abeba, 19 June 1934, FO 371/18025.

113. Minute J1846 by Mr. Wallinger, n.d., but commenting on rumors about fighting between Ethiopian and Italian forces at Welwel, as reported in Barton to FO, Addis Abeba, 2 Aug. 1934, ibid.

114. Minute J2260 by Wallinger, 27 Sept. 1934, ibid.

115. Minutes J2287, 1 Oct. 1934, ibid.

116. FO to Barton, London, 5 Oct. 1934, ibid.

117. Drummond to Simon, Rome, 12 Oct. 1934, ibid.

118. Simon to Drummond, London, 25 Oct. 1934, ibid.

119. Clifford to Colonial Office, Ado, 25 Nov. 1934, FO 371/19100.

120. Rava to minister, Mogadishu, 27 Nov. 1934, IFM/MAI, Serie Affari Politici, busta 23.

121. Same to same, Mogadishu, 3 Dec. 1934, ibid.

122. Same to same, Mogadishu, 4 Dec. 1934, ibid.

123. "Walwal-December 5th 1934," in Collingwood, "Military Progress Report," No. 11, n.d., in Lawrance to Cunliffe-Lister, Sheikh, 17 Dec. 1934, FO 371/19100.

CHAPTER EIGHT

1. Raffaele Guariglia, *Riccordi, 1922-1946* (Naples, 1950), p. 214.

2. Afework to Italian Foreign Ministry, Rome, 10 Dec. 1934, IFM, Serie Affari Politici, busta 23.

3. Mombelli to Herui, Addis Abeba, 11 Dec. 1934, ibid.

4. Haile Sellassie I to Victor Emmanuel III, Addis Abeba, 15 Dec. 1934, ibid.

5. Drummond to FO, Rome, 3 Jan. 1935, FO 371/19000; Ivone Kirkpatrick, *Mussolini: A Study in Power* (New York, 1968), p. 310.

6. As quoted in George W. Baer, *The Coming of the Italo-Ethiopian War* (Cambridge, Mass., 1967), pp. 58-59.

7. William Shorrock, "The Tunisian Question in French Policy Toward Italy," *International Journal of African Historical Studies* 16, no. 4 (1983): 632, 644.

8. William Shorrock, "The Jouvenal Mission to Rome and the Origins of the Laval-Mussolini Accords, 1933–1935," *Historian* 46, no. 1 (1982): 20–35.

9. Compare Jean-Baptiste Duroselle, *La Décadence* (Paris, 1979), pp. 132–133.

10. Lord Vansittart, *Lessons of My Life* (New York, 1943), pp. 132–133.

11. Jean-Paul Garnier, "Autour d'un Accord," *La Revue de Paris* 68 (1961): 112.

12. See, in particular, Chambrun to Laval, Rome, 7 Dec. 1934, Archives of the French Foreign Ministry, "Négociations Franco-Italiennes de 1934–35/1934–38," File 2374–14, Carton 1096. This dossier contains some copies of materials taken by the Nazis to Germany, where they were destroyed or lost. The files of the French Embassy in Rome have nothing whatsoever on the Mussolini-Laval negotiations; Archives of the French Foreign Ministry, Files of the French Embassy, Rome, "Politique extérieure italienne, Rapports Franco-italiens," 1934, File No. 30/1.

13. Alfred Mallet, *Pierre Laval*, vol. 1 (Paris, 1954), pp. 102–103.

14. Pierre Laval, *The Unpublished Diary of Pierre Laval* (London, 1948), p. 34.

15. Laval to Chambrun, Paris, 19 July 1935, FFM, Afrique-Eth., 1930–1940, Conflit Italo-éthiopien, vol. 71.

16. Laval, *Diary*, p. 34. Haile Sellassie understood Laval's reasoning, although he found the logic flawed by the disregard for the international implications of abandoning Ethiopia; Haile Sellassie I, *My Life and Ethiopia's Progress*, vol. 2 (Addis Abeba, 1974), p. 4.

17. Minute N165 by Wallinger, 15 Jan. 1935, FO 371/19101.

18. Minute J403 by Thompson, 1 Feb. 1935, FO 371/19102.

19. Barton to FO, Addis Abeba, 5 Feb. 1935, ibid.

20. Brielli to legation, Dese, 4 Feb. 1935, IFM/MAI, 54/6–17.

21. Kathleen Nelson and Alan Sullivan, eds., *John Melly in Ethiopia* (London, 1937), p. 125.

22. Poem by Tesfa Gebre Sellassie, enclosed in Barton to Simon, Addis Abeba, 3 Jan. 1935, FO 371/19101.

23. Drummond to FO, Rome, 12 Feb. 1935, FO 371/19102.

24. "Une Interview du Roi des Rois," *Paris Midi*, 7 March 1935.

25. Charles-Roux to minister, Vatican City, 15 Feb. 1935, FFM, Afrique-Eth., 1930–1940, Conflit Italo-éthiopien, vol. 66; François Charles-Roux, *Huit Ans au Vatican, 1932–1940* (Paris, 1947), p. 134.

26. Memo. of Conversation between Cav. Farina and Ato Afework, Rome, 17 April 1935, IFM/MAI, 54/34–138.

27. Memo. by military attaché, Addis Abeba, 5 March 1935, FFM, Afrique-Eth., 1930–1940, Affaires politiques, vol. 60.

28. Record of Conversation between M. Bodard and Haile Sellassie, 31 March 1935, FFM, Afrique-Eth., 1930–1940, Projet d'Alliance, vol. 62.

29. See IFM, Fondo di Guerra, 1935–1940, buste 69, 70, 71, 72, 73, 100.

30. See FFM, Afrique-Eth., 1930–1940, Importation d'Armes, vol. 126.

31. Barton to FO, Addis Abeba, 16 May 1935, FO 371/19109.

32. Ramsay to FO, Budapest, 21 March 1935, ibid.

33. Tekle Hawariat to Secretary of the League of Nations, Paris, 17 March 1935, enclosed in Secretary General to the Council of the League and Member States of the League, 19 March 1935, C.126.M.64.1935.VII, as found in FO 371/19106.

34. De Bono to Suvich, Rome, 2 March 1934, IFM, Serie Affari Politici, busta 19.

35. Suvich to Secretary General, Rome, 22 March 1935, enclosed in Secretary General to the Council of the League and Member States, Geneva, 22 March 1935, C.132.M.69.1935.VII, as found in FO 371/19106.

36. Tekle Hawariat to Secretary General, Paris, 29 March 1935, enclosed in Secretary General to the Council of the League and Member States, Geneva, 1 April 1935, C.148.M.79.1935.VII, ibid.

37. High Commissioner to Simon, Cairo, 1 April 1935, FO 371/19107.

38. Serge Groussard, "Entretien avec Hailé Sélassié Ier," *Le Figaro*, part 2, 26 March 1959.

39. "Le Reich a ouvertement offert son appui à l'Ethiopie contre l'Italie," *Le Temps*, 26 March 1935.

40. Elizabeth Wiskemann, *The Rome-Berlin Axis* (London, 1966), p. 63.

41. Esmonde M. Robertson, *Mussolini as Empire-Builder* (London, 1977), p. 111.

42. Minister to Bodard, Paris, 30 March 1935, FFM, Afrique-Eth., 1930–1940, Conflit, vol. 67.

43. Manfred Funke, *Sanktionen und Kanonen* (Düsseldorf, 1970), pp. 47–48.

44. Vinci to minister, Addis Abeba, 15 June 1935, IFM/MAI, 54/25–96.

45. Groussard, "Entretien," part 2, p. 5.

46. William J. Makin, *War over Ethiopia* (London, 1935), p. 204; Jean-Toussaint Samat, *Aux Frontières d'Ethiopie* (Paris, 1936), pp. 76–77, 106–107, 271.

47. Groussard, "Entretien," *Le Figaro*, part 1, 25 March 1959.

48. John H. Spencer, *Ethiopia at Bay* (Alganac, Mich., 1984), p. 39.

49. The Earl of Avon, *The Eden Memoirs: Facing the Dictators* (London, 1962), pp. 241–242; cf. Renato Mori, *Mussolini e la Conquista dell'Etiopia* (Florence, 1978), p. 314.

50. Viscount Simon, *Retrospect* (London, 1952), p. 203.

51. Appunto per S.E. il Sottosegretario di Stato, Rome, 1 April 1935, IFM, Fondo di Guerra, 1935–1941, busta 8.

52. Sir Geoffrey Thompson, *Frontline Diplomat* (London, 1959), pp. 97, 99.

53. Baer, *Italo-Ethiopian War*, p. 122.

54. As quoted in John Connell, *The Office: A Study in British Foreign Policy and Its Makers, 1919–1951* (London, 1958), p. 161.

55. Simon to Drummond, London, 3 May 1935, FO 371/19108.

56. Corbin to minister, London, 16 May 1935, FFM, Afrique-Eth., 1930–1940, Conflit, vol. 68.

57. "Janhoy Speaks to Parliament," *Berhanena Selam*, 18 April 1935.

58. Italian Ministry of War, Communique n. 6, 7 May 1935, enclosed in Drummond to FO, Rome, 7 May 1935, FO 371/19108.

59. Thompson Minute J1738, 8 May 1935, ibid.

60. Memo. of Conversation with Sig. Vitetti, London, 9 May 1935, ibid.

61. Various Minutes, J1792, 13 May 1935, ibid.

62. Aaron L. Goldman, "Sir Robert Vansittart's Search for Italian Cooperation Against Hitler, 1933–36," *Journal of Contemporary History* 9 (1974): 109.

63. Clerk to FO, Paris, 11 May 1935, FO 371/19108.

64. Ladislas Farago, *Abyssinia on the Eve* (London, 1935), pp. 83–85.

65. As reported in Giardini to legation, Harer, 6 June 1935, IFM/MAI, 54/7–18.

66. G. L. Steer, *Caesar in Abyssinia* (London, 1936), pp. 89–106.

67. A compendium of information drawn from messages intercepted by the Italians, IFM/MAI, 181/26–125 and 126.

68. H.M. Consul to FO, Geneva, 20 May 1935, FO 371/19109.

69. Thompson Minute J2125, 1 June 1933, FO 371/19110.

70. As quoted in Drummond to FO, Rome, 21 May 1925, ibid. See chapter 7, n. 17.

71. "Italo-Ethiopian Commission," *The [London] Times*, 3 June 1935.

72. Drummond to Simon, Rome, 1 June 1935, FO 371/19111.

73. Drummond to FO, Rome, 8 June 1935, FO 371/19112.

74. Tekle Hawariat to Secretary General, Paris, 19 June 1935, in Secretary General to the Council of the League and Member States, Geneva, 20 June 1935, C.254.M.126.1935.VII, as included in FO 371/19113.

75. Extract from Cabinet Conclusions N.33 (35), 19 June 1935, ibid.

76. Eden to FO, Rome, 24 June 1935, ibid.

77. Eden to FO, Paris, 27 June 1935, ibid.; cf. Avon, *Facing the Dictators*, p. 232.

78. Minute J2887, 16 July 1935, FO 371/19117.

79. Speech of 18 July 1935, as quoted in *Autobiography*, p. 220.

80. Haile Sellassie, "Le Drame Effroyable que Mon Peuple et Moi Venons de Vivre," part I, *Vu* 432 (24 June 1936): 734.

81. Col. Th. Konovaloff, *Con le Armate del Negus, Un Bianco fra i Neri* (Bologna, 1938), pp. 27, 32.

82. Maj. Gen. J. F. C. Fuller, "A Soldier-Journalist in Abyssinia," in *Abyssinian Stop Press*, edited by Ladislas Farago (London, 1936), pp. 32–33; Geoffrey Harmsworth, *Abyssinian Adventure* (London, 1935), p. 219.

83. Konovaloff, *Fra i Neri*, pp. 36, 40, 44, 45.

84. M. S. Lush, "Notes from Addis Ababa," 12 July 1935, in High Commissioner in Egypt to FO, Cairo, 27 July 1935, FO 371/19121.

85. Pierre Van Paassen, *Days of Our Years* (London, 1939), pp. 293–294; "Haile Selassie," *Paris Soir*, 27 July 1935.

86. Statement by Commandant Listray, Head of the Belgian Military Training Mission, as quoted in Harmsworth, *Abyssinian Adventure*, p. 217.

87. Chatfield to Vansittart, Admiralty, 8 Aug. 1935, FO 371/19123; R. A. C. Barker, "Great Britain, France, and the Ethiopian Crisis, 1935–36," *English History Review* 89 (1974): 297; Arthur Marder, "The Royal Navy and the Ethiopian Crisis of 1935–36," *American Historical Review* 75 (1970): 1328; Rosaria Quartararo, "Imperial Defence in the Mediterranean on the Eve of the Ethiopian Crisis (July-October 1935)," *Historical Journal* 20 (1977): 36.

88. As quoted in Viscount Templewood, *Nine Troubled Years* (London, 1954), pp. 159–160.

89. Memo. by Samuel Hoare, "Points for Consideration by His Majesty's Government in Connexion with the Imminent Discussions Between the United Kingdom, France, and Italy Concerning Abyssinia," n.d., FO 371/19124.

90. Drummond to Hoare, Rome, 13 Aug. 1935, ibid.

91. Tekle Hawariat to Secretary General, Paris, 12 Aug. 1935, in Secretary General to the Council of the League and Member States, Geneva, 14 Aug. 1935, C.312.M.164.1935.VII, as found in FO 371/19125.

92. Eden to FO, Paris, 19 Aug. 1935, ibid.

93. Oliphant Memo. on Mussolini's Reply to President Roosevelt's Message, London, 21 Aug. 1935, ibid.

94. Drummond to FO, 29 Aug. 1935, FO 371/19129.

95. Italo-Ethiopian Commission of Conciliation and Arbitration, "Award of 3 Sept. 1935," FO 371/19131.

96. Eden to FO, Geneva, 5 Sept. 1935, ibid.

97. Same to same, Geneva, 17 Sept. 1935, FO 371/19134.

98. Report of the Committee of Five, in Leger to minister, Geneva, 19 Sept. 1935, FFM, Afrique-Eth., 1930–1940, Conflit, vol. 78.

99. Eden to FO, Geneva, 18 Sept. 1935, FO 371/19135.

100. Laval to Leger, Paris, 19 Sept. 1935, FFM, Afrique-Eth., 1930–1940, Conflit, vol. 78.

101. Drummond to FO, Rome, 21 Sept. 1935, FO 371/19136.

102. *Giornale d'Italia*, 20 Sept. 1935.

103. Haile Sellassie to Secretary General, Addis Abeba, 25 Sept. 1935, in Secretary General to the Council of the League and Member States, Geneva, 25 Sept. 1935, C.384.M.192.1935.VII, as found in FO 371/19138.

104. Eden to FO, Geneva, 28 Sept. 1935, ibid.; Haile Sellassie to Secretary General, Addis Abeba, 28 Sept. 1935, in Secretary General to the Council of the League and Member States, Geneva, 29 Sept. 1935, no numerical classification, as found in FO 371/19139.

105. Steer, *Caesar*, pp. 131–136.

106. Evelyn Waugh, *Waugh in Abyssinia* (London, 1936), pp. 148–149.

107. *Autobiography*, pp. 230–233.

108. Steer, *Caesar*, pp. 138–139.

109. Waugh, *Waugh*, p. 150.

110. Angelo Del Boca, *The Ethiopian War, 1935–41* (Chicago, 1969), p. 44.

111. Drummond to FO, 3 Oct. 1935, FO 371/19140.

112. Drummond to FO, Rome, 5 Oct. 1935, FO 371/19142; Herui to Secretary General, Addis Abeba, 7 Oct. 1935, FO 371/19143.

113. Konovaloff, *Fra i Neri*, pp. 53–61.

114. As quoted in Drummond to FO, Rome, 7 Oct. 1935, FO 371/19144.

115. Makonnan Endlekatchou, *Why Was the Lion of Judah Defeated?* (Jerusalem, 1936), p. 19.

116. Haggai Erlich, "Tigre in Modern History," in *Proceedings of the Seventh International Conference of Ethiopian Studies*, edited by Sven Rubenson (Addis Abeba, Uppsala, East Lansing, 1984), p. 328.

117. War Office Summaries of Intelligence on the Italo-Ethiopian War, nos. 3–26, FO 371/19148.

118. Messages Intercepted by the Italians, IFM/MAI, 181/26–126.

119. War Office Intelligence Summaries for 11 and 22 Nov. 1935, FO 371/19148.

120. League of Nation Minutes, 7th Meeting (Public), 89th Session of the Council, 7 Oct. 1935, A.78.1935.VII, as found in FO 371/19145.

121. Extract from Cabinet Conclusions n. 45(35) of 9 Oct. 1935, FO 371/19144.

122. Memo. by Mr. Thomas, Paris, 7 Oct. 1935, ibid.

123. Hoare to Clerk, London, 11 Oct. 1935, FO 371/19145.

124. Eden to FO, Geneva, 10 Oct. 1935, FO 371/19146.

125. Drummond to Hoare, Rome, 21 Oct. 1935, FO 371/19153.

126. Memo. of Conversation between Laval and Cerruti, Paris, 14 Oct. 1935, in Scammaca to Rochet, Paris, 15 Oct. 1935, FFM, Afrique-Eth., 1930–1940, Conflit, vol. 80; Minute J6790 by Thompson, 25 Oct. 1935, FO 371/19154.

127. Steer, *Caesar*, p. 161.

128. Waugh, *Waugh*, p. 170.

129. Stuart Emeny, "Under Fire with the Emperor," in *Abyssinian Stop Press*, edited by Ladislas Farago (London, 1936), p. 181.

130. Barton to FO, Addis Abeba, 25 Oct. 1935, FO 371/19155.

131. Same to same, Addis Abeba, 1 Nov. 1935, FO 371/19158.

132. George W. Baer, "Sanctions and Security: The League of Nations and the Italian-Ethiopian War, 1935–1936," *International Organization* 27 (1973): 179. See the collection of Italian propaganda posters against sanctions in Mario Giovana, *L'Avventura Fascista in Etiopia* (Milan, 1976), pp. 190–196.

133. Drummond to FO, Rome, 28 Nov. 1935, FO 371/19165.

134. FO to Lindsay, London, 29 Nov. 1935, ibid.

135. Esmonde Robertson, "Hitler and Sanctions: Mussolini and the Rhineland," *European Studies Review* 7 (Oct. 1977): 409–410.

136. Templewood, *Troubled Years*, pp. 179, 182.

137. Hoare to FO, Paris, 7 Dec. 1935, FO 371/19167.

138. Eden to FO, Geneva, 12 Dec. 1935, FO 371/19169.

139. Clerk to FO, Paris, 12 Dec. 1935, ibid.

140. Wilberforce to Leeper, New York City, 13 Dec. 1935, FO 371/19174.

141. Bodard to minister, Addis Abeba, 17 Dec. 1935, FFM, Afrique-Eth., 1930–1940, Conflit, vol. 85.

142. Wolde Mariam to Secretary General, Paris, 12 Dec. 1935, in Secretary General to the Council of the League and Member States, Geneva, 13 Dec. 1935, C.483.M259.1935.VII, as found in FO 371/19170.

143. Templewood, *Troubled Years*, pp. 188–191.

144. "Observations sur les Objections de M. Mussolini aux Propositions Franco-anglais," Rome, 12 Dec. 1935; Italian Embassy to Laval, Paris, 16 Dec. 1935, FFM, Afrique-Eth., 1930–1940, Conflit, vol. 85.

145. *Autobiography*, p. 255.

146. Vansittart, *Lessons*, p. 53.

147. *Autobiography*, pp. 233–235.

148. Konovaloff, *Fra i Neri*, pp. 64–65, 75, 77–78, 82–84.

149. Del Boca, *War*, p. 54.

150. Pietro Badoglio, *The War in Abyssinia* (London, 1937), pp. 15, 50.

151. Bodard to minister, Addis Abeba, 2 Jan. 1936, FFM, Afrique-Eth., 1930–1940, Conflit, vol. 88. According to Alberto Sbacchi, the Italians first used poison gas at Korahe on 10 October 1935, after which it was deployed freely; Alberto Sbacchi, "Legacy of Bitterness: Poison Gas and Atrocities in the Italo-Ethiopian War, 1935–36," *Genève-Afrique* 13, no. 2 (1974): 7–8.

152. War Office Summary of Intelligence, n. 36, 5 Feb. 1936, FO 371/20165.

153. Konovaloff, *Fra i Neri*, pp. 96–100; Kassa to Haile Sellassie, 21 Jan. 1936, IFM/MAI, 181/26–127.

154. Haile Sellassie, "Le Drame Effroyable," part 1, p. 734.

155. Badoglio, *The War*, p. 30.

156. Intercepted Ethiopian Messages, IFM/MAI, 181/26–127.

157. Report of the Asst. Military Attaché, Addis Abeba, 11 April 1936, in Barton to FO, Addis Abeba, 13 April 1936, FO 371/20167; War Office Summary of Intelligence, n. 36, 5 Feb. 1936, FO 371/20165.

158. Addis Abeba News Summary by British Legation, n. 11, 8 Feb. 1936, FO 371/20172.

159. *Autobiography*, p. 251.

160. Emeny, "Under Fire with the Emperor," p. 187.

161. Steer, *Caesar*, pp. 202–205.

162. Ibid., p. 257.

163. Badoglio, *The War*, pp. 77–89 and chapters 9–10.

164. Intercepted Ethiopian Messages, IFM/MAI, 181/26–127.

165. Steer, *Caesar*, p. 259.

166. Badoglio, *The War*, p. 140.

167. "Notes on the Battle of Mai Chio, 31 March 1936, and the Subsequent Retreat of the Emperor's Forces," Addis Abeba, 22 June 1936, in Chargé to FO, Addis Abeba, 22 June 1936, FO 371/20167.

168. Haile Sellassie, "Le Drame Effroyable," part 1, p. 735.

169. The previous several pages were based on *Autobiography*, pp. 272–281; Badoglio, *The War*, pp. 141–144; Colonel Konovaloff, "Notes on the Battle of Mai Chio, 31 March 1936," n.p., n.d., enclosure in Chargé to FO, Addis Abeba, 22 June 1936, FO 371/20167 (hereafter cited as the Konovaloff Report).

170. *Autobiography*, p. 281.

171. Ibid., pp. 283–284; Haile Sellassie, "Le Drame Effroyable," III, *Vu* 434 (8 July 1936): 819.

172. Konovaloff Report; *Autobiography*, pp. 285–290.

173. Bodard to minister, Addis Abeba, 22 April 1936, FFM, Afrique-Eth., 1930–1940, Conflit, vol. 94.

174. Steer, *Caesar*, pp. 356–367; *Autobiography*, pp. 290–291.

175. Barton to FO, Addis Abeba, 30 April 1936, FO 371/20195; Bodard to minister, Addis Abeba, 1 May 1936, FFM, Afrique-Eth., 1930–1940, Conflit, vol. 95.

176. Steer, *Caesar*, pp. 367–369, 371.

177. "Extracts from Reports of Proceedings of H.M. Ships Enterprise and Diana, Concerning the Evacuation of the Emperor of Abyssinia and Party from Djibuti," enclosure in Murray to FO, London, 30 June 1936, FO 371/20197.

BIBLIOGRAPHY

Ethiopians use their praenomens to identify themselves, as the second appellation is their father's first name. Hence Asfa Yilma is Mrs. Asfa, not Mrs. Yilma. Consequently, I shall render the names of Ethiopian authors as given and will alphabetize them by praenomen.

BOOKS

Anderson, Perry. *Lineages of the Absolutist State*. London, 1974.

Arce, Laurent d'. *L'Abyssinie. Etude d'Actualité (1922–1924)*. Avignon, 1925.

Asfa Yilma. *Haile Selassie, Emperor of Ethiopia*. London, 1936.

Avon, the Earl of [Anthony Eden]. *The Eden Memoirs: Facing the Dictators*. London, 1962.

Badoglio, Pietro. *The War in Abyssinia*. London, 1937.

Baer, George W. *The Coming of the Italo-Ethiopian War*. Cambridge, Mass., 1967.

———. *Test Case: Italy, Ethiopia, and the League of Nations*. Stanford, 1976.

Bergsma, Stuart. *Rainbow Empire*. Grand Rapids, Mich., 1936.

Berlan, Eduard. *Addis Ababa, la plus haute ville d'Afrique*. Grenoble, 1965.

Boca, Angelo Del. *The Ethiopian War, 1935–41*. Chicago, 1969.

Bono, Emilio De. *La Preparazione e le Prime Operazioni*. Rome, 1937.

Buccianti, Giovanni. *L'Egemonia sull'Etiopia*. Milan, 1977.

Cassanelli, Lee. *The Shaping of Somali Society*. Philadelphia, 1982.
Cassels, Alan. *Mussolini's Early Diplomacy*. Princeton, N.J., 1970.
Charles-Roux, François. *Huit Ans au Vatican, 1932–1940*. Paris, 1947.
Cimmaruta, Roberto. *Ual Ual*. Milan, 1936.
Connell, John. *The Office: A Study in British Foreign Policy and Its Makers, 1919–1951*. London, 1958.
Dunckley, Fan C. *Eight Years in Abyssinia*. London, 1935.
Duroselle, Jean-Baptiste. *La Décadence*. Paris, 1979.
Eisenstadt, S. N. *The Political System of Empires*. Glencoe, Ill. 1963.
Farago, Ladislas. *Abyssinia on the Eve*. London, 1935.
Felice, Renzo de. *Mussolini, il Duce, gli Anni del Consenso*. Turin, 1974.
Forbes, Rosita. *From Red Sea to Blue Nile*. New York, 1925.
Frangipani, Angenore. *L'Equivoco Abissino*. Milan, 1936.
Funke, Manfred. *Sanktionen und Kanonen*. Düsseldorf, 1970.
Giovana, Mario. *L'Avventura Fascista in Etiopia*. Milan, 1976.
Guariglia, Raffaele. *Riccordi, 1922–1946*. Naples, 1950.
Haile Sellassie I. *My Life and Ethiopia's Progress*. Vol. 1. Addis Abeba, 1973. Edited and translated by Edward Ullendorff as the *Autobiography of Emperor Haile Selassie I, 'My Life and Ethiopia's Progress,' 1892–1937*. Oxford, 1976.
———. *My Life and Ethiopia's Progress (Hywetayna Yeetyopia Armaj)*. Vol. 2. Addis Abeba, 1974.
Harmsworth, Geoffrey. *Abyssinian Adventure*. London, 1935.
Herui Wolde Sellassie, Blattangeta. *Biographie. Sa Majesté Hailé Sélassié Premier, Empereur d'Ethiopie*. Addis Abeba, 1930.
———. *Mahdere Berhan Ha-Ager Japon* (The example of light, the country of Japan). Addis Abeba, 1931.
Hodson, Arnold Wienholt. *Seven Years in Southern Abyssinia*. London, 1927.
Imbakom Kalewold, Alaka. *Traditional Ethiopian Church Education*. New York, 1970.
Juniac, Gontran de. *Le Dernier Roi des Rois: L'Ethiopie de Hailé Sélassié*. Paris, 1979.
Kapuściński, Ryszard. *The Emperor: Downfall of an Autocrat*. New York, 1983.
Kirkpatrick, Ivone. *Mussolini: A Study in Power*. New York, 1968.
Konovaloff, Col. Th. *Con le Armate del Negus, Un Bianco fra i Neri*. Bologna, 1938.
Laval, Pierre. *The Unpublished Diary of Pierre Laval*. London, 1948.
Levine, Donald N. *Wax and Gold: Tradition and Innovation in Ethiopian Culture*. Chicago, 1965.
Makin, William J. *War over Ethiopia*. London, 1935.
Makonnan Endlekatchou. *Why Was the Lion of Judah Defeated?* Jerusalem, 1936.
Mallet, Alfred. *Pierre Laval*. Vol. 1. Paris, 1954.

Mantel-Niećko, Joanna. *The Role of Land Tenure in the System of Ethiopian Imperial Government in Modern Times.* Warsaw, 1980.

Marcus, Harold G. *The Life and Times of Menelik II: Ethiopia, 1844–1913.* Oxford, 1975.

Maydon, Maj. H. C. *Simen: Its Heights and Abysses.* London, 1925.

Mikhailovich, Alexander. *Always a Grand Duke.* New York, 1933.

Mori, Renato. *Mussolini e la Conquista dell'Etiopia.* Florence, 1978.

Nelson, Kathleen, and Sullivan, Alan, eds. *John Melly in Ethiopia.* London, 1937.

Nicopoulos, Demetre. *Addis Ababa ou Fleur Nouvelle.* Marseilles, 1923.

Paassen, Pierre van. *Days of Our Years.* London, 1939.

Perham, Margery. *The Government of Ethiopia.* New York, 1948.

Pétridès, Pierre. *Le Héros d'Adoua: Ras Makkonen, Prince d'Ethiopie.* Paris, 1963.

Powell, Alexander. *Beyond the Utmost Purple Rim.* London, 1925.

Rebeaud, Henri. *Chez le Roi des Rois d'Ethiopie.* Paris, 1935.

Rey, C. F. *Unconquered Ethiopia as It Is Today.* London, 1923.

Robertson, Esmonde M. *Mussolini as Empire-Builder.* London, 1977.

Rochat, Giorgio. *Militari e Politici nella Preparazioni della Campagna d'Etiopia.* Milan, 1971.

Samat, Jean-Toussaint. *Aux Frontières d'Ethiopie.* Paris, 1936.

Sandford, Christine. *The Lion of Judah Hath Prevailed.* New York, 1955.

Seligman, Edwin R. A. *The Economic Interpretation of History.* 2d ed. New York, 1907.

Simon, Viscount [John Allsebrook]. *Retrospect.* London, 1952.

Skinner, Robert P. *Abyssinia of Today.* London, 1906.

Smith, Dennis Mack. *Mussolini's Roman Empire.* New York, 1976.

Spencer, John H. *Ethiopia at Bay.* Alganac, Mich. 1984.

Steer, G. L. *Caesar in Abyssinia.* London, 1936.

Susmel, Edwardo, and Susmel, Duilio, eds. *Opera Omnia di Benito Mussolini.* Vol. 27. Florence, 1959.

Suvich, Fulvio, et al. *Il Processo Roatta.* Rome, 1945.

Templewood, Viscount [Samuel John Gurney Hoare]. *Nine Troubled Years.* London, 1954.

Thompson, Sir Geoffrey. *Frontline Diplomat.* London, 1959.

Vansittart, Lord [Robert Gilbert]. *Lessons of My Life.* New York, 1943.

Virgin, Gen. Eric. *The Abyssinia I Knew.* London, 1936.

Waugh, Evelyn. *Waugh in Abyssinia.* London, 1936.

———. *When the Going Was Good.* London, 1948.

Wellby, Capt. M. S. *'Twixt Sirdar and Menelik.* London, 1901.

Wiskemann, Elizabeth. *The Rome-Berlin Axis.* London, 1966.

Worsley, Peter. *The Three Worlds.* London, 1984.

Wylde, Augustus B. *Modern Abyssinia.* London, 1901.

ARTICLES

"Abyssinia." *Near East,* 4 May 1931.

Aleme Eshete. "The Influence of the Capucin Bishop of Harer (1900–1940), Mgr. Andre Jarosseau on Taffari Makonnen, Later Emperor Haile Sellassie." *Ethiopian Journal of Education* 7 (1975).

Baer, George W. "Sanctions and Security: The League of Nations and the Italian-Ethiopian War, 1935–1936." *International Organization* 27 (1973).

Bahru Zewde. "Economic Origins of the Absolutist State in Ethiopia." *Journal of Ethiopian Studies* 17 (Nov. 1984).

———. "The Fumbling Debut of British Capital in Ethiopia: A Contrastive Study of the Abyssinian Corporation and the Ethiopian Motor Transport Company Ltd. In *Proceedings of the Seventh International Conference of Ethiopian Studies,* edited by Sven Rubenson. Addis Abeba, Uppsala, East Lansing, 1984.

Barker, R. A. C. "Great Britain, France, and the Ethiopian Crisis, 1935–36." *English History Review* 89 (1974).

Coquery-Vidrovitch, Catherine. "La Mise en Dépendence de l'Afrique Noire: essai de periodisation, 1800–1970." *Cahiers d'études Africaines* 16 (1976).

Crummey, Donald. "State and Security: Nineteenth-Century Ethiopia." In *Modes of Production in Africa: the Precolonial Era,* edited by D. Crummey and C. Stewart. Beverly Hills, 1981.

Daniel Ayana. "Some Notes on the Role of Village Schools in Planting Protestantism in Wollega, 1898–1935." In *Collected Papers of the Eighth International Conference of Ethiopian Studies.* Vol. 2, B-E. Institute of Ethiopian Studies, Addis Abeba University, 1984.

Dessalegn Rahmato. "Political Power and Social Formation Under the Old Regime." In *Collected Papers of the Eighth International Conference of Ethiopian Studies.* Vol. 2, B-E. Institute of Ethiopian Studies, Addis Abeba University, 1984.

Edwards, Jon R. " 'And the King Shall Judge': The Capitulary Regime in Ethiopia, 1908–1936." In *Proceedings of the Seventh International Conference of Ethiopian Studies,* edited by Sven Rubenson. Addis Ababa, Uppsala, East Lansing, 1984.

———. "Slavery, the Slave Trade, and the Economic Reorganization of Ethiopia, 1916–1935." *African Economic History* 11 (1982).

Ellis, Gene. "The Feudal Paradigm as a Hindrance to Understanding Ethiopia." *Journal of Modern African Studies* 14 (June 1976).

Emeny, Stuart. "Under Fire with the Emperor." In *Abyssinian Stop Press,* edited by Ladislas Farago. London, 1936.

Erickson, Olle. "Education in Abyssinia." *Africa* 5 (1932).

Erlich, Haggai. "Tigre in Modern History." In *Proceedings of the Seventh International Conference of Ethiopian Studies,* edited by Sven Rubenson. Addis Abeba, Uppsala, East Lansing, 1984.

"Faits divers." *Le Semeur d'Ethiopie* 7–8 (Aug.-Oct. 1910) and 7 (Aug. 1911).

Fuller, Maj. Gen. J. F. C. "A Soldier-Journalist in Abyssinia." In *Abyssinian Stop Press*, edited by Ladislas Farago. London, 1936.

Garnier, Jean-Paul. "Autour d'un Accord." *La Revue de Paris* 68 (1961).

Garretson, Peter. "The Naggadras, Trade, and Selected Towns in Nineteenth and Early Twentieth Century Ethiopia." *International Journal of African Historical Studies* 12, no. 3 (1979).

Geshekter, Charles L. "Anti-Colonialism and Class Formation: The Eastern Horn of Africa Before 1950." *International Journal of African Historical Studies* 18, no. 1 (1985).

Goldman, Aaron L. "Sir Robert Vansittart's Search for Italian Cooperation Against Hitler, 1933–36." *Journal of Contemporary History* 9 (1974).

Haile Sellassie. "Le Drame Effroyable que Mon Peuple et Moi Venons de Vivre." Parts 1 and 3. *Vu* 432 (24 June 1936) and 434 (8 July 1936).

Harlan, Harry. "A Caravan Journey Through Abyssinia." *National Geographic* 47 (1925).

Hoben, Allan. "Perspectives on Land Reform in Ethiopia: The Political Role of the Peasantry." *Rural Africana* 28 (Fall 1975).

Horvath, Ronald J. "Addis Ababa's Eucalyptus Forest." *Journal of Ethiopian Studies* 6, no. 1 (1968).

Iadorala, Antoinette. "The Anglo-Italian Agreement of 1925: Mussolini's 'Carte Blanche' for War Against Ethiopia." *Northeast African Studies* 1, no. 1 (1979).

Keefer, Edward. "Great Britain and Ethiopia, 1897–1910: Competition for Empire." *International Journal of African Historical Studies* 6 (1973).

McCann, James. "Children of the House: Slavery and Its Suppression in Lasta, Northern Ethiopia, 1916–75." In *The Suppression of Slavery in Africa*, edited by Suzanne Miers and Richard Roberts. Madison, forthcoming.

————. "Ethiopia, Britain, and Negotiations for the Lake Tana Dam Project." *International Journal of African Historical Studies* 14 (1981).

————. "The Political Economy of Rural Rebellion in Ethiopia: Northern Resistance to Imperial Expansion, 1928–1935." *International Journal of African Historical Studies* 18 (1985).

McClellan, Charles W. "Land, Labor, and Coffee: The South's Role in Ethiopian Self-Reliance." *African Economic History* 9 (1980).

————. "State Transformation and Social Reconstruction in Ethiopia: The Allure of the South." *International Journal of African Historical Studies* 17, no. 4 (1984).

Marcus, Harold G. "Disease, Hospitals, and Italian Colonial Aspirations in Ethiopia, 1930–1935." *Northeast African Studies* 1, no. 1 (1979).

————. "The Embargo on Arms Sales to Ethiopia, 1916–1930." *International Journal of African Historical Studies* 16, no. 2 (1983).

————. "Genesis of an Ethiopian Monarch: Haile Sellassie, 1916–1918." *Horn of Africa* 3, no. 4 (1980–1981).

————. "The Infrastructure of the Italo-Ethiopian Crisis: Haile Sellassie, the

Solomonic Empire, and the World Economy, 1916–1936." In *Proceedings of the Fifth International Conference of Ethiopian Studies*, edited by Robert L. Hess. Chicago, 1979.

———. "Review of Haile Sellassie I, *My Life and Ethiopia's Progress*. Vol. 1, edited and translated by Edward Ullendorff, Oxford, 1976." *International Journal of African Historical Studies* 10 (1977).

Marder, Arthur. "The Royal Navy and the Ethiopian Crisis of 1935–36." *American Historical Review* 75 (1970).

Markakis, John, and Asmelash Beyene. "Representative Institutions in Ethiopia." *Journal of Modern African Studies* 5 (1967).

Marx, Karl. "The Eighteenth Brumaire of Louis Bonaparte." In *Karl Marx and Frederick Engels, Selected Works*. New York, 1969.

"Mgr. Jarosseau, vicare apostolique des Gallas." *La Croix* 1–2 (Jan. 1925).

Moore, W. Robert. "Coronation Days in Addis Ababa." *National Geographic* 59 (1931).

Osgood, Wilfred H. "Nature and Man in Ethiopia." *National Geographic* 54 (1928).

Pankhurst, Richard. "The Hedar Baseta of 1918." *Journal of Ethiopian Studies* 13, no. 2 (1976).

"Le Prince Taffari. Fils du Ras Makonnen." *Le Semeur d'Ethiopie* 6 (July 1910).

Quartararo, Rosaria. "Imperial Defence in the Mediterranean on the Eve of the Ethiopian Crisis (July-October 1935)." *Historical Journal* 20 (1977).

"Ras Tafari of Abyssinia." *Near East*, 10 July 1924.

Rebeaud, Henri. "Au Service du Négous [Récit inédit]." I. *Tous les Vendredis*, 8 March 1935.

Rémond, Georges. "L'Agonie de l'empereur Ménélik." *Le Correspondant* 244 (25 July 1911).

Rey, C. F. "Abyssinia of Today." Parts 1–3. *Journal of the Royal African Society* 20, 21, 22 (1922–1923).

———. "A Recent Visit to Gudru and Gojjam." *Geographical Journal* 16 (1926).

Robertson, Esmonde. "Hitler and Sanctions: Mussolini and the Rhineland." *European Studies Review* 7 (Oct. 1977).

Rubenson, Sven. "The Genesis of the Ethio-Somali Conflict." In *Proceedings of the Fifth International Conference of Ethiopian Studies*, edited by Robert L. Hess. Chicago, 1979.

[Sandford, Col. D.] "Abyssinia and the League." *Near East*, 20 Sept. 1923.

Sbacchi, Alberto. "Legacy of Bitterness: Poison Gas and Atrocities in the Italo-Ethiopian War, 1935–36." *Genève-Afrique* 13, no. 2 (1974).

Shiferaw Bekele. "Prince-Merchants and Tujars: A Preliminary Study of Class Evolution (c. 1900–1935)." In *Collected Papers of the Eighth International Conference of Ethiopian Studies*. Vol. 6, P-S. Institute of Ethiopian Studies, Addis Abeba University, 1984.

Shorrock, William. "The Jouvenal Mission to Rome and the Origins of the Laval-Mussolini Accords, 1933–1935." *Historian* 46, no. 1 (1982).

———. "The Tunisian Question in French Policy Toward Italy." *International Journal of African Historical Studies* 16, no. 4 (1983).

Southard, Addison. "Modern Ethiopia." *National Geographic* 59 (1931).

Spencer, John H. "Haile Sellassie: Leadership and Statesmanship." *Ethiopianist Notes* 2, no. 1 (1978).

———. "Haile Selassie: Triumph and Tragedy." *Orbis* 18 (Winter 1975).

Tedeschi, Salvatore. "La Carrière et les idées de Heruy Wäldä-Sellasié (1878–1938)." In *Trois Essais sur la Littérature Ethiopienne.* Issued by Bibliotèque Peiresc. Antibes, 1984.

Tekalign Wolde Mariam. "The Slave Trade in the Economy of Jimma." In *Collected Papers of the Eighth International Conference of Ethiopian Studies.* Vol. 7, T-2. Institute of Ethiopian Studies, Addis Abeba University, 1984.

Tessema Ta'a. "The Basis for Political Contradictions in Wollega: The Land Apportionment Act of 1910 and Its Consequences." *Northeast African Studies* 6, no. 1–2 (1984).

Triulzi, Alessandro. "Italian Colonialism and Ethiopia." *Journal of African History* 23, no. 2 (1982).

Vedovato, Giuseppe. "Gli Accordi Italo-etiopici dell'Agosto 1928." *Rivista de Studi Internazionali* 22 (1955).

Villari, Luigi. "The Italian Case." *Journal of the Royal African Society* 34 (1935).

NEWSPAPERS (IN CHRONOLOGICAL ORDER)

"Slavery in Ethiopia." *Westminster Gazette,* 18 Jan., 1 and 2 May, 6 June 1922.

"S.A.I. Le Ras Taffari à Aden." *Le Courrier d'Ethiopie,* 18 Nov. 1922.

"Un Brut Incroyable." *Dépêche Coloniale,* 2 May 1924.

"L'Invraisemble peut être Vrai." *Dépêche Coloniale,* 3 May 1924.

"Ras Tafari in Paris." *The [London] Times,* 17 May 1924.

"Black Ruler Thanks Parisians." *Daily Express,* 17 May 1924.

"Le Prince d'Ethiopie à Bruxelles." *Le Soir* (Brussels), 24 May 1924.

"Freeing the Slaves." *Westminster Gazette,* 9 June 1924.

Bolitho, William. "Ras Tafari in Paris." *Manchester Guardian,* 17 June 1924.

"Our New Royal Visitor." *The Observer,* 6 July 1924.

"Prince Tafari of Abyssinia." *The [London] Times,* 7 July 1924.

"Ras Tafari Arrives." *Manchester Guardian,* 8 July 1924.

"Ras Tafari at the Tower." *Daily Express,* 9 July 1924.

"Un entretien avec le Ras Tafari." *Echo de Paris,* 30 August 1924.

"Prince Tafari's Plans." *The [London] Times,* 9 Oct. 1924.

"Reform in Ethiopia." *The [London] Times,* 20 June 1925.

Editorial. *Washington Post,* 8 Aug. 1926.

Editorial. *Berhanena Selam,* 16 Sept. 1926.

"Der Maria-Therasien Thaler" and "La Situation en Ethiopie." *Correspondance d'Ethiopie,* 21 July 1927.

"Abyssinia Sees Independence at Stake in Tsana Dispute." *New York Times,* 13 Nov. 1927.

"Abyssinian Dam Flurry Called Publicity Bid." *New York Herald Tribune*, 13 Nov. 1927.

"The U.S. Insists on Open Door in Abyssinia." *San Francisco Chronicle*, 13 Nov. 1927.

"Two African Visitors Entertained by Harlem." *New York World*, 20 Nov. 1927.

"La cérémonie de Courronnement du Négous Tafari Makonnen." *Correspondance d'Ethiopie*, Dec. 1928.

"Motor Cars in Abyssinia." *Morning Post*, 1 Feb. 1929.

"Proclamation." *Berhanena Selam*, 17 April 1930.

"Une étude retrospective des achèvements de la régence." *Le Courrier d'Ethiopie*, 16 May 1930.

"The Inauguration of a Bridge at Akaki, near Addis Ababa." *Berhanena Selam*, 24 Sept. 1931.

"Ogaden Expedition." *Berhanena Selam*, 31 Dec. 1931.

Editorial. *Berhanena Selam*, 5 May 1932.

"The Judgment of Ras Hailu." *Berhanena Selam*, 30 June 1932.

"Small Incident in Debre Markos, Gojam." *Berhanena Selam*, 20 Oct. 1932.

"In the Ogaden." *Berhanena Selam*, 5 Nov. 1932.

Zelleke Tachbele. "Unity." *Berhanena Selam*, 28 Dec. 1933.

"Eritrea." *Berhanena Selam*, Part 1, 20 Sept. 1934; Part 2, 18 Oct. 1934.

"Une Interview du Roi des Rois." *Paris Midi*, 7 March 1935.

"Le Reich a ouvertement offert son appui à l'Ethiopie contre l'Italie." *Le Temps*, 26 March 1935.

"Janhoy Speaks to Parliament." *Berhanena Selam*, 18 April 1935.

"Italo-Ethiopian Commission." *The [London] Times*, 3 June 1935.

"Haile Selassie." *Paris Soir*, 27 July 1935.

"Etiopia." *Giornale d'Italia*, 20 Sept. 1935.

"Haile Sellasie and His Family." *Bath Weekly Chronicle and Herald*, 10 and 19 Oct. 1936.

Monfried, Henri de. "Vers les Terres hostiles d'Ethiopie." *Le Petit Parisien*, 6 July 1938.

"L'Oeuvre de Mgr. Jarosseau." *Le Petit Parisien*, 6 July 1938.

Groussard, Serge. "Entretien avec Hailé Sélassié Ier." *Le Figaro*, Part 1, 25 March 1959; Part 2, 26 March 1959.

UNPUBLISHED PUBLIC AND
PRIVATE ARCHIVAL DOCUMENTS

The Public Record Office, London

Foreign Office 403/255
Foreign Office 371/
2593, 2594, 2595, 2853, 2854, 2855;
3125, 3126, 3494, 3495, 3496, 3497;
4394;

5503, 5505;
7146, 7147, 7148, 7152;
8410;
9985, 9988, 9989, 9990, 9992, 9994;
10871, 10872, 10874, 10875, 10876, 10877, 10878;
11560, 11561, 11563, 11564, 11565, 11566, 11574;
12339, 12341, 12342, 12343, 12349, 12350, 12351;
13101, 13103, 13112, 13830, 13831, 13833, 13834, 13840;
14587, 14588, 14592, 14595, 14596, 14598;
15382, 15384, 15385, 15388, 15389;
16102, 16989, 16995, 16996, 16997;
18025, 18028, 18029, 18030, 18031;
19100, 19101, 19102, 19106, 19107, 19108, 19109, 19110, 19111, 19112, 19113, 19117,
   19121, 19123, 19124, 19125, 19129, 19131, 19134, 19135, 19136, 19138, 19139, 19140,
   19142, 19143, 19144, 19145, 19146, 19148, 19153, 19154, 19155, 19158, 19165, 19167,
   19169, 19170, 19174;
20165, 20167, 20172, 20197.

United States National Archives

Records of the Department of State relating to the Internal Affairs of Ethiopia, 1910–1929, three volumes, on microfilm.
Decimal Files of the Department of State, 1930–1949: 884.00, 01, 01A, 001—Selassie, 002, 03, 154, 2, 20, 24, 242, 4016, 42A—Work, 51, 515, 5151.

National Records Office, Khartoum, Sudan

Palace, Class 4/Box 4/File 13.

Historical Archives of the Italian Foreign Ministry, Rome

Affari Politici, 1914–1918: File 1145/2, 1145/3, 1114/2.
Archivio Politico, 1916–1920: File 66/1135, 66/1145–3.
Archivio degli Affari Politici, 1919–1930: Pacci 1020, 1024, 1025, 1026, 1027, 1028, 1029, 1031, 1035, 1036.
Serie Affari Politici, 1931–1935: Buste 2, 6, 13, 19, 20, 21, 23.
Fondo di Guerra, 1935–1941: Buste 5, 8, 69, 70, 71, 72, 73, 100.
Ex-Ministry of Italian Africa: File 37/11, 54/3–71, 54/4–3, 54/6–17, 54/7–18, 54/12–34, 54/13–37, 54/13–39, 54/14–44, 54/20–64, 54/24–64, 54/25–93, 54/26–98, 54/26–99, 54/26–100, 54/31–124, 54/31–128, 54/34–137, 54/34–138, 54/36–147, 54/37–149, 54/37–150A, 54/37–150B, 54/38–158, 54/38–159, 181/26–125, 181/26–126, 181/26–127.

Archives of the French Foreign Ministry, Paris

Guerre, Affaires politiques générales, Ethiopie: Vols. 1617, 1619, 1620, 1621, 1622, 1623, 1624, 1625.
K-Série, Afrique, 1918–1930, Ethiopie: Vols. 6, 7, 8, 9, 10, 12, 13, 14, 15, 16, 17, 18, 19, 20, 29, 34.

K-Série, Afrique, 1930–1940, Ethiopie: Vols. 59, 60, 61, 62, 65, 66, 67, 68, 71, 78, 80, 85, 88, 94, 95, 126, 129, 134, 135.

Négociations Franco-Italiennes de 1934–1935/1934–1938, File 2374–14, carton 1906.

Archives de la Ambassade de France à Rome, "Politique extérieure italienne, Rapports Franco-italiens 1934, No. 30/1, 1934.

Papiers domestiques de Léonce Lagarde

Archives of the Capucins, Province of Toulouse, Toulouse, France

Archives de la Mission:
Vicariat apostolique des Gallas, 1846–1925
Journal de Mgr. Jarosseau
Correspondance Jarosseau.

National Library of Ethiopia, Addis Abeba

The Collected Letters of Tafari Makonnen, Books One and Two.

UNPUBLISHED THESES, ESSAYS,
DISSERTATIONS, AND MANUSCRIPTS

Ababa Kiflayasus. "The Career of Liul Ras Imru Hayla Sillase." B.A. essay. Addis Abeba University, 1973.

Aby Demissie. "Lij Iyasu: A Perspective Study of His Short Reign." B.A. essay. Addis Abeba University, 1964.

Adugna Amanu. "The Ethiopian Orthodox Church Becomes Autocephalous." B.A. essay. Addis Abeba University, 1969.

Alem Mulaw. "Begemdir and Simien (1910–1930)." B.A. essay. Addis Abeba University, 1971.

Aleme Eshete. "A General Survey of Ethiopian Feudalism." Conference paper. Addis Abeba University, 1976.

Asrat Tassie. "The Status and Role of the Ethiopian Parliament: A New Appraisal." B.A. essay. Addis Abeba University, 1971.

Bairu Tafla. "Education of the Ethiopian Makwannent in the Nineteenth Century." Seminar paper. Addis Abeba University, 1972.

Blackhurst, Hector. "A Community of Shoa Galla Settlers in Southern Ethiopia." Ph.D. diss. University of Manchester, 1974.

Cooper, Adi, et al. "Class, State, and the World Economy: A Case Study of Ethiopia." Conference paper. University of Sussex, 1975.

Edwards, Jon. "An Introduction to Foreign Office File 915: The British Consular Court in Ethiopia, 1912–1938." London, 1981.

Garretson, Peter. "A History of Addis Ababa from Its Foundation in 1886 to 1910." Ph.D. diss. University of London, 1974.

Gebre Egzabieher Elyas. "YeTarik Mestawasha, 1901–1922 E.C." Unpubl. ms., No. 23. National Library, Addis Abeba, n.d.

Gizachew Adamu. "A Historical Survey of Taxation in Gojjam, 1901–1969." B.A. essay. Addis Abeba University, 1971.

Hamilton, David Napier. "Ethiopia's Frontiers: The Boundary Agreements and their Demarcations, 1896–1956." Ph.D. diss. Trinity College, Oxford University, 1974.

Kenefe-Regb Zelleke. "The Episode of Eyasu Menelik (1896–1935)." Conference paper. Lund, 1982.

Levine, Donald N. "Individualism in Feudal Ethiopia." Conference paper. Addis Abeba University, 1976.

———. "Legitimacy in Ethiopia." Conference paper. American Political Science Association, 1964.

Maaza Bekele. "A Study of Modern Education in Ethiopia: Its Foundation, Its Development, Its Future, with Emphasis on Primary Education." Ph.D. diss. Columbia University Teachers College, 1966.

Marse Hazan Wolde Qirqos. "BaDagmawi Minilik Zaman KeYahutna KeSamehut." Unpubl. ms. Institute of Ethiopian Studies, Addis Abeba University, probably 1938.

———. "YeZaman Tarik Tezzetaye BaNegesta Negastat Zawditu Zamana Mangist." Unpubl. ms. Institute of Ethiopian Studies, Addis Abeba University, n.d.

McCann, James. "Households, Peasants, and Rural History in Lasta, Northern Ethiopia, 1900–35." Ph.D. diss. Michigan State University, 1984.

McClellan, Charles W. "Politics and Change in Ethiopia's Southern Periphery—Darasa in the 1920s and 1930s." Conference paper. Stanford University, 1982.

———. "Reaction to Ethiopian Expansionism: The Case of Darassa, 1895–1935." Ph.D. diss. Michigan State University, 1978.

Mehari Yohannes. "Debra Markos Awraja-Gojjam. Local Administration: The Role of Traditional Elements." B.A. essay, Addis Abeba University, 1970.

Negussay Ayele. "Is There Feudalism in Ethiopia?" Conference paper. Addis Abeba University, 1976.

Tesfaye Ababe. "The Life and Career of Dejjazmatch Takala Walda Hawariat." B.A. essay. Addis Abeba University, 1971.

INDEX